D0210728

STRANGE
CONTAGION

ALSO BY LEE DANIEL KRAVETZ

Supersurvivors

STRANGE CONTAGION

*Inside the Surprising Science
of Infectious Behaviors and Viral Emotions
and What They Tell Us About Ourselves*

LEE DANIEL KRAVETZ

HARPER WAVE
An Imprint of HarperCollins*Publishers*

FIRST EDITION

Library of Congress Cataloging-in-Publication Data

Names: Kravetz, Lee Daniel, author.
Title: Strange contagion : inside the surprising science of infectious behaviors and viral emotions and what they tell us about ourselves / Lee Daniel Kravetz.
Description: New York : Harper Wave, 2017. |
Identifiers: LCCN 2016058761 (print) | LCCN 2017020424 (ebook) | ISBN 9780062448958 (eBook) | ISBN 9780062448934 (hardback)
Subjects: LCSH: Collective behavior. | Contagion (Social psychology) | Social psychology. | BISAC: PSYCHOLOGY / Emotions. | PSYCHOLOGY / Social Psychology. | PSYCHOLOGY / Interpersonal Relations.
Classification: LCC HM866 (ebook) | LCC HM866 .K733 2017 (print) | DDC 302--dc23
LC record available at https://lccn.loc.gov/2016058761

ISBN 978-0-06-244893-4

17 18 19 20 21 LSC 10 9 8 7 6 5 4 3 2 1

To Alec and Chloe
We catch each other.

CONTENTS

AUTHOR'S NOTE

I chase narratives for a living. As a science writer, when I seek out stories I'm really looking for specific qualities: a struggle to understand and classify human behavior; unique characters confronting high stakes, moral dilemmas, and a question of personal culpability; heroes facing opponents; and oftentimes a situation in which life hangs in the balance.

In 2009, these qualities announced themselves within a twenty-five-square-mile expanse delineated by the trappings of Silicon Valley, homeland for technology pacesetters surrounded by abundant icons of immense wealth, as well as luminous environmental conditions ideal for cultivating revolution. Palo Alto, California, found itself in the middle of an extraordinary psychological outbreak when numerous students from a single high school died by suicide. This was not the result of a pact; in most cases the children didn't know one another. Even more confounding, on paper at least, they had everything going for them: They came from loving families and environments of plenty. Each was popular, valued, talented, and happy. They were also thriving in one of the highest-ranked public schools in the country. Despite these considerations, something switched within the minds of relatively well-adjusted people, leading inexorably to moments in which each chose to step in front of an oncoming commuter train.

Unlike other narratives I have pursued, though, this time the stakes were personal. The people I interviewed were neighbors. The train that killed these students ran not five minutes away from my apartment. I saw the community's outpouring of grief. I witnessed the town scramble to understand why this was happening. And then there were my own worries to contend with, as well as my growing intellectual curiosity.

Examining events through social contagions, the ways in which others influence our lives through catchable thoughts, emotions, and behaviors, was the only method I found to both understand and describe the events as they transpired. Learning this language, however, first required me to redefine *contagion*, to separate the menace from the meaning. Through the epidemiologist Gary Slutkin, who I came to know well during my search for answers, I learned to view social contagions as neither inherently good nor bad. Instead, he said, they lead to either positive or negative consequences. He reminded me that a social contagion's intent doesn't exist under scrutiny, and that *good* and *bad* are not scientific words. Our job is to understand them deeply, he said, and everything that they influence—such as the way we raise our children, engage in commerce, scale ideas, educate the youth, and care for the sick—so that we do what we can to improve well-being.

The science of social contagions suggests that influence travels through observation. It rides on cues in the environment and traverses the space between people on both spoken and written words. Telling the story of this tragedy, then, meant creating a potential vector for everything it purported to illuminate and protect people from. How was I going to write about something I wasn't supposed to write about without increasing the risk of others catching it?

I decided to go about this with a careful and delicate investigation, undertaking a balancing act of reportage and empathy. I adhered to media guidelines proposed by the US surgeon general and the Annenberg Public Policy Center of the University of Pennsylvania. I avoided romanticizing facts, neither turning victims into martyrs nor insulting their memories. I managed to do so by recognizing early on that this particular story of Silicon Valley was not the story of specific individuals but that of the collective. While, thankfully, few will ever experience the tragedy of this suicide cluster, we have all seen social contagions at work in our lives: we need only look at stock market sentiment to know that greed is communicable, or count the number of campus shootings to watch violence spread. Personal drive, happiness—even our innate senses of generosity, courage, and work ethic—are as transmissible to others as the flu. Researchers from Yale University to the Department of Defense and the Pentagon have invested millions to understand and channel this science, because social contagions covertly impact all elements of our lives, from memories to moods, and often do so beneath the surface of our awareness. My own investigation became a haunting example of just how high the stakes can be, and my goal became one of understanding not *why* these things matter to us all but *how*.

In telling this narrative of Palo Alto, I hope that we can better understand the ways in which each of us, despite physical boundaries, is truly linked to one another. By uncovering this largely covert yet highly commonplace world of social contagions, we recognize their importance as well as the ways in which they contribute to the trajectories of our lives. We learn how to guard against the ones that can lead to potentially harmful outcomes, like hysteria and fear. We come to understand how to spread the ones that lead to healthy results, such as happiness and resilience. We acquire the ability to direct them in order to create the relationships, the community, and the culture we desire.

Given the infectiousness of thoughts, the stickiness of the most subtle of emotions, and the transmissibility of others' behaviors, the chronicle of what transpired in this small town, which just happens to be one of the biggest towns in the world in terms of innovation and scaling of new ideas, will prompt us to take better stock of the invisible forces that sway us. It will also allow us to gain insight into those we ourselves propagate. Ultimately, my hope is that this tale of Silicon Valley will spread a catchable sense of personal responsibility for one another in a world that demands so much of it.

THE VALLEY OF THE SHADOW

"Second verse, same as the first."
—TRADITIONAL

Chapter 1

ARRIVAL, PART I

We've been in the new apartment for a week. My wife, six months pregnant, belly large in a turquoise blouse and hair cut short, arranges the terra-cotta planter pots on the balcony. I'm in the living room, flattening and folding empty cardboard moving boxes. Over the past decade I've become pretty competent in this routine of packing and unpacking. In our twenties we moved around a lot, for work, for graduate school, for adventure and opportunity, living in Boston, New York, and briefly Baltimore, followed by a fifteen-month sojourn in San Francisco. We've decided that 2009 will be the year that we settle down and create a permanent home in which to raise a family. My wife began looking for a job that would bring us out of the city. My work as a freelance science writer unmoored me from any particular location, thus her offer from Google moved us from the trendy Mission District to the sleepy hamlet of Palo Alto.

An ambulance siren is going off maybe a mile away. Another siren closely trails behind it. "I wonder what's going on out there," she says offhandedly. I finish making my morning coffee in the kitchen, and with mug in hand I head to the balcony where she is looking over the railing. "There must be an accident nearby."

Even before entering the low heat of the summer I can hear the traffic that's gathered two stories below. Just beyond our apartment complex, maple trees block the partial view we have of Hoover Tower rising above Stanford University, a pink-hued emblem of the region and those who have brought to it a touch of wunderkind in the form of geniuses, masterminds, idea incubators, and dream originators. Below us, cars collect along El Camino Real and east along Oregon Expressway toward the interstate. The streetlights cycle through from green to red and the traffic doesn't budge. Somewhere overhead a helicopter thumps the sky.

Later that evening I read online that the bumper-to-bumper traffic was due to a fatality not on the road but on the Caltrain tracks close by. The casualty halted the lines for hours. Delayed commuters scrambled for alternate routes to work, causing an ugly cascade of backups on the roads. While I'd been deconstructing our moving boxes up in our apartment, down below a boy named Jean-Paul "Han-Wei" Blanchard, a junior at nearby Henry M. Gunn High School, was walking off of the campus. He'd moved along Arastradero Road, past dozens of tidy, brightly painted homes, crossed the wide span of El Camino Real, and, in broad daylight, stepped onto the railroad.

We've been in town for less than a week, but I'm still certain that a train hitting and killing a local student is unusual in Silicon Valley, where the spectrum of intellect runs a parallel track to a kind of acceptable madness of professors, scientists, writers, investors, and entrepreneurs who run this distinct Bellevue of ambition.

The news is doubly unusual given the particular school the boy attended. By academic measures the students at Gunn High—and all the schools in the area, for that matter—are among California's brightest. In the past five years, Gunn High in particular has boasted more National Merit Scholarship Program semifinalists than 90 percent of schools in the country. Recently, half of its students took roughly two thousand Advanced Placement tests for college credit, 93 percent of whom scored three or higher on a scale of one to five. These are the kind of facts people in this town like to quote, especially those who've moved here expressly so that their children can take advantage of the public school system.

But for a couple of days the litany of academic praise ends. Short sound bites and tiny paragraphs in local newspapers carry the unusual story of the boy's death. People talk about it. Then they stop talking about it. They return to their lives, and I return to unpacking.

IT HAS BEEN three weeks since Blanchard's suicide when all of the trains on the Caltrain line receive an emergency order to stop. Passenger cars in the night stagnate at points along their routes. The Santa Clara County coroner investigates what appears to be another body on the same length of tracks near Gunn High.

Reporting on the incident within hours of her death, media reveal that authorities have recovered Sonya Raymakers, a graduating senior preparing to attend NYU's prestigious theater program in the fall. The town is already beginning to speculate about her motivation. People point to the region's ethos of scholastic pressure, its common burden to achieve, its unspoken but understood dictum of success at any cost. They consider the effects of undiagnosed or undisclosed mental illness. They talk about copycat behavior.

Growing up, you heard about kids who died by suicide, but oftentimes these tragedies were isolated situations, happened behind closed doors, and remained private family affairs. These two events, however, took place in an unbelievably open fashion, practically forcing public outcry and reflection. I don't know much about the pathos of suicidal thinking, but I can't help but wonder if there is a connection between the two children. Then again, reading into these tragic moments might simply be an exercise in attempting to reason away the unreasonable.

Even as a relative newcomer to this community and stationed on the sidelines of grief, I find myself caught up in the shock. At the same time, the natural distance of my station grants me some perspective. I watch the town absorb the wave without it knowing quite what to make of its power or source. People in turn pivot to focus on everyday tribulations, relying on the trajectories of life as usual to steady them from the blow; no one can stand to have this glue mucking up the chambers of their heart.

And neither can I, frankly. I'm about to be a father. The most pressing personal issue at the moment is the nursery I have to build. I frame illustrations and hang the pictures from blue ribbon on the walls. Climb a stepladder and lock metal rings through heavy curtain fabric. Stand before sections of a white crib spread out on the floor like kindling, uncertain how to decipher the instructions or interpret how the pieces fit together.

Chapter 2

MIRROR/MIRROR

When my son is born, I wrap him in folds of a thin and gauzy blanket and place his warm body in the crook of my wife's arm, where he will remain, more often than not, for the next three months.

He is enamored with her. Endlessly stares into her face. Watches her eyes widen and her mouth turn out big expressions. He responds to her as though engaged in conversation, his own eyes opening wide, and his mouth mimicking her smile.

From our first moments, our understanding beyond the womb is dependent on our natural instinct to mirror. We are built to receive and perceive cues, to understand displays of happiness, fear, and sadness, and to create with others a harmony of movements. While writing *The Expression of the Emotions in Man and Animals*, Charles Darwin observed the collective makeup of human countenance. Despite age, ethnicity, and gender, people articulate the same state of mind as someone they observe. Every person is unique, and yet by way of a smile, a frown, a grimace, a wince, they hold universal commonality. Expressions cue recognition and activate in us similar empathetic responses. Remarkably, the mechanism for mirroring others takes place so fast and automatically it's nearly imperceptible.

The social psychologist Elaine Hatfield credits this to a kind of automatic attunement bred by a nonconscious imitator within each of us. We capitalize on moments during which the mind registers the tiniest flickers of expression from the world around it, activating a primal process of reflecting and aligning.

I watch my son, a face surrounded by folds of a moon-colored blanket, his eyes gray as old nickels. His brain is wired to register a kind of neural Wi-Fi, unconsciously picking up cues from other people. Through clusters of mirror neurons, the amygdala instantly reacts to prompts of facial expressions, creating a mental response that mimics what it believes it's seeing.

While we're left scratching our heads about why two children took their own lives, in watching this enthralling exchange between my son and his environment, I'm beginning to think that mirroring might be a large part of the puzzle. I'm now assembling a new science-based framework to help put recent events in context. It's built on a foundation of social contagions, or discrete infectious characteristics found within the makeup of the school and, perhaps, the town that feeds it.

Is it possible that the two students mirrored specific thoughts? The evolutionary biologist Richard Dawkins calls this particular kind of social contagion a *meme*: "When you plant a fertile meme in my mind you literally parasitize my brain, turning it into a vehicle for the [idea's] propagation in just the way that a virus may parasitize the genetic mechanism of a host cell." I find his virus parallel to be rather apt. Contagious thoughts mimic natural laws like those overseeing the mutation and transmission of germs. Under the right circumstances, corralled within perfect conditions, thoughts spread, catch, activate, and—through certain people—proliferate to others. Like biological viruses, which begin to amass abilities, interact with our bodies, and replicate along the way, thoughts begin with random cues, gestures that harm nothing, and interact with the psychological characteristics of the host. And while biological viruses are dependent on taking over a cell to work, thoughts implant in people and are absolutely dependent on taking over the mind.

In terms of how we unconsciously spread our thoughts to others, the scientists Nicholas Christakis at Yale University's Human Nature Lab and James Fowler at the University of California, San Diego, suggest that this particular kind of social contagion crosses the transom by relying on elaborate and complex relationship networks that "branch like lightning bolts, forming intricate patterns throughout human society." Which thoughts people mirror depend on the makeup of the community in which they exist. This is why certain groups of friends consider dissolving their marriages within two degrees of separation of another divorcing couple, why the stock market fluctuates on the suggestion of trouble, and why children struggle under the weight of outsized achievement expectations in school. In this case, maybe the two students from Gunn High caught ideas around achievement or failure.

Thinking about the work of French anthropologist Gustave Le Bon, I'm reminded that thoughts are not the only type of social contagion that exists. Influence runs deeper than ideas alone, and I find myself wondering how infectious *behaviors*, like those accompanying parenting trends or an exceedingly strong work ethic, might be behind the mystery of these two young students.

Le Bon proposes that the wisdom or dysfunction of those around us supersedes that of the individual. A person "immersed for some length of time in a crowd soon finds himself . . . in a special state, which much resembles the state of fascination in which the hypnotized individual finds himself in the hands of the hypnotizer," he writes. Standing close to others exposes us to all manner of behaviors, like impulsiveness, irritability, a lack of capacity to reason, the absence of judgment, and the exaggeration of sentiments that unyoke us from our own and more conventional social norms.

Given this, it isn't difficult to apply the psychology of contagious behavior to what's happening in Palo Alto. It's feasible, I suppose, that we're witnessing the result of hive mentality, a malady of toxic crowd-think and dangerous conduct. Kids wind up adopting the prevailing standards of those around them, an impetuous, unwelcome, and indiscriminating imitation, a mirroring of blind impulse. The more people there are who mirror a behavior within a particularly insular and dense community, the more these prominent features catch. The initiator's gender and age relative to the population matters. So does the personality of the observer, a ratio of extroversion to introversion, and one's natural response to the burden of conformity.

In addition to staggeringly contagious thoughts and behaviors, I also consider how *emotional* contagions might play into this situation, like feelings associated with personal expectations that spread and catch among peers. An automatic lockstep synchronization of countenance, body movement, language, and attitudes is responsible for emotion infection rates that hardly stop at just one-to-one spread. Emotions radiate outward like an atomic blast across groups of people, each member receiving and mirroring everything that accounts for the full spectrum of the human emotional experience.

Each one of these influences rings true, yet none of them perfectly matches the phenomenon at Gunn High. I—and the rest of Palo Alto—want to be able to point to one specific cause, but the more I investigate, the clearer it becomes that diagnosis will not be that simple. So, rather than look at each type of social contagion in isolation, I'm now left considering the possibility that we have witnessed the merging of highly communicable traits, catchable phenomena mixing together as a perfect storm, a "strange" contagion comprising many common phenomena silently passing between people.

Perhaps this is not the result of any one type of social contagion—thought, behavior, or emotion—but a terrifying consequence of *all of them together.*

Chapter 3

A PERFECT TEMPEST

I meet Roni Habib at a class for new fathers. Relying on a safety-in-numbers approach, we gravitate toward one another, becoming fast compatriots united in a struggle to learn how to swaddle, soothe, and diaper. Hearing his personal story over time, I come to find that hope is never far removed from his boyish face and his warm eyes. Habib carries himself with contentment and amiability, as well as a manner of brashness that instills confidence in his students at Gunn High. This is especially true whenever circumstances oblige him to relay troublesome news, as they do once again and for a third time in fewer than three months.

At the start of the new academic year, an incoming freshman named Catrina Holmes becomes another teenage fatality on the train tracks close to the school.

The following Sunday morning as we pack up after our parenting class, Habib divulges, "I don't know what to tell my econ students." Is he supposed to facilitate conversation about it, discourage rumination over it, or encourage his classes to put their heads down and carry on like nothing's wrong? "Between you and me, I can't stop thinking about it."

Like Habib, since Holmes's death I've found myself caught

in a kind of mental loop, too. As a new parent, it is far too easy to place myself in the shoes of grieving fathers. I imagine walking past an empty bedroom, and the unfathomable heartache residing within that emptiness. Whenever the local news radio station reports on Holmes's passing, I turn up the volume in my car in anticipation that someone has come forward with new information to share that will stop what seems to have become a deadly cycle. The experts repeat their refrain. The town, they say, is experiencing a suicide cluster—that place, time, and mental illness connect all three cases.

Alongside horror, these incidents admittedly stoke in me a kind of inquisitiveness, too. I'm familiar with Palo Alto's reputation for intellectualism, its wealth, and the promise it offers its children. All of these things make a cluster in this town seem all the more implausible. These kids have such bright futures to live for.

Visiting a Stanford University library while gathering research for another article, I find myself pulling up academic studies on suicide clusters instead. One of the more noteworthy instances I happen across is a case in 1984 in which a young Austrian businessman jumped in front of an oncoming Viennese subway. His behavior set into motion a string of copycat suicides at a rate of roughly five per week for nearly a year.

I run across the story of a pop singer named Yukiko Okada. Her 1986 suicide led to dozens of copycats in Japan, a phenomenon that became known as Yukiko syndrome. In another I read that, well before any of these scenarios, there was a famous Chinese silent film actress, Ruan Lingyu, who died by suicide in 1935, sparking a collective national grief so profound that three women killed themselves while participating in her funeral procession.

When the writer Johann Wolfgang von Goethe published

his novel *The Sorrows of Young Werther* in 1774, readers shot themselves in line with the actions of its protagonist. Two hundred years later, the sociologist David Phillips suggested that media exposure glamorizing a single suicide not only predicted additional deaths but also that they would take place in the same manner. You ran into the Werther effect, as Phillips called it, when vulnerable people mimicked graphic, detailed coverage surrounding the event. Each story has resulted from a kind of spontaneous mirroring effect within groups of people. The method of transmission looks familiar; it's the very thing that Elaine Hatfield, Richard Dawkins, and Gustave Le Bon were writing about, if not specifically about how to stop it from occurring.

Reading on, I'm glad to learn that communities have halted clusters before. To address the subway suicides in Austria, a prevention task force speculated that Vienna's oversaturated media attention was somehow transmitting deadly thoughts, behaviors, and emotions. Those who had never thought about completing suicide, let alone by jumping in front of subway cars, were unconsciously catching the idea and engaging in heretofore unthinkable actions. The theory went that the strange contagion event in Vienna was propagated by media exposure, and so, to stop it, the city needed to curb its coverage. The plan worked. Once publishers removed any mention of train deaths from the front pages, the rate of copycats dropped by 80 percent.

The curbing method so triumphantly stopped this mirroring that the US surgeon general and the Annenberg Public Policy Center created nonbinding guidelines on how media were to talk about suicide in a way that would not make it look viable or attractive to susceptible people. I learn from the Stanford archives that researchers from the university's Division of Child & Adolescent Psychiatry and Child Development are working with regional media to keep stories about the deaths by Gunn High students brief and off of the front pages. They are convincing editors to seek advice from prevention experts rather than pursue quotes from police or first responders. They are also encouraging reporters to refrain from describing fatalities in lurid detail.

These guidelines seem to be working, too. Every week that goes by without another incident supports the effectiveness of this curative method. The town picks up the pieces of a tragic summer, catches its breath, and makes the motions of carrying on until the motions feel somewhat genuine.

THE RAINY SEASON is upon us when a sixteen-year-old named William Dickens becomes the fourth train fatality from Gunn High. I slow my car a couple of blocks away from my apartment and turn off the radio after the report finishes airing.

This isn't like Vienna.

The standard media cure method isn't working in Palo Alto. By tempering their coverage, Austria's media stopped the localized suicide cluster; despite adhering to the same media standards at home, children from Gunn High are still taking their lives. The strange contagion in Palo Alto proves itself utterly unique and scary as hell. Where I initially found examples in the archives that comforted me—communities that experienced and stopped suicide clusters—that logic doesn't seem to hold true here and I don't understand why.

So I return to the science, hunting for deeper insight. I pull studies by social psychologists like Peter Totterdell, Albert Bandura, Peter Salovey, and John D. Mayer. Their work begins to create for me an unusual picture: Palo Alto is unique. The search for a cause is developing into a hunt for the specific conditions amalgamating in a particular time and place, a fusion of environment, temperature, mutation, and host. Maybe it's the town's particular brand of stress or, as some suggest, its teaching philosophies, its rumored "Tiger mom" culture emphasizing high levels of academic achievement, or the result of dozens or more qualities unique to this place and coming together within the rage of a perfect tempest.

In the eye of this storm exists Gunn High, an otherwise self-contained system relatively spared from crime and violence. The most affluent families in the country populate the neighborhoods within the school district's boundaries. Parents of Gunn High students work at nearby Hewlett Packard, NASA's Ames Research Center, Facebook, Tesla Motors, Google, and Stanford University. More than a third of these households have a family member who has earned a higher degree. In this striking setting, none of the usual explanations or preventative measures for this horror apply. For instance, the greatest frequency of teenage suicide in the world is a consequence of living in troubled inner cities and some of the poorest places, while Palo Alto remains among the wealthiest. Obviously, responsible media coverage hasn't stopped the cluster. Neither has the school's implementation of preventative safety measures, like supplemental on-site therapists. Nothing about this population points to the unlikely formation of a suicide cluster within it, and yet the death toll continues to climb.

I want to know why.

AT GUNN HIGH, Roni Habib has also been hunting for answers. He searches for the reasons that are leading young people from his school to take their lives. One day after our last parenting class, he and I stop for breakfast together. For a while, we sit at a small table on the patio at Printers Cafe in the late morning sunlight. Just beyond the roundabout a block up the street, a

Caltrain whooshes past with a couple of blasts of its horn. Everyone in Silicon Valley recognizes that high-pitched, pained, and elongated detonation of sound.

Many of the students who died over the summer and fall have passed through Habib's economics class at one time or another. I ask him how the rest of the students are faring at the high school. Hard to tell, he says. Obviously they're scared and sad, but they're also guarded. Maybe too guarded. Stoic, even.

His stare grows distant as he says this, and his voice softens a little. Each death finds him questioning whether he might have been able to do anything more to identify trouble or stop it from transpiring. He knows this school system, knows these kids, knows the breed of students Gunn High cultivates—both from the perspective of a teacher and as a onetime student. Before becoming an educator, back when he was an underclassman at Gunn High, he and his friends talked about modeling the path of Silicon Valley tech legends. They were going to become engineers, make their fortunes, and retire young. Unfortunately, Habib was a terrible engineer, couldn't figure out coding, hated the math, and was unfulfilled by the undertakings of life in front of a computer monitor. While his friends went on to work for start-ups and launch tech companies, he fell into teaching. Education suited him much better than tech anyway. It doesn't hurt that his height, a looming six-foot-three, and the gravity of his voice, tinged with its Israeli lilt, provides him with effortless classroom authority. At thirty, he easily negotiates the river between students and teachers. More than most people, he feels he's in a position to notice a young person's distress, yet he's registered none of the signs.

He remembers his students fondly to me. Jean-Paul Blanchard was popular, smart, and well loved. He had a pretty girlfriend. "He was the last person anyone suspected of harboring suicidal thoughts," he says, weary and uncertain. Sonya Raymakers was the theater department's head designer and sort of a mother hen to the drama kids. She even babysat some of the faculty's own children. Catrina Holmes hadn't matriculated into Gunn High yet, so Habib hadn't had her in his class. William Dickens he describes as a sweet boy, athletic, a star on the swim team.

"It's gotten bad," he sighs. "People are scared for their kids. Naturally, everyone's pointing fingers." The resonance and pitch of disparate accusations against the school administration is beginning to overshadow Gunn High's sterling academic character, its placement among the top 1 percent of public high schools in the country. Personally, he doesn't think the school or overarching academic protocols are behind the cluster. As for what's actually behind it, underneath it, operating inside it, he honestly doesn't know. And despite all of the expert research and statistics pointing to possible or even likely explanations, he suspects the truth is that in this case *nobody* knows.

But he's building a theory.

Chapter 4

A PARTICULAR PREDILECTION
FOR CATCHING

Habib ends breakfast with an invitation to visit him at Gunn High. I take him up on his offer in late January 2010. We are sitting now in Habib's simple office in Gunn High's administration building. It's lacking in legroom and walking space, and the air smells like old carpet. I wonder if he worries, as I do, for his own newborn son. "I know this sounds like science fiction," I start, "but do you think our kids can catch whatever's going around?"

And it does sound strange, the supposition coming out of my mouth, as though factors beyond our control could really have so much sway in dictating how we act, think, and feel. Still, all we have are facts and the conclusions we try to draw from them.

The facts now include another name. A week earlier, county authorities recovered the body of a nineteen-year-old recent Gunn High graduate named Brian Bennion Taylor on the train tracks, 150 yards north of the crossing where four other students have already taken their lives since last May. He had been a varsity wrestler and tennis player and the recipient of a presidential service award. He was also nominated to be the senior home-coming prince.

If five well-off and seemingly adjusted all-American kids walked in front of trains, then what says *our* all-American kids aren't going to be subject to whatever forces shaped that decision? Then again, just because a few people died by suicide doesn't mean that every child is subject to the stimuli that promote such extremes. Logically, it's unlikely our children, many years from now, will mimic this behavior. Yet, when it comes to suicide, rationality plays no part.

"I don't think so," Habib says, hesitantly. "I hope not, anyway."

He has spread his lunch out on a brown paper bag before him on a vintage teacher's desk that makes this room feel more dated than any other part of the school I've seen so far.

"Then again," he muses, biting into his cheese sandwich, "Silicon Valley's particularly adept at making things catch."

HABIB'S THEORY INTRIGUES me. Making things catch takes artistry. It involves a balance of substance, precise timing, a favorable environment, and a bit of theater. To Habib's point, Silicon Valley exists to scale great products. Its track record remains unmatched. The Audion vacuum tube, audio oscillators, personal satellites, premium electric vehicles, social media and smartphones, the popularizing of thirty-dollar hoodies and work attire of denim and T-shirt cotton—all of these things have caught. Traits that define the way Silicon Valley works, that make innovation more possible—thinking big, creating transparency, developing the peer-to-peer sharing economy of Uber and Airbnb—these things, too, have caught.

Silicon Valley is also responsible for producing the deaths of five young people in six months. As for reasons why—*why* here and *why* now—there are seemingly no points to hear that people haven't already made dozens of times. They say that the suicide cluster is the result of symptoms of this unique culture of wealth in a community built of innovation-driven economics. Or a malady of an obscenely ambitious work ethic. Or the bug inherent in new technology that allows media to stoke the spread of bad ideas. Some say it's the toxicity of a frenzy effect. The pestilence of irrational hysteria. The infection of bad attitudes. A side effect of the kind of leaders we model. Others put forward it's the fever of parental expectation and personal determination. The petri dish of American acculturation taken to its extreme. A plague of extreme anxiety and depression the likes of which few have seen before.

Of course *each* of these thoughts, behaviors, and emotions is a contagious phenomenon, and there's no reason to believe that some if not all of them are culprits in creating this strange contagion event. If Silicon Valley is better than other places at making things catch, maybe, says Habib, the same mechanisms are behind the cluster. As to what those mechanisms are, we talk about an element of unconscious attunement at play here that has always served the region well. This very insight allows Silicon Valley companies to innovate, read market demand, and oftentimes exceed it better than almost anyone else.

Meanwhile, the train passes through Silicon Valley, and the suicide rate in the town of Palo Alto, caught in this seemingly endless loop, is on its way to rocketing five times beyond the national ten-year figures.

After lunch, Habib takes me on a tour. I fall for the campus immediately. The buildings of Gunn High, trim the color of jasper, roof of faded shale, are separated by walkways open to the sky, to the fog moving across smoky-green trees, to the traffic sounds off of Foothill Expressway. The school merges so perfectly with the hinterlands, the surrounding flat houses built cheaply, as was the sensibility of their 1950s construction when energy was inexpensive and copper was in short supply, then updated over the years with state-of-the-art accoutrements.

We lean against a short retaining wall in one of the concrete quads. From there, we watch masses of kids fill every open space, some in large roving huddles, others walking alone, heads down, feet working fast to get to their classes on time. There are so many things that neither Habib nor I want to acknowledge. Our natural response is to pretend that everything will be fine, to ignore the worry and the risk and to believe things will work out, because this town is all about solving seemingly unworkable problems. And it will figure this one out as well.

Despite this faith, I feel the great weight of regret bare down on my chest as the students move across the campus. Beyond my journalist's penchant for analysis, I personally need to understand if there's a solution, an aspect of this monster we just aren't seeing yet that might clue us in to its vulnerability. I want to know that these students are going to be safe. I want to protect my son.

If Habib thinks about the five deaths for too long, the self-assuredness in his eyes fades, his stare grows distant, and his lips tighten. While he's not clear what's causing his students to harm themselves, he does believe the situation is a creature of Silicon Valley's own making, a golem constructed out of the region's best and worst qualities. It recalls for me the writing of Anne McWhir, who scrutinizes the manner in which the author Mary Shelley fashions a creature of resurrected flesh and organs and bones, a train wreck of disparate bodies connected as a whole, and whose knowledge of the world comes by "reiterating" and "replicating" the behaviors around it. "In the process [the monster] may teach us something . . . about our own situation as teachers and as students."

Above all, if children acquire their knowledge by reflecting the world around them, then unconscious mirroring is how we learn to be human, how we learn to live. What kinds of examples are we setting?

THE UNCONSCIOUS IS the realm in which all of the elements that make up this strange contagion event operate, under the surface, just beyond our awareness. Each component soundlessly shuffles from person to person and spreads at exponential rates with chilling and extraordinary consequences. The unconscious is also perhaps the most divisive and revolutionary theoretical concept since the Babylonians added zero to the Sumerian counting system.

Unconscious mirroring is much more than intuition, instinct, or even sympathy, which are based on what we speculate others might be experiencing. Rather, social contagions are perfect emulations of others' thoughts, behaviors, and emotions. It's the difference between empathizing with a friend's feelings of joy, and actually experiencing the same sensation of warmth, an accelerated heart rate, and a release of endorphins ourselves. Yet I find the most fascinating, and at once the most unsettling, part to be that we have no idea we've caught these experiences, or that they are running our lives in the background like a computer's operating system.

The unconscious suggests a separation between awareness and a far more powerful process that runs in the shadows. The unconscious is automatic. It's instinctual. It provides insight into almost everything we do and everything we believe we know about the world. It is the oldest knowledge our minds possess, a vast and mysterious collection of memory. "What we find is that our brains have colossal things happening in them all the time . . . ," writes the neuroscientist David Eagleman. "Most of what we do and think and feel is not under our conscious control." Maintaining the conscious self, he explains, is vital but merely a fraction of the mind's responsibilities. Instead, it focuses much of its energy on monitoring our inner lives.

Yet a rich history exists between the invisible, unknowable unconscious and those trying at once to define and to access it. Early characters in the narrative of modern psychology, such as the physician and physiologist Wilhelm Wundt, believed that the mind perceives its own processes. But the late-nineteenth-century physicist Hermann von Helmholtz championed the theory that the brain is more than meets the mind's eye. Consider how the theater lulls its audience into a trance of false perception, how it convinces the mind that characters on the stage are real, how its representations induce in us genuine weeping and laughter. This separate and unknowable part of the knowing brain, he claimed, was the work of the unconscious. When Sigmund Freud created a topographic map of this ancient edifice, he further delineated the conscious, the unconscious, and the preconscious to justify how the mind operates outside of its own grasp. Salvador Dalí and Max Ernst claimed to have tapped the unconscious in order to create surreal and odd biomorphic dreamscapes of cracked eggs, insect carapaces, headless bodies, and disturbances in nature. John F. Kihlstrom at the University of California, Berkeley, and other explorers of the unconscious mind now suggest that subliminal perception, implicit memory, and hypnosis can access it.

The unconscious, contend some, thinks only in the present. Others suggest its lens lacks the sensitivity to distinguish the line between fiction and reality. Still others define the unconscious as a monitoring system, the National Security Agency of our inner world that observes every experience we have and records even while we sleep, or as a guidance system, an enhanced GPS that feeds us maps and also tells us where to go.

And now there are those who suggest it is the reason why five kids from a rich suburb in Northern California jumped in front of oncoming trains: social contagions of desperate ideas, fatal behaviors, and diverse emotions tapped the unconscious through subtle cues and neurological triggers.

All of this leads to an inescapable understanding that there's certainly more beneath the surface feeding this strange contagion. Perhaps, I figure, the unconscious has a role to play in stopping it as well.

Chapter 5

A QUEST IN FARNEST

Not long after my visit to Gunn High, I place a call to Yale University. The Human Nature Lab there has taken the lead in making some of the most significant findings on social contagions to date. Nicholas Christakis, the lab's director, entrenches himself in the study of the interplay between them and the people they infect.

It's difficult to quantify how much of what we do is achieved by our own volition versus what we unknowingly pick up from others, he tells me, his voice low and steady. We can't comprehend, for instance, the number of social contagions we pick up in a given day, let alone across a life span. Notwithstanding, the outcome of Christakis's decades of research shows that social contagions are so powerful that they shape the landscape of every domain of our lives. And this hidden system of influence, he says, connects us all.

Along with his collaborator James Fowler, Christakis suggests in a wide-ranging report on networks and human behavior that thoughts, behaviors, and emotions have *flow*. Their influence spreads beyond a single person to affect many others within relative proximity to one another. Using observational regression-based models and actual experiments, they have proven not only that social contagions happen but also how they happen, influencing everything from voting behavior to public health interventions.

For instance, in one experiment they mapped hundreds of village households in Honduras and discovered a connection between those who tangentially observe violence and those who go on to perpetrate it themselves. In another experiment, they identified seventy-five villages in rural India and delineated the specific types of social influence that led communities to adopt the use of hygienic latrines. Through these and other cases, they've also shown that peer effect and interpersonal influence spread kindness, alcohol addiction, loneliness, and even political mobilization.

"What we know about the connectedness of people on the planet would suggest a kind of global influence of a single individual that seems very implausible," they observe in their study of social networks and human behavior. Yet the phenomenon is far more plausible, and common, than we often realize, Christakis tells me today. Some lead to negative consequences. Others are incredibly beneficial for us. One social contagion causes people to "catch" smoking. Another allows people to unconsciously catch cooperation. There are others still that manipulate economic growth and personal wealth. Most important, social contagions afford people immense power over others. This includes the ability of a person to project, and of others to catch, qualities that, in some, counter that supreme instinct to survive.

I know that exposure to suicide alone does not make the act of taking one's life spread. Psychiatrists have alluded to the contributions of environment and personal temperament as other potential factors. They've also implicated treatable mental health issues and cultural communication barriers. When one takes into account the added influence of interacting thoughts, behaviors, and moods flowing across personal networks, one begins to witness a cascade of mounting factors that can become crushing.

Despite the dangers inherent in some social contagions, Christakis has learned to recognize all of them as connectors of life rather than the erosion of it. Citing the universities of Yale, Harvard, and Pennsylvania, he reminds me that happiness connects people by up to three degrees of separation, and that a sad acquaintance doubles our chances of becoming unhappy ourselves. Secondhand stress connects first responders to victims. Psychologists share the nightmares of the Holocaust survivors they treat. Post-traumatic stress disorder cascades across no fewer than three generations, connecting people to a single event by more than a century. In the workplace, stamina connects employees in collaboration efforts and alliance building. Social contagions among members of sports teams connect players in camaraderie and bring about better game results.

I consider this deluge of information, adding each fragment of imparted knowledge to the stockpile I've been amassing since last summer. My eyes slide over a question I've jotted in the margin of my yellow notepad.

I ask Christakis outright if Silicon Valley has, with its unique proficiency at producing things that catch, the ability to create a cure to help Palo Alto defend itself against this unprecedented strange contagion event.

He reflects on this for a moment. He doesn't have a definitive answer, though. Instead, he tells me that the best evidence he's seen suggests there's a chance, and that it is certainly a question worth exploring.

As a kind of structure for this exploration, he encourages me to look at other strange contagions outside of Palo Alto and examine the ways in which people have caught, contained, and treated events in the past. Somewhere, someone has asked the same questions I'm asking. Somewhere, others have struggled with strange contagions. Somewhere, people have grappled with them and have found solutions.

Part II

THE PERFECT MODEL

"Children have never been very good at listening to their elders, but they have never failed to imitate them."

—JAMES BALDWIN

Chapter 6

HOW TO START A CONTAGION

The international code for London leads to a busy signal and then to a wrong number. Finally, after a series of electronic beeps, a delicate and bookish voice answers the line. I feel capricious and hesitant knowing I've connected with the British psychologist Gerald Russell, who started one of the most significant strange contagion events in history: bulimia.

Christakis had suggested that I reach out to him, and it doesn't take me long to understand why. Like our own strange contagion, Russell's involved young people, accusations of parental pressure, and problems with media exposure. Like Palo Alto's strange contagion, an eating disorder comprises many different social contagions. Oxford University identified eating disorders as one part idea contagion, proliferating thoughts and skewed beliefs about body image and perfectionism. Bard College found that they are also one part behavioral contagion: they spread the act of starvation and nutrient depletion. The University of Minnesota described eating disorders as one part emotional contagion, spreading feelings of helplessness, hopelessness, anxiety, and depression.

For a while, Russell and I speak about the nature of eating disorders and the unique portal to history they offer. Triangulating regions, trends, and cultures, he takes me back to 700 BC, when wealthy Romans facilitated endless feasting with occasional purging. In eastern deserts, ancient Egyptians expunged their bellies to avoid illness. In China, dynasties practiced dangerous food restriction. The path leads to the plains of Africa, where tribes dieted to the point of near starvation. Arriving at the sixteenth century, women plagued with wasting disease were burned at the stake. Throughout history, the transmission of eating disorders was often tied to religious and cultural extremes. Pious European women during the Renaissance limited their food intake to reach a higher plane of spirituality. As the cultural rebirth came to an end in the late seventeenth century, physicians and psychiatrists recorded an uptick in young women who appeared as "skeletons clad with skin." Two centuries later, researchers suggested anorexia was the result of hormone imbalances, endocrine deficiencies, tuberculosis, or a pituitary issue called Simmonds' disease. Presenting at the Clinical Society of London in October of 1873, Sir William Gull said that eating disorders primarily affected women with dysfunctional families, a position that by 1930 evolved to combine emotional, biological, and cultural components.

"That's where I stepped in," says Russell with jovial heft. In 1972 a woman checked into London's Royal Free Hospital to be treated for anorexia. "I found her symptoms to be unique. They didn't match the diagnostic criteria for anorexia at all." Unlike his emaciated patients with sallow skin and big eyes, Russell's new patient was of average weight. Her face was full. Her cheeks were pink as the skin of an onion.

She was the first of roughly thirty instances of this unusual condition that crossed the threshold of his clinic over the next seven years. Each person presented with perplexing purging behaviors secondary to binge eating. Russell wasn't dealing with anorexia nervosa, he realized, but something as yet undefined by psychology or medicine. In fact, he had stumbled upon a condition that science had yet to see in large numbers or identify at any time in the long history of eating disorders. *Psychological Medicine* published Russell's ensuing paper on these unusual cases. In it he described the key features of this novel mental illness he was now referring to as bulimia nervosa. Many in the scientific community objected to Russell's conclusions, pointing to the limited and problematic sample size he'd used. At the time, however, there were simply too few cases for Russell to draw from. The pool in the 1970s was just too small.

As bulimia gained further diagnostic legitimacy in 1980 with its inclusion in the third edition of the *Diagnostic and Statistical Manual of Mental Disorders*, Russell ruefully tracked its unexpectedly swift spread across Europe and North America, where it infiltrated college campuses, affecting 15 percent of female students in sororities, all-women dormitories, and female collegiate sports teams. The disease moved through the halls of American high schools, where binging, fasting, diet pill use, and other eating disorder symptoms easily clustered. He chased its dispersion across Egypt, where the number of new cases grew to 400,000. In Canada, it swelled to 600,000. In Russia, 800,000. In India, 6 million. In China, 7 million. In the UK, one out of every one hundred women was now developing the disorder.

"It makes you wonder if maybe bulimia wasn't a new eating disorder, that it was always there and people just didn't notice it or talk about it before your paper came out," I offer.

Russell demurs politely. If the hidden afflicted numbered as overwhelmingly high as they now seem, surely the condition would have made itself known well before he—or anyone, for that matter—identified it. "You might suggest it required somebody to come along and put two and two together before people felt safe talking about bulimia, but I don't believe that. Until then, the disorder was extremely rare. But after 1980 it became widespread in a very short period of time. Once it was described, and I take full responsibility for that with my paper, there was a common language for it," he says. "And knowledge spreads very quickly."

With this knowledge, Russell's discovery took on characteristics of a pandemic that was set to claim 30 million people, but neither he nor anyone could do a thing at that point to stop it. He was confronted, he says, by a problem of entropy, a gradual decline into disorder with devastating implications for social contagions: once they are out, they are virtually impossible to rein back in again.

Even so, a single academic journal article and a mention in a dense diagnostic manual read mostly by psychology professionals doesn't quite explain to me how bulimia leapt from a few isolated cases to infect people across the globe. Russell agrees: we are missing a critical connection between academia and everyone else.

Following the debut of bulimia nervosa in the *DSM-III*, the University of Chicago put out a press release publicizing its own rather novel data on a kind of sequela of anorexia. *Mademoiselle* and *Better Homes and Gardens*, among other popular women's magazines, took the press release and described the effects of a new "binge-purge syndrome" making inroads into American culture. With Russell's data proliferating among diagnosticians, and the term itself entering the lexicon through trendy magazines with wide distributions, cases of bulimia rose steeply. Once people realized they were able to eat whatever they wanted and as much as they wanted without a weight consequence, binging and purging became the new strategy for weight management. It was no coincidence that these unhealthy and harmful behaviors took hold at the same time that obesity—which Christakis and Fowler have found to be as contagious as any eating disorder—doubled in the US.

The theory of media's culpability in the spread of social contagions is not a new one. Psychologists studying the developmental psychopathology of eating disorders have led dozens of controlled experiments finding a near-perfect link between mass media and eating disorder symptoms. The question in my mind now isn't whether media have a part to play in replicating social contagions; if we were able to purge ourselves of certain conduits of influence like media itself, we might have an easier time stopping transmission. Rather, I question just how big a part media actually play in spreading them.

To answer that, Russell refers to an exceptional case that transpired in the Republic of Fiji. By the mid-1990s, he says, bulimia was rampant across industrialized parts of the world, but not so much in developing countries. The Harvard Medical School associate professor Anne E. Becker figured that cultural context likely accounted for this barrier to transmission. To test her theory, she sought out a place completely isolated from Western influence. In all of Fiji's history, the republic had yet to report a single case of someone suffering from an eating disorder. That all changed in 1995.

"What happened in 1995?" I ask Russell.

Melrose Place, he says. *Xena: Warrior Princess. Beverly Hills, 90210.*

"That was the year the first television arrived to the island republic."

After just three years of exposure to shows like *Seinfeld* and *ER*, 11 percent of Fiji's adolescent girls admitted to Becker that they had purged their food at least once to lose weight. In that time, the risk of developing an eating disorder jumped from 13 percent to 29 percent. More than 80 percent revealed that television influenced them or their friends to be more conscious about body shape or weight. By 2007, 45 percent of girls from the main island reported purging their food.

Becker also found that the effect of media exposure went beyond eating disorders. She recorded an increase in personal ambition based on certain characters that viewers watched on television. In one of her studies, 80 percent of the girls said they planned to eschew traditional agrarian jobs for professional careers, specifically those that only wanted thin women. The republic also experienced a rise in the social contagion of emotional strain among teenage girls. Fiji's society was changing quickly, and psychological problems accompanied these massive cultural shifts as media transmissions carried along even more social contagions.

All of this seems like an awful lot of blame to heft onto mass communication, I comment. Is the answer to understanding and stopping the spread of social contagions really as simple as curbing media and their messages? And if so, why hasn't it worked for curbing the strange contagion event in Palo Alto?

"As that very elegant Fiji study by my American colleague found, media matters. But the truth often requires us to dig a bit further," Russell replies, then remarks, with a bit of cunning, "Of course it's not about media. It's about *awareness*."

Chapter 7

STUMBLING UPON A CURE AND
ITS UNINTENDED CONSEQUENCE

The writer Johann Wolfgang von Goethe writes that in nature we never see anything in isolation but everything in connection with something else, which is before it, beside it, under it, and over it. It is a growing awareness of these connections that has me thinking quite a bit about the stark picture Gerald Russell painted of strange contagion events, illustrating the way a little exposure can lead to large effects like a global pandemic of bulimia. I'm finding it difficult to comprehend the full deleterious influence of awareness. Russell has explained that we acquire eating habits by watching characters on television, by noticing the way our friends eat or the images they post online, and by unconsciously registering subtle cues in the culture itself. I can accept that exposure creates opportunity for the spread of social contagions, but how then does one defend against *awareness*? You can't go through life closing your eyes and shutting your ears.

In the case of five teenagers jumping in front of trains, I see Palo Alto trying to defend against awareness. In the beginning, students tied memorial ribbons to wire gates. Affixed hand-scrawled messages on folded sheets of paper to the wooden sides of school buildings. Wove bunches of wildflowers into chain-link fences around the baseball field. Drew memorials to their friends in thick chalk lines on campus walkways. Penned essays and published op-eds about the classmates they've lost. But mental health experts were quick to point out that acknowledging the suicides risked passing the seed of influence on to others. Commemorations threatened to turn the dead into martyrs and activate in some a desire to achieve the same attention. It seems absurd, but the more we make people aware of the problem, the more we expose others to it. Talking about the suicides is dangerous. If awareness is the biggest vector for a social contagion, a lack of awareness should stop it. And yet, at this suggestion, there's a tickle in the back of my head, the cynic eager to get out: to say nothing of strange contagion events like bulimia or the suicide cluster is to simply ignore a problem, and problems like these typically don't go away on their own.

Following my chat with Russell, I seek out a copy of a dissertation written in the early eighties that includes one of the first-ever references to a condition resembling bulimia, as well as an effective treatment for it. The author is the psychologist Deborah Brenner-Liss. She used to work at an eating disorder clinic in New York and is now running a small private practice in San Francisco.

Brenner-Liss's office is big and bright and staged like the studio set of a television show about a psychologist, with a plush sofa and big armchairs deliberately placed to provoke a conversation, a divulging, a confession. She is lean, with a small chin, pronounced cheeks, and slender shoulders. The lines in the skin of her face run deep.

She recounts a now-familiar story of bulimia's genesis and its spread, along with her own exploration of the early literature on binging and purging. Like Russell and Becker, Brenner-Liss found that once the condition started appearing in the media, it spread unrestrained. "Our intentions as researchers and practitioners fighting bulimia were good," she emphasizes. "We wanted to get the word out about it to help professionals understand that this exists, and to rally to find effective ways to treat it." That was the task: to find a way to halt the spread.

As Brenner-Liss speaks to me about the early attempts to stop bulimia, it calls to mind the story of Marseille, France, in 1720, when the merchant ship the *Grand-Saint-Antoine* arrived to port with freights of foreign silks and cottons and the body of a Turkish passenger who perished by bubonic plague. Once moored, the ship hoisted a bright yellow flag. Today it's known as a yellow jack. Ships raise the banner to alert passersby that the vessel is under disease quarantine. Despite confinement, however, within days new cases of plague inundated hospitals and killed thousands of locals. To contain the spread and warn incoming ships of peril, the port raised more bright yellow flags along the waterfront's docks, piers, and cargo platforms. They fluttered on the Mediterranean wind atop masts of fishing vessels and trade ships. The maritime basin was soon awash in yellow. Still the plague spread as though it rode on the very breeze that stirred them. Believing it moved through heavy vapors, the town stoked perpetual fires to cleanse the air. People sniffed herbs and dosed themselves with paste made from drugs crushed, mixed, and doused in honey. These desperate attempts to counteract the deadly effects of the invisible illness failed to contain it, and so the people of Marseille erected a wall of stone across the countryside and purged the town of its sick. They would hold off the contagion by depriving it of hosts and starving it out of existence. But the wall of Marseille ultimately failed, too. Instead of purging the illness from the town, the protective wall trapped people inside with infected fleas and rats, the true vectors of the illness. Within the quarantined district, 50,000 people contracted the *Yersinia pestis* bacterium and died.

Thankfully, we're more familiar with the causes and methods for the spread of communicable disease than we were in the eighteenth century. Unlike the plague, however, catching an eating disorder has nothing to do with microbes, and we need something more creative than antibiotics to stop it. As Brenner-Liss describes desperate measures to find a treatment for bulimia, she relates some harrowing facts. For instance, today 60 percent of people who receive treatment for eating disorders recover, sustaining a healthy weight and normal diet, she tells me. Another 20 percent make partial recoveries. Brenner-Liss is among them; as Gerald Russell was writing about an ominous variant of anorexia and the University of Chicago was putting out press releases, she was one of the first Americans to both develop the symptoms of bulimia and the earliest to receive treatment for them.

I joke with her that in Silicon Valley we call the people who first try new technology *early adopters*. "That's what I am, then," she says, giving me a fleeting, jaunty look from her sofa chair, the white collar of her blouse riding high up on her neck. She's an alpha user. A beta tester. A pioneer of early cures designed to stop a strange contagion event.

She speaks with me about her earliest experiences with compulsive overeating and purging, as well as finally encountering a successful treatment. Her personal story tracks remarkably well to the cultural fulcrum toward perfect models, *Playboy* centerfolds, beauty pageant contestants, and television actresses, as well as the rise of diet products in the seventies and eighties that perpetuated the desire and means to achieve these looks. Not only did the media come to glorify a slender ideal, they also emphasized its importance, and the importance of appearances in general that went into shaping identity, gender roles, values, and beliefs. To treat this perfect storm of catchable body image standards, openness to restrictive eating behaviors, and feelings of despair, pugilists of this pandemic would, in due course, introduce prosocial media campaigns to reinforce healthy body weight, antidepressants, and evidence-based psychotherapies.

In the early days, however, with very few options for treatment available to her, Brenner-Liss sought out support groups, meetings of eight or ten people who exhibited similarly unique eating behaviors as her own. Some members of these groups exercised obsessively. Others dosed their bodies with laxatives. Many presented with chipped teeth, eroded stomach linings, brittle hair. Despite their symptoms, what connected them all was a purposeful act of engaging in that most delicate of equations, seeking the balance between consumption and depletion, impulse and restraint.

"Whatever it was we were doing in those living rooms, I suddenly found I was starting to get better," she reveals. The curious curative nature of these support groups went well beyond talking, relating personal experiences, and offering empathy. There was something about being in the presence of others who were trying to eat healthfully and also engaging in nourishing activities that began influencing healthy behaviors in her. These tightly knit, highly influential social networks fostered her motivation for positive behavior changes and stoked the stamina in her to stay in the fight.

In other words, she says, members of her support group, by virtue of simply attending the meetings, were *catching healthier eating behaviors* from each other, along with motivation, resilience, and hope by way of observation and unconscious mirroring. Although they didn't know it at the time, members of

Brenner-Liss's support group were combating the social contagions contributing to bulimia with *other* social contagions.

I consider the idea that perhaps we can do the same in Palo
Alto. Assuming we can identify which social contagions are in
the mix, we can use helpful ones to counteract those contributing to the rise in suicide.

Support groups would go on to gain popularity in the eighties in greater numbers than ever before, as researchers at the
University of Illinois found empirical evidence reinforcing what
might be considered their contagious benefits. As a practicing
psychologist today, Brenner-Liss has incorporated group therapy and peer support networks into treatment for her own patients with eating disorders, with great success. "What I've been
able to do with our groups is to subtly invite healthy competition toward recovery," she tells me. Social contagions work in
their favor.

And yet, I've come across an impassable contradiction.
To a layperson, this sounds a lot like exchanging one idea for
another—simple enough. But all of this creates a very different
portrait about the connection between exposure, knowledge,
and cures from the one Gerald Russell presented me. I explain
Russell's theory of awareness to Brenner-Liss, how he believes
that even unconscious exposure to an idea, a behavior, and an
emotion spreads them. No matter how recovery-focused one
keeps support groups, sometimes an *unhealthy* competition
erupts, he said. For every person whom support groups cure,
others leave group therapy after having developed worse symptoms than those they had when they entered it. Bulimia is so
contagious that support groups and in-treatment facilities designed to help patients are also primary spreading agents.

Further inquiry only seems to justify Russell's troubling
conclusion. In 2004, Great Britain's National Centre for Eating

Disorders reported that inpatient treatment and specialist units serve to create opportunities for exposure to the worst cases, allowing participants to catch more severe eating disorder symptoms, dangerous behavioral modeling, and harmful attitudes toward treatment that perpetuate well beyond the formal group therapy. Peeling back the processes even further, the psychiatrist Walter Vandereycken examined ethnographic reports and qualitative investigations to find that sitting within close range of others exposes people to the worst cases and leads patients to unintentionally contend for the worst symptoms. Treatment, he reported, can do more damage than good by allowing the harsher and crueler strain to jump to new hosts.

Where Gerald Russell finds a threat in exposure, Brenner-Liss finds healing and a road to the remission of symptoms. Are media and group exposure vectors for spread, I continue to wonder, or are they vectors for treatment?

"Maybe it's a little of both," she offers. The same processes of mirroring and unconscious competition that allow people to encode dangerous thoughts, behaviors, and feelings from others might just be the very same that spread beneficial social contagions.

"Then what tips the scale?"

"Personal susceptibility. Environment. The unknown." She shrugs her shoulders.

Riding the train home later that afternoon, I organize the frayed threads of new information into my evolving model to try to best explain the strange contagion at home. I mull over the mechanisms that allow unique people to share universal expressions and similar empathetic responses to one another. Automatic attunement guides us to unintentional mirroring of thoughts, behaviors, and feelings, phenomena that share a language perceptible on a level of the invisible, unknowable unconscious. I consider the findings of Brenner-Liss, who, like others, trusts that awareness is a vessel for treatment and cure. Yet, as Russell and Baker discovered, awareness will exacerbate a strange contagion event the same way that spreading knowledge about bulimia helped to triple the frequency of new cases in ten- to thirty-nine-year-old females between the late 1980s and early 1990s. The rate dipped a bit as treatment caught up with the illness, but the number rose steeply again in 1992, shortly after Princess Diana publically disclosed her battle with bulimia. Her revelation brought tremendous awareness to the condition. It corresponded both with an uptick in people seeking treatment for the first time as well as an explosion of new cases as the strange contagion spread further than ever.

Christakis was right: this scenario, this conceptual template to help guide my investigation, is a perfect model to compare with ours and to help me understand the kind of dynamic we're facing. But I've come away conflicted. Looking at contagious eating disorders has shown me that strange contagion events are far more nuanced and complicated than I expected at first. Stopping a social contagion sometimes means using tools of remission and transmission, exploiting a cure that also spreads the disease. Ultimately, it's a numbers game: you save some, lose others, and hope against hope that in the end we come out ahead.

Part III

THE FRENZIED

"I suppose I have found it easier to identify with the characters who verge upon hysteria, who were frightened of life, who were desperate to reach out to another person. . . ."

—TENNESSEE WILLIAMS

"We find that whole communities suddenly fix their minds upon one object and go mad in its pursuit; that millions of people become simultaneously impressed with one delusion, and run after it, till their attention is caught by some new folly more captivating than the first."

—CHARLES MACKAY

Chapter 8

A DILEMMA OF CONTAGION

An outbreak is imminent.

My son is now six months old. I've started dropping him off in the mornings at Google's infant center, near my wife's office and just off of the search giant's Mountain View campus. The playroom is set within a capacious space fashioned with meshed canopies for shade, dozens of organic gardens, and kitchens stocked with all-natural foods. The playroom is lined with baskets of fruit plucked from the center's orchards, and natural wood toys made of blocks and pegs and wheels. It's a kibbutz by way of Whole Foods.

Before he was born, my wife and I visited child care facilities all over town, scoping them out as we had college campuses for ourselves years earlier. We asked questions of each center with the thoroughness of inexperienced parents who knew so very little about why we were asking these questions at all, only that it seemed somehow right to carefully inspect the infant rooms for signs of neglect. To search out the reassuring smell of talcum. To learn the composition of the chemicals they used to clean the surfaces. To know the rate they were going to change diapers and how often they were going to feed him.

The Google children's center was one of the most impressive

we'd seen. To get in, we put our names on a years-long waiting list with hundreds of other families vying for a space. We only managed to get a spot on a technicality. The center was opening a new infant room, and to secure our admission we agreed to pay tuition for ninety days before our son was old enough to actually attend. As painful as this was on our wallet, we agreed the price for admission was worth avoiding the emotional cost of letting this opportunity slip away.

Our son has been at the children's center for a couple of weeks, when one of the infant/toddler teachers hesitantly approaches me during pickup one afternoon. She's wondering if I have a few minutes to talk privately with the center's director. I feel that hot, loose wire of worry start to vibrate in my chest. I leave my son on a blue mat in the middle of the playroom, the loop of his collar damp from the drool of teething.

Outside, I meet up with a short woman with red hair and raw red nostrils from a cold she's had all winter. We move away from the rooms to an empty playground, out of earshot of anyone else, and she smiles timidly.

A couple of days before we started dropping off our son, she says, another child in his room went home with mouth herpes.

"This sounds like a common cold sore," my wife later reasons, always the rational party in our two-person congress. "What's to worry about?"

True, I say, but the director thought it was important to tell us for some reason, and she's provided me with just enough information for me to be concerned. Exposure to herpes before the age of one, I've now learned, puts children at risk for developing painful sores all over their bodies. The virus also causes outbreaks throughout the child's life and can scar. The cycle of an occurrence is reliably two weeks, a sequence that begins with the formation of a blister and ends when the virus goes dormant. During that time, the center bans an infected child from attending. Yet the real problem is that a person is most contagious right before a blemish appears. There's no way to know that a baby is passing the virus along until it is too late to do anything about it. Meanwhile, the child can now mouth any toy and drool on every kid in the nursery.

"We can't just leave him here," I argue. Undoubtedly, we have a responsibility to protect our son. I feel an urge to throw my body over his like a force field. True, none of the other parents are pulling their children from the room. Maybe they aren't aware of how dire this situation is. Or perhaps, I reason, they are just waiting for one family to make the first move. I weigh the option of yanking my son out of the program against the worry that doing so might be a clear overreaction. By fleeing, we might start some kind of stampede, a revolt that finds parents perhaps needlessly transferring their children to other programs. I certainly don't want to humiliate or isolate the infected baby, either. Still, if it will mean sparing other children from the risk of catching this virus, maybe I have an obligation to ignite this frenzy.

The children's center has procedures in place to mitigate the risk and keep children healthy. They clean the nursery with extra care, doubling down on wiping the surfaces with biodegradable, USDA-certified plant-based cleaners and a volatile organic compound-free water-based agent infused with lime and cypress oils. They dip the toys in baths of lemon juice and hydrogen peroxide. They replace the mattress covers with fresh linens and wear rubber gloves when handling toys that the child, whoever he or she is, has mouthed. Since the staff isn't at liberty to identify the carrier by name, this just means I'm going to have to spend the next few weeks eyeballing the playroom until I notice the pox. Then I'll know whom to avoid; then I can make my baby safe.

It isn't difficult to figure out who the carrier is. About two weeks later, a baby girl in the room develops a small lesion on her upper right cheek. Knowing the source does little except rile my anxiety.

I'm going to protect our son.

He's at risk.

I'm acting ridiculous.

I'm conflicted.

Even in the heat of the herpes outbreak, I'm aware that ours is a problem of privilege. We are lucky to have my wife's job, and equally fortunate to have access to the kind of services living in Silicon Valley provides. And, yes, it is unapologetically an upper-class problem, the choice between leaving our son at this dazzling center and transferring him to another. This much I do know: rich or poor, we are collectively responsible for the well-being of these children, yet the right thing to do remains elusive.

One afternoon as I pick up my baby from the nursery it occurs to me that another child, a little girl, has been suspiciously absent all week. I ask one of the teachers about it. She flashes a look that tells me everything I need to know. Despite the center's best efforts, the virus has claimed its second victim.

Do I feel horrible and guilty and ashamed for my inaction? I do, because on some level I know there are things I might have done differently to influence others, to sway them even on an unconscious level. Wielding the power of fear-based hysteria might have prompted parents to pull their children, sparing the second infant who caught the virus, and those who might catch it still. Instead, I've done nothing. With my inaction I've failed to protect them.

Chapter 9

SHIFTING STRATEGIES, I TURN TO
TRACKING HYSTERIA

Not long after permanently pulling my son from the child care facility, I'm back on the campus of Gunn High. I pass golf carts parked under a canopy for maintenance workers and posters promoting the upcoming spring musical. Classes have just let out for the afternoon, and the walkways are teeming with students.

My investigation into a cure for the strange contagion event has recently shifted direction a bit. Bulimia, my early model for the investigation, only highlighted how difficult it is to treat the problem head-on without encountering its remarkable defense mechanisms. Tools of treatment become tools of spread.

Instead, I've determined that I need to attack this more strategically. The task has now become one of identifying the specific social contagions contributing to the strange contagion event in this town. Only once we identify them might we counteract them. In my conversation with Nicholas Christakis, he spoke about the way in which thoughts, behaviors, and emotions catch. He called it flow. My new supposition is that if Palo Alto were able to stop the flow of enough individual social contagions, maybe it could bring down the beast itself.

Of course, uncovering the mechanisms behind individual social contagions becomes problematic, considering that each behaves according to its own rules. Contagious weight gain spreads faster among women than men, for instance, whereas gender matters little with social contagions like emotional burnout. Making social contagions even more difficult to track is the fact that they don't operate in a vacuum. They interact with each other. Also, not every idea, behavior, or emotion spreads as easily as others. Which things catch, and how far they spread, varies, adding more complexity to the puzzle.

I came away from the experience at my son's child care center with an idea about where I should look first: hysteria, a natural consequence of this roiling and churning storm. Today I'm at Gunn High to learn how hysteria manifests here and to what effect.

This is only my fourth visit, but I've already intuited the goodness of these students and the enormity of their capabilities. There is also something hard in their eyes, and a flatness that better belongs to people two or three times their age, people who have lived long enough to experience disappointments and heart-bursting ache. Since kids from here started dying, many have.

The students present themselves to the world as a series of mismatched illusions. I find it nearly impossible to resolve the contradictions, of which there are many. Deborah Brenner-Liss facilitates therapy as far south as Silicon Valley, this place I am coming to know as one of extremes. "The kids in Palo Alto, they have a different temperament than kids in other places," she'd said when we'd met. "Young people are running as fast as they can, and at younger and younger ages. They're trying to achieve in all areas, even those that are internally inconsistent and very difficult to reach." There was fear in her voice when she said this and I sensed disappointment. Having lived in this town for a little more than half a year now, I've noticed that dissonance as well: a kind of adulthood superimposed on the bodies of babes. The kids at Gunn High, barely out of elementary school and halfway to graduating from the Ivy League universities many are so determined to attend, are on the path to reach some unprecedented level of success, stacking their transcripts with AP courses and extracurricular activities, stuffing their résumés, and looking to the future with hope and with worry.

Then again, maybe I am reading these kids wrong. When I ask students about their lives at Gunn High, they usually say all of the right things: grades don't matter; social support is their safety net; self-care is important; a rich life is one defined by relationships and love, not money or success. I believe that *they* believe they are telling me the truth. I will also come to believe that, for many of them, the opposite is also true. The grade point average that bears so much credence in the school becomes both an encumbrance and the yardstick by which one measures one's value and worth in many other settings. Good friends and good times come easily, but they also come at the expense of time better spent on refining oneself, sharpening one's acumen, polishing the sheen to outshine all the others in a field already defined by its exuberance. I question what it is about this town that invites such extremes and wildly varying contradictions. For the kids of Palo Alto, everything that doesn't matter matters to the core.

As for what vulnerabilities distinguish the living from those who have ended their lives, I'm not entirely sure. Not yet anyway, even as I am coming to better know their stories. One of the children who died liked working with cloth and fabric, looping thread through buttons, infusing character into dramatic plays through costumes and design. One was a varsity team wrestler, aggressive on the mat, a master at sprawls and pins, at throwing his body and countering the weight of another. One played tennis, lunged and volleyed, grunted and sweat and leapt. One was active in student affairs, listening to ideas, learning to work within systems and how to challenge them. Despite our individual experiences at the high school and beyond it, the fact remains that each of us is equally susceptible to social contagions flitting about among the mundane and the ordinary plots of daily life. Every moment offers great potential for mirroring others, the opportunity to incorporate and map foreign instincts and desires onto our own personalities. I'm learning that, despite any personal differences, the language of social contagions speaks to all of us, and that includes each of the students at Gunn High.

I am on campus today to meet with one of the people who knows these students well. His name is Paul Dunlap, and he has taught English and drama for twenty years at the high school. I learned about him shortly after he began sponsoring a student-led watchdog group for signs of suicidal thinking and psychological trouble called ROCK: Reach Out. Care. Know.

A broad-framed man with a military-style crew cut awaits me in his surprisingly expansive classroom. Empty desks fan out in a weblike pattern. He folds his long body into one of these student-size tables.

Dunlap tells me that, prior to the first suicide, he'd attended two, and only two, emergency all-staff meetings at Gunn High. The first assembly alerted teachers to the September 11 terrorist attacks in 2001. The second meeting was to inform the staff that a United States–led military coalition had moved into Iraq, signaling the start of war. Those intermittent emergency assemblies have since become semi-routine, beginning with the

shocking train fatality of Jean-Paul Blanchard late last school
year. By early 2010 "we all started looking at everyone and wondering who's next," he tells me. "There's that feeling you get,
looking around, like: Are we going to see everyone tomorrow?"

In an article for *San Francisco* magazine, the writer Diana
Kapp framed the growing tension within the town in terms of a
rising hysteria pushing the community into panic. In my mind,
it actually seems to be a kind of double hysteria, part witch
hunt for a scapegoat and part fear frenzy. Because no one knows
who is going to be next, one has to assume anybody might be.
Responding to these fears, the Children's Health Council, a
kind of think tank and multidisciplinary treatment center for
school-age kids, will later invite nearly sixty psychologists and
educators to form a suicide call-to-action committee. Religious
leaders from a dozen denominations have already hosted numerous town symposiums. The school district, civic leaders, and
parents, worried and angered and panicked, foster a fear about a
dark phenomenon taking the town's kids.

Nurturing the contagious frenzy of hysteria is the fact that
for every student who has died, people have pulled others off
the rails before the train has struck. By now, 3 percent of young
people in Palo Alto are making serious attempts on their lives.
The number of completed deaths by suicide in this town bar-
rels toward a twentyfold increase in less than a year. Therapists are treating four dozen Gunn High students for suicidal
thoughts. It is enough to fuel hysteria among even the most
measured of us.

Dunlap describes the worry in Palo Alto and says he feels
that it's intensifying. Silicon Valley nonprofits specializing in
emotional health receive more requests today than ever before.
Gunn High has tapped the country's best-known adolescent
psychologists and is bringing in the National Peer Helpers

Association to train counselors. Each death has heightened the stakes and the sense of impending doom. It's not just the school but the town, too, he says, that is swept up in a kind of sponta-neous frenzy, reacting to this series of horrible events. Dunlap doesn't want to admit he is powerless, that we are at a loss for actions and desperate for resolution. So instead he's created a ritual for his room. "We enact it at the end of every class," he says. "I have my students turn to their neighbors and promise each other they're going to see each other again." It's really the only thing he is able to think to do.

HYSTERIA FEEDS ON our capacity to imagine the worst. Even amid improbability, our belief in the inevitable seals us in our certainty that something bad is coming, is already here, is un-stoppable.

Like many people, I first heard about hysteria in connection with the witch trials of Salem, Massachusetts. When I view the trials today through the lens of functionality and psychol-ogy, I see a town's desperate attempt to relieve the paranoia and anxieties associated with periods of rapid social and economic changes. Historical accounts from the seventeenth century play heavily on the myth of a frenetic female condition that Hip-pocrates in ancient Greece called wandering womb. When the playwright Arthur Miller writes about young girls taken by hysterics in *The Crucible*, he represents this furious state with a show of children acting as though they are cornered animals, screaming and writhing, infected by a kind of mania. In college, I read Gustave Flaubert's *Madame Bovary*, which described hys-teria's telltale signs of dizziness, anxiety, feelings of suffocation, instability, melancholia, and boredom. In *The Turn of the Screw*, Henry James portrays a governess's slow decent into madness as a fever of fear, paranoia, and hallucinations. Even Lady Brett

Ashley's flirtatiousness, promiscuity, and independent spirit might have signaled symptoms of hysteria in Ernest Hemingway's *The Sun Also Rises.*

An epidemic of hysteria stormed nineteenth-century Europe, where it landed one out of every five people in French madhouses. The neurologist Jean-Martin Charcot's investigation into hysteria looked upon the condition as a physical illness caused by hereditary defects. He began a fruitless search for a dysfunction of the central nervous system. Hysteria, he theorized, was the result of a mysterious lesion hidden somewhere within the body that caused a psychological illness. Charcot was also among the first to use hypnosis to demonstrate how hysteria and the mind were innately connected. His model led the psychiatrist Hippolyte Bernheim to interpret hysteria as an exaggerated reaction to stress. Because people are highly suggestible beings, he wrote, under the right conditions anyone can succumb to hysterics.

Hysteria, he continued, takes on the qualities of a social contagion, with the ability to manifest and spread over populations by way of mere suggestion. Sigmund Freud, in adopting Charcot's hypnosis technique, regressed patients to the origins of their symptoms. So remarkable was this power of suggestion that Freud claimed he was able to cure hysterical convulsions, paralysis, blindness, and fits. I can't imagine it was lost on Freud that suggestibility, which allowed him to treat hysteria, was the very same mechanism that led to hysteria in the first place.

In reading account upon account of hysteria throughout history, one of the things that becomes painfully evident is the effectiveness of fear as its unwavering catalyst. I think about this, and about Paul Dunlap's fear of the future and of the unknown. Since our conversation, I've found myself back in the archives to try to discover how other towns ensnared in strange contagion events have assuaged fear-based hysteria. My research turns up numerous stories.

The one that sticks with me, that turns in my head, is the case of Fishers, Indiana. In 2004 its residents gathered in a small municipal building to talk about the fear of an imminent terrorist attack by Al Qaeda operatives on their rural home. With national security focused on the terror threats in big cities, people worried extremists might instead look for unprotected targets. Perhaps a grocery store in Kansas. An amusement park in Texas. A mall in Nebraska. The worry was so real that the CIA held terrorism briefings with small-town law enforcement officials designed to empower rural areas to defend themselves. The Department of Homeland Security even provided resources and counterterrorism training. It didn't matter that a threat of international terrorism in Fishers never existed, or that there was no evidence at any time to suggest the town was a target. However unfounded, the fear itself was real.

That's because fear is a powerful social contagion from which no one is entirely immune. As casual observers of life, our internal instrumentation, our antennae, our infrared understanding of the world, registers the way in which others respond to everyday objects and situations. Fear in particular trades in a unique currency, a kind of superstitious magical thinking that offers people a sense of control in situations that warrant none. It explains why we toss salt over our shoulders. Why we burn effigies.

For the first months after my son was born, his fears were uncomplicated. It occurs to me that the things I fear seem to increase with age, countering the conventional wisdom that states we grow braver with experience and time. Yet, the more time we spend among others, the greater the opportunity emotions like fear have to infiltrate our minds. In the eighties, the researchers

Michael Cook and Susan Mineka once compared two groups of monkeys and their responses to snakes. When encountering a snake, the facial expressions of wild rhesus monkeys indicated fear, and most primates fled confrontation. But laboratory-raised monkeys, isolated from fear-based behavior and sheltered from the knowledge of potential danger, remained calm and even became playful around snakes. The fearful monkeys, raised among other primates in the jungle, exposed to their fear-based responses, literally aped others' dread.

Fear also leaps between people, something I come to see as a communicable bridge between individuals built on terror and forged through expressions, gestures, and tone. While all communicable emotions create in others a kind of feedback loop of memory and feelings, I've learned that fear in particular transmits in ways beyond the usual subtle and otherwise imperceptible cues. In 2008, Stony Brook University, endeavoring to discover something exceptional about the social contagion of fear, collected the underarm sweat of inexperienced skydivers after their first jump from an airplane. They then placed two types of sweat into nebulizers—one with fear-based sweat—and tasked experiment volunteers to inhale. The areas of the brain associated with fear, the hypothalamus and the amygdala, lit up when the volunteers unknowingly inhaled the fear-based sweat, indicating to the university lab "that there may be a hidden biological component to human social dynamics."

Fear, whether transmitted by pheromones or through direct or indirect observation, proves to be one of the more impactful social contagions. I understand this fear. Back home I think we all do. We worry about raising our youth under the specter of dead children and whatever it is that's led them to choose to take their lives. The stigma now attached to Palo Alto makes us fearful. If viruses are death, then fear is a ghost, roaming, haunting, and possessing us. Here, demise on a singular length of railroad has not stoked enough fear to keep people from seeking out the crossing. Yet there is a stigma to this place now, an undeniable reservation sticking in our chests, as though the spirit of this place might someday take our children from us.

Of course, as Roni Habib once pointed out to me, the reality is that most children are safe from suicidal thinking. Yet sometimes fear has a way of becoming a self-fulfilling prophecy. Even if our fears are unreasonable, they can lead us to make choices that will actually cause the thing that we are avoiding. Parks become dangerous places when people avoid them out of fear of being attacked by criminals, yet nothing invites criminals to an area better than an empty park. This effect transpires within us as well. Fear triggers a response in the brain, which is in itself an undesirable outcome. It trips the circuitry in our minds, manipulates the cells, activates neurotransmitter production, and alters hormonal states. The cascade of physiological and behavioral reactions continues, increasing blood flow, activating the limbic system, and awakening the brain's anterior and medial hypothalamus. Our heart rates increase to pump blood through our bodies, and when all else fails our blood pressure drops, reducing circulation, causing a fainting response akin to playing possum.

It isn't difficult to allow my thoughts to drift into that small place where fear mutates from sensible into something far more irrational. I tell myself fear is only irrational if the threat isn't real.

THREE HUNDRED MILES from Palo Alto rests the site of one of the most damaging fear-based social contagions in modern history. It's a story I've heard, but I've never before seen parallels or its significance to my own. Perhaps more important, it's the site where a social contagion also ended.

It started in a sparse agricultural haven thirty years ago. The differences between the sleepy county of Kern, California, and that of Silicon Valley, in both pace and industry, are vast. Yet back in 1982, Kern County and Silicon Valley had a surprising amount in common. Both valleys were high-density agricultural regions filled with almond groves and orchards of oranges and apricots. The two regions were also about to grow rapidly in population, albeit for different reasons. While Kern County rode high on oil production, Silicon Valley was investing in semiconductors and a trade war with Japan. They diverged even more, however, in terms of the kind of culture these changes nurtured. That same year *National Geographic* magazine noted that Silicon Valley was suddenly appealing to a tremendously striving, intellectually oriented population of workaholics who risked falling prey to alcoholism, divorce, and depression. "'Burn out,'" it reported, "has become a common valley syndrome, for not all can maintain the winner profile."

Far away from these developments, in a quiet Kern County neighborhood, the step-grandmother of two young children leveled gruesome charges against their parents, Debbie and Alvin McCuan. In separate police interviews with the children, both presented investigators with testimony alleging sexual abuse and bizarre details involving satanic cult rituals. Their statements ensnared another local family, too, the Kniffens. The two accused parties stood trial and received a combined sentence of a thousand years in prison.

The winds of hysteria stirred. Just south, in Los Angeles County, the mother of a toddler accused a McMartin preschool worker named Raymond Buckey of killing animals, satanic worship, and hosting orgies involving the molestation of her young son. This led to the longest and most expensive trial in US history up until that time. Police sent a form letter to McMartin parents encouraging them to quiz their children about possible abuse they may have experienced. The investigation led to another 360 individual counts of satanic cult ritual abuse.

Parents accused a day care center handyman in Malden, Massachusetts, named Gerald Amirault of molesting their son. Nine other children came forward about a secret room in the child care center where the handyman made them watch him perpetrate animal sacrifices. Testimony led to Amirault receiving a forty-year sentence in state prison. Detectives did not have to look far to find more cases in the state. In nearby Pittsfield, Bernard Baran Jr. was arrested in October 1984 and sentenced to three life terms based on similar charges.

That same year, in Miami, Florida, a court convicted a man named Frank Fuster for sexually molesting children in his care. Nineteen other children came forward with stories involving snakes and abusers wearing scary masks. Janet Reno, then the Dade County state attorney, landed a conviction and life sentence for the accused.

Devil worshippers were discovered operating in day care centers in the Bronx; in Maplewood, New Jersey; in Great Neck, Long Island; in Spring Valley, California. Seven adults in Edenton, North Carolina, were arrested in 1989 after child rape and satanic ritual abuse allegations surfaced, leading to sentencing of all defendants. A gruesome account in Austin, Texas, led to the conviction of Frances and Dan Keller, accused of offering blood-laced Kool-Aid to children, exhuming bodies in cemeteries, and dismembering a cadaver. For these abuses, all too insane to be believed, the Kellers served twenty-one years in prison. The plague of ritual devil worship and child sex abuse then hit Martensville, Saskatchewan, where a woman who ran a babysitting service and day care center was accused of sexually abusing more than a dozen children in connection with running a satanic cult called the Brotherhood of the Ram. Authorities uncovered similar cases in São Paulo, Brazil, and then in communities in France, Italy, and New Zealand.

Back in Kern County, a task force continued to land dozens of convictions. By the time witnesses started recanting their stories, some defendants had already spent decades behind bars.

As it happened, just prior to the first accusations leveled against the McCuans and the Kniffens, county social workers received dubious training materials that erroneously suggested satanic ritual abuse was also a factor in child sexual abuse. This is a fairly natural response, the kind of phenomenon that commonly plays out whenever personal bias clouds our judgment of someone or a situation. That is, it's easy to see signs when you know what you're looking for, even if there's nothing there to see.

In the Los Angeles McMartin preschool case, the original accuser was later diagnosed with acute schizophrenia, and one of the children involved in the case later retracted his testimony. The charges against Gerald Amirault relied on testimony from children coerced by questionable and highly suggestive interrogation techniques, as was testimony in the case against Frank Fuster in Miami that invited suggestible children to make believe. In other cases, the accusations stemmed from interpersonal disputes among neighbors as well as testimonies that relied on paranoia cascading across the community.

Courts later determined that charges and convictions were obtained because of the prominent force of hysteria. From such inauspicious beginnings sprung a contagion of fear that contaminated populations the world over. And yet, somehow, the world managed to bring this terrifying chapter to a close.

In determining how the country dampened the contagion

of fear-based hysteria, I discover something rather surprising. While a strange contagion is perfectly capable of causing contagious hysteria, hysteria itself *causes* strange contagions. It happened in Fishers. It happened in Kern. And it's happening in Palo Alto.

Chapter 10

DISCOVERING THE WRONG
RESPONDERS

A line from James Baldwin's *The Fire Next Time* keeps running through my mind: "Generations do not cease to be born, and we are responsible to them because we are the only witnesses they have." At the start of my investigation, Nicholas Christakis told me that if his experiences studying social contagions have taught him anything, it's that, given their great power to influence people, we have an even greater responsibility to be mindful and take care of one another. What matters more, however, is *how* we manage to do that. Sometimes going after the source of hysteria is the very thing that perpetuates it.

To make his point, Christakis told me about a case of hysteria that happened in Tanzania in the early sixties. The symptoms manifested within a mission-run boarding school where girls, for no apparent reason, started laughing and couldn't stop. This was no mere schoolroom disruption, Christakis said. The condition moved from classrooms to dormitories, infecting students throughout the academy without prejudice. The story illustrates the devastating swiftness with which anxiety-based, tic-like mass psychogenic illnesses can grip ordinary, everyday people. Three months after the onset of symptoms, the social contagion of unbridled, impulsive laughter swept up 60 percent of the school. As for how to care for the students, the academy was at a loss.

With no idea what to do to stop the spread and save their children, administrators closed the academy. The strategy accomplished two things, Christakis said, neither of which was stopping the outbreak. Instead, its drastic response convinced the country that the affliction was genuinely dangerous. Moreover, by sending frightened students home, the hysterical laughter was free to spread. Ten days after the school's closure, the first of two hundred cases of the laughter contagion caught in the Nshamba village complex and, later, at a girls' middle school in the village of Ramashenye. Medical investigators descended into these hot zones, testing for toxins and infections. The Uganda Virus Research Institute at Entebbe examined blood for biochemical, bacteriological, and microscopic abnormalities and assessed for the creation of viral antibodies. Scientists also collected rainwater from local wells and streams and examined bananas, beans, and meat sources. These avenues of inquiry led nowhere. But the *Central African Journal of Medicine* continued to chart the laughter epidemic's rapid spread, along with a "considerable fear among the village communities."

Psychologists later noted something unusual, Christakis continued, a direct connection between the school closure, these formal investigations, and the laughing symptoms themselves. "How we respond and care for each other matters," he said. "Hysteria in particular spreads by the way we witness authority figures responding to it."

Investigators would later run into the same problem in Fishers, Indiana, where the town was preparing to defend itself against what they feared to be an imminent terrorist attack.

They called in the FBI and analysts from the CIA's Directorate of Intelligence, which dispatched counterterrorism experts to Fishers. The local police chief, Homeland Security officials, the Secret Service, and other federal, state and local law enforcement agencies led public hearings. If there was ever any doubt that terrorists were plotting against Fishers, these overblown countermeasures suggested that maybe the danger wasn't so unfounded after all. Administrators attempting to show that they were taking the threat seriously, by virtue of their presence, only wound up confirming for the worried populace that there was something truly wrong, and signaled a legitimacy to their concerns. The most logical response to squelching hysteria merely hastened its dispersion.

In Kern County, each guilty verdict validated the belief that these fears were not only real but also necessary. Not that I can blame the community members. Placed in their position, I might have succumbed to the same hysteria, an automatic reaction to protect my son. I realize that the tissue connecting all of these stories, in fact, is fashioned out of the most natural of instincts: to look after our children. This impulse impelled me to pull my son from the Google child care facility for reasons innocuous and rather tame.

We respond to these dangers, real or otherwise, by throwing all of our resources at the problem—calling in the CIA, the EPA, the FBI, perhaps even the CDC—and hoping that one of these Hail Mary measures works. Only in the end do we come to find that there was nothing wrong to begin with, and that these overblown responses have done little but fan the flames. There was nothing wrong in Tanzania. A handful of girls took on somatic symptoms of stress. There was no terror threat in Indiana, just heightened speculation. And there was never any danger of running afoul of satanic cults in Kern

County child care centers, only hypervigilance and volumes of misinformation.

The historian Norman Cohn writes that true believers can endow hysteria with such confidence, energy, and ruthlessness that it will attract into its wake vast multitudes of people who are themselves not at all paranoid but simply harassed, hungry, or frightened. I believe this is true. Yet, to really understand mass hysteria, we have to look at the nature of human behavior, the way logical people become overwhelmed by fear and caught up in the snare of excitement, how easily we can fashion and twist frenzy, how effortlessly it moves from person to person, untethering the most stable of us, cracking the foundations on which we so heavily rely. Hysteria legitimizes the improbable and supersedes the logical. In so doing, it becomes a self-replicating system. A day care crisis creates the need for an organized response. It generates jail sentences and produces media attention. It creates hysteria that reinforces a belief in a problem that never existed in the first place. The process cascades in a never-ending loop, a mirror-like recursion.

Our responsibility to one another is to seek out the facts rather than so easily give in to the frenzy. The fix is logic over myth. In Tanzania, the investigators could go home. The CIA and Homeland Security officials could stay in Washington, DC, instead of visiting Indiana. The task forces hunting and prosecuting innocent people in Kern County and other places could disband. With no evidence to believe symptoms are real, they will completely vanish. Evidence supersedes fear. A contagion is eradicated.

I'VE FILLED THE gas tank of my Mazda, cleaned the windows with three swipes of the windshield mop, and am headed into the Central Valley. I drive through the towns of Wasco and

Buttonwillow here in Kern County. It is an exercise in examining a place's extraordinary banality: the houses are plain and the lawns well tended. One house has a basketball hoop in its driveway. On the next block, a line of parked minivans distinguishes the street. A high school football field's tall turf lights rise in the distance. At the same time, I see nothing extraordinary here that even hints it possessed a unique ability to scuttle such a destructive social contagion, though clearly all traces of it are long gone. Nothing about this place suggests to me it was once the progenitor of a vicious plague of panic.

During the two days I spend in Kern County, the people I meet here—those who are old enough to remember living through that period of heightened paranoia and those who concede that it happened with low, knowing nods—often state their belief that this dark chapter is far behind them. Nothing like this mindless fear, the kind that sets a system on autopilot and then takes a hammer to the control panel, has happened in the county in decades. There's no reason to suspect that it will ever happen here again.

Yet, thirty years after the child care hysteria in Kern County was put to rest, an understated distrust continues to thrive under the surface, as noted by one mother who discloses to me that she still hesitated before putting her child into day care only a year ago. A land assessor I speak to remembers an uncle and aunt of his who fell under suspicion of being cult members in the eighties. To avoid jail, they skipped town and joined the circus. On some level he's always known the accusations were bogus. And yet there is, he says, a suspicion within the family. What if it is even a little bit true?

These anecdotes tell me that a social contagion like hysteria may run its course, but it leaves indelible marks on the culture and its collective memory. Back home, in the unsteady wake of the student suicides, panic leads the district to hire well-regarded mental health specialists. A consortium of faith leaders, doctors, and police produce nearly two dozen initiatives to create a supportive atmosphere for Palo Alto children. The town weighs the creation of volunteer track watchers to stand guard at the rails. The school district mulls a system-wide mental health curriculum and a suicide-awareness training program for all faculty. Schools are overhauling their homework policies to lower student stress. They shift first period to allow the students to get a bit more sleep. I don't know if these measures are necessary or if they're overblown responses. Some of these measures seem only logical.

Then again, what if these school district maneuvers—manifested out of our frantic need to regain control and bolstered by a feeling that we have so little of it—only reinforced the thought that every child is in danger of catching the kind of desperation that leads to suicide? In which case, we're simply perpetuating a false belief that, like fear, can quickly become a self-fulfilling prophecy, heightening anxiety and stress responses. Not unlike the double-edged sword of awareness, stopping this social contagion becomes yet another catch-22. To stop it, we must act. To act, we cannot stop it.

Yet stopping hysteria is crucial. And it is possible, through measured and fact-based responses. At the same time, if what I've found here in Kern County is any indication of what will happen once we snuff out hysteria at home, then the memory of what's happened in Palo Alto may still doom us to lasting fear, uncertainty, and suspicion for generations to come.

Chapter 11

TRACKING NOCEBOS AND THE MYSTERY OF THE DEKALB COUNTY WINDMILLS

t isn't until I'm moving through the low canyon of Altamont Pass on my drive home from the Central Valley that it occurs to me that there's still an element of this social contagion left unresolved. It's the very thing that makes Palo Alto's situation different from those in places like Kern County and Tanzania. If hysteria tends to spread fast, far, and wide, why aren't towns outside of Palo Alto worried about the risk of suicide affecting their children to the same degree we are? Palo Alto is unique, but not so unique that other places, especially those in Silicon Valley sharing the same demographic characteristics, populated by wealthy, tech-driven, highly ambitious people, are not subject to the same factors. The nearby towns of Los Gatos, Los Altos, and Menlo Park also report suicides, although none are responding quite like Palo Alto is. In fact, some places are turning away help from social services, which is either the most rational and measured response possible or an act of mind-boggling denial. In either case, hysteria in Palo Alto remains confined within its finely drawn borders.

My flight lands at Chicago Midway International Airport on a gray wintery morning. I pull out of the rental car lot and drive sixty-three miles west, to the sleepy province of DeKalb County, where brown and gray barns scatter across northeast Illinois farmland. Small townships delineate the countryside, once run through by the Zephyr streamliner trains. Winter is heavy on the cold ground, with old soot-colored snow and sparse, empty trees. Over the past few years, big flatbed trucks loaded with blocky generators have exited Interstate 55 and driven provisional roads scratched into the geography. They've unloaded 126 wind turbine towers that now rise against the county's skyline. Together the turbines generate enough electricity to power 50,000 homes.

People closest to the four-hundred-foot-tall turrets receive more than just electricity. The turbines interrupt their sleep patterns. They also generate faint ringing in their ears. Emissions cause pounding migraine headaches. The motion of the vanes also creates a shadow flicker that triggers disorientation, vertigo, and nausea.

Grievances against wind farms are not exclusive to DeKalb County, with a perplexing illness dogging many a wind turbine project. Similar complaints have surfaced in Canada, the UK, Italy, and various US cities like Falmouth, Massachusetts. In 2009 the Connecticut pediatrician Nina Pierpont offered an explanation. Wind turbines, she argued, produce low-frequency noises that induce disruptions in the inner ear and lead to an illness she calls wind turbine syndrome. Her evidence, now largely discredited for sample size errors, a lack of a control group, and no peer review, seemed to point to infrasound coming off of the wind farms. Since then more than a dozen scientific reviews have firmly established that wind turbines pose no unique health risks and are fundamentally safe. It doesn't seem to matter to the residents of DeKalb County, whose symptoms are quite real.

The professor Mark S. Micale writes that hysteria is an alternative form of communication, a proto-language for people who otherwise might not be able to speak or even admit to what they feel. Understanding hysteria comes down to deciphering what a social contagion, in its proto-language, is saying. Wind farm hysteria is, at its core, a conversation led by those fighting bitterly to keep the turbines off their land, a position that grew so contentious that it provoked in some a psychosomatic response.

The science behind this unique and primitive conversation can be traced to the early sixties, when the physician Walter Kennedy experimented with the placebo effect. Kennedy marveled over the way an inert sugar pill induces positive health results. To this day the exact mechanisms behind the placebo effect continue to perplex even while they prove useful in changing the neural circuitry and complex chemical makeup of the brain in up to 80 percent of patients. Mental focus, personal expectations, the environment in which a patient receives the placebo, and even the shape, size, and color of the pill itself lead people to experience genuine pain relief, lower blood pressure, and better moods. Placebos are so influential that, in one of the more fascinating effect studies, Harvard researchers found that deception, which figures largely into making patients believe they are taking a real pill, is not necessary. Investigators in a groundbreaking 2010 examination came clean and told patients they were going to be taking placebo pills. Nevertheless, participants reported twice as much symptom relief as the group of patients that received no treatment at all.

But it was back in 1961 that Kennedy discovered a particular kind of placebo, a social contagion that worked on a massive scale. Instead of inducing positive effects, the *nocebo reaction*, as he came to call it, allowed for the equivalent inert sugar pill to cause people to experience unpleasant effects. As a field of study, nocebos went on to provide physicians and psychologists with a new understanding of the power of the mind. Doctors in 2006 falsely told Parkinson's patients they were switching off their brain pacemakers, and soon enough their Parkinson's symptoms increased. In 2010, researchers at Sapienza University of Rome asked a group of lactose intolerant people to drink milk. Even though they were really given glucose, nearly half experienced pain. Later, Harvard's Program in Placebo Studies and Therapeutic Encounter at Beth Israel Deaconess Medical Center in Boston confirmed that the nocebo effect was more widespread than anything they had ever seen with placebos and powerful enough to induce nausea, stomach pains, fatigue, vomiting, muscle weakness, colds, ringing in the ears, memory disturbances, and other unfavorable health outcomes.

Like placebos, they take advantage of our highly suggestible nature. They rely on intellectual, emotional, and physical vulnerabilities. The sugar pill is often a single object we come to ritualistically, and obsessively, ruminate over until the expectation of poor consequences brings on symptoms. Negative expectations ramp up the pain regions of the brain, the anterior cingulate cortex, the prefrontal cortex, and the insula. The nocebo effect influences the brain's neurotransmitters, which regulate our moods. In one case study, researchers observed a person who was attempting to complete suicide by swallowing twenty-six pills. Not realizing that they were sugar tablets, the subject experienced dangerously low blood pressure based solely on the belief that the overdose was going to be deadly. After the subject learned he'd ingested an inert substance designed to have no effect, the symptoms disappeared. Our bodies are not naturally immune to the mind any more than they are to most viruses.

The residents of DeKalb County bought into the idea that these turbines cause physical harm. I question what it is we buy into at home—the frenetic optimism around Palo Alto's education system, about the stamina of our children, and about the power of place. Perhaps the culture of Palo Alto is a kind of nocebo, too, the Silicon Valley equivalent of wind turbine farms. The town manifests the false idea that the very act of residing in Palo Alto produces negative health consequences in its kids—that the town cultivates pressure, stress, and oversized personal expectations. Just as the people in Kern County maintain a sense of uncertainty about the status of child molesters among them, a *what-if* exists within the population of Palo Alto. I am as guilty as anyone of hosting this uncertainty. Something irrational in me worries that the town will adversely influence my son—that as we move him through its school system, he'll internalize, as we all do, demands both spoken and silent. The nearby municipalities outside of Palo Alto aren't responding the same way because Palo Alto *is* the nocebo. Real or perceived, the crippling pressure of high expectation, an enormous personal burden to achieve a level of perfectionism, and other traits we are led to believe Palo Alto has taken on are what's led its children to become depressed, anxious, numb to pleasure, and suicidal.

Once again it falls on the community to set the record straight, to deliver accurate and scientifically sound facts, and to help the rest of us avoid buying into this hysteria, believing that this town brings harm to its children. The natural decibel level of fear is high, so rational voices, with rational answers, must speak louder. The town isn't going to make our children catch anxiety, depression, a belief in uncompromising promise, skyrocketing expectations, heart-bursting loneliness, or suicidal thinking. And yet I think back to the studies I've read about patients knowingly swallowing sugar pills and continuing to report medical benefits or health impairments. Awareness, as Gerald Russell told me, is paramount to spreading a strange contagion like bulimia. But now it's clear that, not only do we have to worry about concrete facts like the mechanics of binging and purging to spread a strange contagion, but we also have to contend with awareness based on false beliefs, facts that are not facts at all but remain, nonetheless, those that people hold deeply.

Despite assurances that the wind farms are perfectly safe, regardless of the facts people have read and in some cases have come to fully believe, there remains suspicion, because people are getting sick, and people are laid out, and people are afraid.

I'm in DeKalb County to see if the windmills will make me feel any different. I know they are harmless, and yet the mind is far more powerful than the knowledge it holds. My heart rate will accelerate. I will feel the pinch of a migraine behind my eyes. A wave of nausea will knock me down.

But I feel nothing.

I give it some time. Drive through the small town of Genoa. Grab a bite to eat at a sandwich shop off Route 64 in Sycamore.

None of these effects has taken hold yet.

As hysteria is a kind of psychosis, I suppose it's possible to catch madness. In his short story "The Quantity Theory of Insanity," the writer Will Self considers a scenario in which there is only a limited amount of saneness in the world. Lunacy moves like a virus from person to person, latching onto individuals for brief periods of time before letting go and jumping into the next body. People are living their lives, going to work, raising their families, and waiting for their turns. Here I am, moving across the land of wind turbines, waiting for the madness to grip me. And here we are, existing in Palo Alto, still waiting for the madness to let us go.

Part IV

THE MOTIVATORS

"God, how we get our fingers in each other's clay. That's friendship, each playing the potter to see what shapes we can make of each other."

—RAY BRADBURY

Chapter 12

DISCOVERING THE
"HARD DRIVE" VIRUS

This town pushes people to push harder. That's the belief as Roni Habib frames it for me. It's as though, he suggests, his students have contracted a caffeine-like stimulant that engenders a disconnect with reality, that gets the heart rate pumping furiously, that inculcates a dependency on this personal drive, that numbs them, and that yields a dampening anhedonia. The exhaustion that threatens to overtake them is one they will fight to push, push, push through.

Right now as we talk, Habib is locking their grades for the semester, rating and ranking his students. He's logging their scores like diagnoses. "Everyone points to the fact that these kids are driven," he says. "They want to succeed. They'll always go the extra mile." He sees this far more now as a teacher than he did as a student at Gunn High, but it was part of the culture here even back then in the late nineties, this pervasive desire to take the hardest classes and to do so as though you're in the middle of an intense competition. Or an all-out war. I've heard it said in different ways from other teachers in town, from social workers, from therapists, from students, from parents. A researcher at the Hasso Plattner Institute of Design at Stanford

I spoke to spent a year visiting high schools around the country, gathering information ahead of a research project. He told me he'd never seen anything like the kind of personal drive rousing students at Gunn High.

Hysteria is driving fear and hypervigilance through this town, but something else is driving these kids. There's fear, yes, of failure and uncertainty, but there's something richer, too.

"It's more than kids thinking it's the Ivy Leagues or bust," Habib says.

"It's a personal challenge," I offer.

"No, it's more like they've caught a sense that it's in their best interest to work like mad," he clarifies. "Generally speaking, it's all they've ever known."

And it's obvious why: this contagious work ethic—the kind that drives the creation of better products, better workplace environments, better leadership models, better transparency across processes, and better product iterations—is the philosophy of Silicon Valley, a shining example of innovation that is also a place where employees log sixty- to eighty-hour work-weeks, motivated by a basic intention, *to do it better.*

The characteristics of Silicon Valley's unspoken mantra might be responsible for instilling in children super-high expectations, extreme drive, hyperfocus, or perfectionistic tendencies. Still, I wonder about the validity of these claims. And in the end, is one's tendency to catch motivation really so bad?

So I peel back stratas of history overlaying this place by re-visiting the development of the first vacuum tube by the Federal Telegraph Company and the founding of corporations like Magnavox, Hewlett Packard, and Varian Associates. The seeds of a deep-seated work ethic sprouted from this bedrock. But this kind of extreme drive to succeed doesn't belong to a single unique culture, and it never has. The professor of philosophy

Musa Owoyemi presents the tenets of a strong work ethic as a series of contrasting associations, beliefs about the moral superiority of hard work over leisure, pride over carelessness, sacrifice over extravagance, earned over unearned income. It is about a commitment to working hard, he writes, and doing so for the purposes of wealth, societal obligation, the betterment of the community, and, as some contend, rewards in the afterlife. Judeo-Christian memes about the value of a strong work ethic influenced capitalists across Northern Europe in the sixteenth century and spread to America through the Germanic immigration.

Eventually, US fortitude and the principles of the Protestant work ethic intertwined and created the American myth of the self-made person, one who starts from nothing and becomes someone of value and importance through ability, resourcefulness, and resilience. In both boardrooms and classrooms, a belief in a work ethic transmits through peer modeling and proselytizing. People naturally adopt ideas and standards when they have either an economic or an educational motive for doing so.

The business writer Eric Chester highlights the better transmissible characteristics of a contagious strong work ethic—things like positive energy, professional attire, ambition, integrity, and gratitude—which people can, and do, unconsciously catch from others. The positive spillover improves bottom lines and becomes a hidden driver of great performance.

But the opposite is also true. Writing on social and emotional learning, the psychologist Daniel Goleman finds that a poor work ethic introduces a kind of social virus to an otherwise cohesive and well-functioning system. It threatens to impede motivation. Stunt creativity. Halt learning. Maim cooperation. It also stokes conflict. In scenarios where team members are dependent on one another, a person with a poor work ethic triggers a natural move to restore balance. As a result, group members collectively, and often unconsciously, reduce the amount of work contributions all around. From here, a subtle and automatic cascade occurs. Over time, a single person with a bad work ethic can create a company-wide atmosphere of problematic behavior. The social contagion spreads from one team to many teams. Businesses lose more than half a trillion dollars a year due to diminished employee motivation and burnout, which wreaks havoc on productivity, recruitment, and training costs. The more exposure people have to those infected by a bad work ethic contagion, the more it spreads.

It doesn't help matters that an employee with a poor work ethic has a natural advantage in groups. A 2006 study in the journal *Research in Organizational Behavior* suggests that negative attitudes are heavier than positive ones. Because not every social contagion carries equal influence, the lowest, poorest-functioning teammate, the person who's short on agreeableness and functioning, determines the performance of an entire group. If I were to add a number score to every member of a team according to positive or negative work ethic, the most negative among them would singlehandedly predict overall group performance better than the average personality score. In fact, the most cooperative and hardworking person among the group will have a rough time counterbalancing a singular bad influence.

Yet, even taking into account the unequal weight of social contagions, I learn that the scale itself does not always work the way we might assume. Sometimes a positive work ethic is as damaging as a negative one. This happens when it fosters company cultures like some in Silicon Valley, predicated on what the executive director of the Markkula Center for Applied Ethics at

Santa Clara University notes is the most intense, competitive, 24-7 environment in the country. Corporations lauded for their free restaurants and on-site massage services also employ people willing to work excessively long work hours to achieve prohibitively high standards.

Transforming conscious choice into an unspoken, authorless zeitgeist, the culture of Palo Alto eventually ingrained the social contagion into its DNA. While noting that nothing directly links strong work ethic to children who decide to kill themselves, there is still a suspicion that a culture producing such pressure to achieve, exerted through the encouragement of an exceedingly strong and intense work ethic, has been at the very least a factor in pushing the teenagers in my town to hit a wall. Like a hacker who abuses a flaw in the system to upload a computer virus, the social contagion of work ethic exploits inherent vulnerabilities. It takes advantage of the only weakness the cascade of otherwise beneficial ideas and behaviors possesses: the tendency for students to mirror a desire to breach the highest standards and achieve beyond any rational measure of accomplishment. Added to this is a troubling tendency for some to ruminate over failing to reach an arbitrarily high level of success.

The mantra of a strong workforce—*I must work longer, labor harder, reach higher*—becomes the chant of young people worried about their places in the world, a contagion that proliferates freely among children who harbor the best intentions, to thrive, to succeed, and to, above all, do and be better.

THERE'S A RATHER famous story in Palo Alto about two college students who roomed together as undergraduates at the University of Pennsylvania. Elon Musk would go on to head, among other companies, Silicon Valley–based giants PayPal, Tesla Motors, and SpaceX. Adeo Ressi would found a hyperlocal news platform that he sold to America Online, as well as a Web development firm and a Silicon Valley–based start-up incubator called the Founder Institute. The narrative conjures up a kind of destiny-spinning myth in which, for a time, two inchoate charismatic leaders lived under one roof. It's as though there was something uniquely contagious in their house, a kind of hard-driving work ethic virus floating in the air that each caught. The truth, of course, is that there exists nothing so extraordinary. However, their home did harbor something unique, a surplus of a style of thinking and behaving that was particularly motivating to those around them and to each other.

I find myself thinking about this story after my most recent conversation with Habib. If students are catching the culture's contagious work ethic, then I want to know which entities are most responsible for driving them toward this institutionalized frenzy. I start to look at the types of companies and leaders who are capable of cuing people in to both healthy and harmful epidemics of motivation. Ressi and Musk, I reason, exemplify entrepreneurs who encourage people through the social contagion effect of charismatic leadership, the epoxy banding everyone from employees to future investors together in pursuit of a singular vision. The passion for building something new and innovative is a powerful rallying cry. An entrepreneur's leadership style can be persuasive, and through unconscious mirroring it can also be a vital factor in an individual's, as well as a corporate venture's, triumph or failure. Even if someone doesn't deliberately go about trying to spread contagious zeal, the writer John Hersey suggests that leaders hold positions of unavoidable infectiousness. The most infectious will naturally transfer to others the desire for an individual to commit to an idea, a philosophy, an endeavor. One's passion aligns thoughts, behaviors, and emotions; it fuels innovation, persistence, and accomplishment.

In many ways this phenomenon of top-down contagious enthusiasm is remarkable only in its banality. Obviously, exuberant leaders inspire others. And yet its apparatus, its middling sway, remains one of the most overlooked factors in organizations large and small. While examining the cause of company collapses in America, Germany, and Japan, the executive recruitment firm Egon Zehnder discovered that a CEO's failure often has little to do with competence, knowledge, or lack of experience. Those who failed were hired on the basis of their IQ and business expertise—but fired for lacking the ability to win over their board of directors or inspire their employees. Leaders who possess the ability to control and express their emotions well, and thoughtfully handle interpersonal relationships among stakeholders, remain the most successful at aligning teams and spreading a productive work ethic. Their interactions with people create a nonverbal duet of mutual empathy and understanding. They stoke personal drive in others without uttering a single word, conveying sentiment through subtle, nonverbal channels like the pace and timing of a conversation as well as body movements. Charismatic leaders are particularly good at listening deeply and responding to what others feel, say, and do. Their gauge for interpretation is also highly accurate. They tune in to what someone else feels and thinks with stunning exactness. In so doing, they have a remarkable ability to pass along contagious zeal, impart their ambition to others, and inspire pride.

If there is a worrisome flip side to contagious charismatic leadership, it exists at the apex where intention and outcome meet, where people catch the aspiration and hard-driven work ethic of the leaders in their midst. We'll toil for longer hours and dedicate more energy to achieving their vision. As the Wharton professor Adam Grant highlights in his book, *Originals: How*

Non-Conformists Move the World, when Polaroid founder Edwin Land was developing the instant camera, he once worked for eighteen days straight without even changing his clothes: "Just like the Silicon Valley founders . . . [Land's] focus was rather on whether [employees] would value generating novel ideas and dedicate themselves to the mission. Surrounded by others who shared the same passion and goals, his employees felt a strong sense of belonging and cohesiveness. When you're bonded that strongly with your colleagues in your organization, it's hard to imagine working anywhere else."

Work ethic, for better or worse, springs from a leader's ability to spread fervor for reaching a level of triumph. In the best cases, leaders stimulate in people creative thinking, problem-solving abilities, and enhanced task involvement. In the worst cases, contagious charismatic leadership is so powerful that it tilts an entire culture toward an impossible work ethic, raises standards staggeringly high, perverts interpretations of greatness, and pushes an idea of perfection so hard that it threatens to tear the best of us asunder.

Chapter 13

ON THE TRAIL OF
THE MOTIVATION LAB

Like all strange contagion events, the makeup of the one in my town is unique and continues to prove its complexity to me. The ingredients I've collected thus far repeat in my head—fear, hysteria, work ethic, transmissible zeal—but none of these components directly addresses the issue of personal susceptibility. Why are these specific social contagions so catchable? As unique as Palo Alto's situation is, there is something about these social contagions, and others, that makes each of us vulnerable to their sting. I worry it's something central to our human constitution.

Not long after Habib turns in his grades for the semester, I take what I've learned about contagious work ethic and book a flight to Philadelphia. From there, I catch an early morning train that brings me to 30th Street Station. In terms of scale and grandeur, its grand platform is beyond any on the Caltrain line back home. The ones I know lack this station's natural stone veneer and its lofty coffered ceilings that muffle the sound of voices and shoes *click-clacking* across the marble. The sign in the center of this station springs awake with a rapid, trill-like sound as the large split-flap display announces arriving trains for Boston, Harrisburg, and New York.

Its rotating tiles of letters and numbers create the impression of a flowing motion across the dark face of the display. The mechanical whir of the sign triggers a rush of commuters that hungrily swarms the gates to the trains. At some point in the history of commuters, this has become the way of train riders everywhere, a Pavlovian response creating a kind of contagious urgency and cuing a torrent of movement. I can't help but watch this interplay under the new light of social contagions, the way thoughts, behaviors, and emotions cascade through group culture.

I leave 30th Street Station on foot and walk a bridge across the Schuylkill River. Its banks are hemmed with lines of oil-hued railroad tracks. The trains lumber across the brown earth beneath the overpass. I stuff my hands in my winter coat pockets as a line of russet- and rust-colored container cars clanks by. The approach to the Wharton School leads me west of the University of Pennsylvania's main campus. The streetlights are draped with banners promoting an exhibit on ancient Panama at the Penn Museum called BENEATH THE SURFACE. To find this answer, beneath the surface is where I'm headed. It's the place where dread and panic, good and bad influences, and hard-driven work ethic all tread.

Slipping quietly into a multilevel rotunda, I watch Adam Grant finish leading an undergraduate class on organizational behavior. He is a youthful professor dressed in blue jeans, a black T-shirt, and bright blue tennis shoes. His head is shaved close, his expression one of enduring thoughtfulness. I've sought him out because Grant's research is at the forefront of work motivation and leadership. Oddly, despite teaching in a school dominated by economists, he's landed at a surprising place in terms of the one social contagion he grudgingly propagates. "The study of economics pushes people toward a selfish extreme," he tells me after his class lets out. More to the point, he says, "The scholarship of economics is responsible for spreading a contagion of greed."

The Cornell University economist Robert H. Frank has discovered many examples of this, Grant says. Consider that professors of economics give less to charity than professors in other fields. Or that students of economics are more likely to practice deception for personal gain. Then there's the fact that students majoring in economics routinely rate greed as generally good, correct, and moral. In fact, says Grant, simply thinking about economics chips away at one's sense of compassion for others. Studying economics also makes people become less giving and more cynical. Students who rank high in self-interest might self-select for degrees and careers in economics-related fields, but by learning about economics they wind up catching more extreme beliefs than those they possess when they first register for class. By spending time with like-minded people who believe in and act on the principle of self-interest, students of economics can become convinced that selfishness is widespread and rational. Self-interest becomes the norm. Individual players within the whole unconsciously model and catch behaviors, in turn pushing ethical standards.

Grant's argument draws me back to something Deborah Brenner-Liss said to me at her office in San Francisco months earlier. She explained that the young people in Palo Alto have a unique temperament, a penchant for running as fast as they can to reach their prizes, and they are doing so at younger and younger ages. Since then I've encountered this, too. A fifteen-year-old student I spoke to in Palo Alto once told me about an idea for an electric car battery she was developing in her garage with some of her friends. Without compunction, she stated flatly the device was going to save electric car manufacturing companies billions. Her exit strategy was to sell the battery technology to Elon Musk. A seventeen-year-old I met was building a data storage system he hoped to bring to market before going to college in a year. A sixteen-year-old I spoke to was foregoing college to join his friend's online clothing start-up, which had already attracted angel investors. Another high school student was creating an online social network, adding confidently, without a shred of diffidence, that his product was going to crush Facebook—a belief that sprung from either great naïveté or the deep-seated mind-set of champions.

So many of these lofty dreams are driven by intellectual and creative desires to better the world. Just as many, however, are motivated by the goal of making as much money as possible. Between studying and tending to extracurricular activities, kids are developing prototypes, learning the complexities of marketing, practicing the skills of networking, and sharpening their abilities to design and develop business plans to present to venture capitalists. It's remarkable really: upon meeting these teenagers, I remember thinking about where my life might have taken me if I'd applied even a fraction of the energy they are devoting to such ambitious causes.

But behind the story of constructive ambition lies the other story of cultures high on the contagion of economic-spread avarice with a long history of producing societal and personal downfalls. In seventeenth-century Amsterdam, for instance, the market went mad selling tulips as a desire for these exotic plants reached astronomical heights; sellers rushed to make a fortune, ratcheting up the price of Switsers tulips by more than 1,000 percent before the world's first speculative bubble inevitably burst and caused a market collapse. An economic bubble driven by greed, runaway debt, and consumer credit preceded the stock market crash of 1929. In the late 1990s, hungry entrepreneurs rushed to Silicon Valley to make their fortunes against the surface tension of a hyperinflated dot-com bubble, which popped in 2000 and drove the American economy into a recession. The global economic downturn of 2008 was also heralded by market gains propagated by greedy home mortgage lenders.

I imagine taking this information back to Roni Habib, telling him that he can no longer teach economics to his students at Gunn High because it makes them catch greed, and then awaiting the incredulous silence sure to follow. "We can't eliminate economics classes any more than we can avoid seeing the effects of economics in play everywhere," I say to Grant. "So where does that leave us?"

He cautions me, however. I'm not looking at the problem correctly. While the specialty of economics indeed spreads greed, there is actually something more foundational at the heart of all social contagions. This is not an issue of economics but an issue of commonality, he says. Greed is one of the most common traits on the planet. Its universality is the very thing that makes everyone respond to the stimuli of economics, which simply triggers that trait. Lights it up. Turns it on. It's a cue that activates a widespread quality within each of us. It begs the question, if something as universal as economics can cue a social contagion like greed, what other triggers are influencing the children back home, and can we identify them before it's too late?

TO COMPLETE THIS picture, I realize I have one more stop to make. I've got to track down a place known as the Motivation Lab.

To find it, I board an Amtrak train from Philadelphia and head north. I arrive ninety minutes later at New York's Penn

Station. As I cross the dimly lit grotto of this subterranean place, every few seconds the changeable text announces arrivals and departures, the black and white tiles flipping with an illusion of cascading scales. I ride the escalator up to Eighth Avenue, entering into a citywide laboratory of greed, charismatic leadership, resilience, drive, hope, fear, and frenzy undergoing infinite sequences of catching and spreading.

Inside a gloomy NYU building, I make several quick turns down dull hallways lined with doorknobs of tarnished brass. At the end of a corridor, an entryway opens into an empty room with a lamp, a coffee table, and a second door, a room within a room. I rap on the doorframe and step inside to a warm space—bright, even—endowed with a bit of natural light from the windows.

This is where I find Peter Gollwitzer.

He calls me over with a little wave. "Come in, come in."

He's seated at a small table, and I settle in a chair across from him. He's handsome, solemn, mid-sixties, with pale skin and short hair as white as textbook paper. Our table is in the middle of a roomy office, and there is a sofa and chairs set up to my left. There are pictures on the wall above it, capturing a winter scene. On the other side of the room hangs a set of different pictures, images of brightly colored buildings. There's a smell of floor wax.

"You want to know how motivation affects action," Gollwitzer says, speaking softly. His tone is deliberate as well as imbued with a German timbre. "You're interested in how strong the effect is."

"I am."

"You want to know how people catch motivation, yeah? How people arrive at strong goals, catch them from other people, and how they go on to translate those goals into action."

Yes, and more, I say. I want to know why the Palo Alto kids are so responsive to specific social contagions and what we can do to identify the triggers.

He watches me, unblinking. Takes off his glasses, which have thick black frames. Turns them in his hands.

"You want to talk about primes."

Chapter 14

WE HAVE A PROBLEM OF PRIMES

n the Motivation Lab, where the heat moves through old pipes, I'm getting an idea about where Gollwitzer fits in within a long line of psychologists like William James, Clark Hull, Robert M. Yerkes, and John Dillingham Dodson, pioneers in the drives, incentives, and arousals that provoke people to chase their goals. One of their more widely accepted theories about motivation suggests people choose to pursue goals as long as they believe that the outcome is attainable, that it's attractive, and that it's socially desirable. But as a senior researcher at Munich's Max-Planck-Institute for Psychological Research, Gollwitzer found that, even if people have the belief that a goal is feasible, oftentimes they don't act on it.

Now at NYU, his Motivation Lab designs tools and strategies to translate a person's desire into a strong goal commitment using primes: words, sounds, or objects that unconsciously convince people to accept new thoughts, behaviors, and emotions. Early behaviorists like Hull and James spoke about primes in terms of the power of suggestion and the process of guiding a person's goals through hypnosis. Later experiments at the University of Connecticut modified that a bit, suggesting instead that verbal and nonverbal cues influenced people using *waking suggestion*, or non-hypnotic suggestibility. This, says Gollwitzer, is how people unconsciously catch goals from one another. The process of making someone catch a goal involves, among the usual behavioral mimicry, subtly exposing people to specific primes, or cues. They plant good and bad ideas in our minds that quietly germinate and eventually motivate the body to engage in the pursuit of them.

Gollwitzer tells me he can fairly easily make people catch some goals and behaviors without their knowledge—things like assertiveness, flexibility, docility, aggression, and the motivation to be more successful. In the lab, his process involves subjecting people to a sophisticated series of words hidden in writing prompts, or furtively revealing specific images and sounds to people that might seem innocuous but in reality implant ideas or behaviors. If he wants to increase a person's attention to detail, he uses a technique called embodied priming. By assigning a pre-task game of connect-the-dots, he slows down the subject's processes. In another kind of lab manipulation, words like *fast* or *accurate* flash so rapidly between images on a screen that they are imperceptible to the eye, yet they prime a subject to work faster or more slowly.

He and his colleagues once set up an experiment that asked participants to read a short scenario about a man planning to go on vacation. In one slightly different version of the story, he included information about the man's job on a farm, details that implied, but never explicitly mentioned, a goal of earning money. Next, every participant was asked to perform a short task. They learned that if they finished the task on time they would be invited to participate in *another* task in which it was possible to earn money. The participants in the goal condition—those who had information about the main character's job—worked faster and exerted more effort to reach the last task than those in the control condition. In other words, perceiving another person's goal-related behavior, in this case working on a farm to make money, led readers to catch and pursue a similar goal, even though it meant the participants pursued it in a different way from the farmer. Far more fascinating to Gollwitzer was that this effect was *automatic*. Encoding the goal required no specific instruction.

"I'm guessing these primes happen naturally outside of the lab, too."

"That's actually where things get interesting," he says. "Beyond the lab, we catch other people's goals through everyday cues. There are some people who say that 99 percent of our lives and actions are the result of unconscious goal pursuit through primes we've registered from others around us."

That means, I muse, that, unbeknownst to me, my goals could really belong to a friend, a person on the periphery, or someone just beyond it. My motivation for ordering a latte from Starbucks instead of one from Dunkin' Donuts this morning might have come from a brand of cup tossed into a trash can I scarily registered out of the corner of my eye. Or perhaps I caught the smell of a brand of coffee on the clothes of the woman at the bodega who sold me my morning paper. Better yet, one of these cues might have sparked the thought that I *needed* a cup of coffee, or that my body was tired from travel, or that I required sustenance at all. What if one such off-the-cuff cue primed me for something more substantial, like my desire to start a family?

I think about the theories Palo Alto has floated about reasons behind the suicide cluster. Gollwitzer would have me believe that primes in the environment are responsible for cuing social contagions like work ethic, ambition, and greed, and our fear-based responses as well. And yet, given everything I've learned about our strange contagion, I have to consider that the mind is strong enough to thwart ideas that are not its own, let alone those that propel it toward self-harm.

Still, the Motivation Lab continues to find evidence to the contrary. Many of our most personal goals are actually those we have inadvertently caught from primes in the community. Not only are goals contagious, but the mind has difficulty deciphering between an intrinsically motivated goal and one that a person has ostensibly picked up from someone else.

For instance, Gollwitzer says, women are more likely to get pregnant from thirteen to twenty-four months after a coworker has had a child. Men's roles in the proliferation of this contagion appear to be negligible, although the pregnant sister of a nonpregnant colleague will transmit the desire to have a child to women in the office within eighteen months of her sister giving birth. In other words, it's possible that a stranger's pregnancy can unintentionally influence another person's desire to have a baby. The mechanisms behind contagious goals go well beyond biological synchronicity, chemical signals that harmonize menstrual cycles, or biological cues from underarm-sweat compounds that provoke fear-based reactions. Gollwitzer is talking about something far more universal, the mundane and the everyday that hide in plain sight that possess the power to activate desires and goal commitments in each of us in both intentional and unintentional ways. "People have become very good at using hidden priming strategies to mold us," he says. Our standard QWERTY keyboard configuration is a beautiful piece of ingenuity specifically created to slow down typists, preventing typewriter jams. The original logo for Jack in the Box included subliminal religious subtext as the O and X came together to create the symbol of the Jesus fish, encouraging an adherence to a certain value system. To convince people to buy a product,

advertisers sell the customers on an environment or an experience, like the image of a modern kitchen instead of the features of a single appliance. During presidential campaign rallies,
color, lighting, and room temperature affect a crowd's energy
and mood. Department stores pipe in fast-paced music, priming
customers to move quickly from rack to rack, goading patrons
to see more inventories and increasing the likelihood they'll find
something they will like.

With this new understanding of primes, the makeup of the
strange contagion at home once again grows in complexity. My
definition continues to evolve. I briefly take stock of what I've
learned, about the delicate balance between treating social contagions and spreading them, about the way hysteria galvanizes
the power of the mind, creating feedback loops of paranoia and
fear. Adding to this classification the fact that objects cause us
to catch thoughts, behaviors, and emotions, this psychological
picture sharpens for me.

With his glasses still in his hand, Gollwitzer points behind
me and says, "That's where I lead team meetings." I turn and
look across the room toward the sofas. On the wall above the
love seat hangs a grouping of black-and-white photos I noticed
when I first arrived. I look at the pictures in their frames and
recognize Battery Park, the Hudson River slogging by in the
background. A dusting of snow clings to metal gate rails.

"So often our conversations get heated, so I asked a photog-
rapher to give me pictures that can cool us down."

Before I can fully process this, he directs my attention to his
work desk against a wall near the center of the office. My eyes
fall on the poster above it, an image of mismatched rooftops.
Some are made of brick, some of wood. Each pops with bright
color. "That's for me," he says. "It primes me for creativity."

I shake my head: he's intentionally set these primes for

himself, to unconsciously coax his moods, to guide his behaviors, to foster his strengths, to mitigate his weaknesses.

Just then I notice another poster on the wall, this one directly beside us. With a finger I gesture to the image of big glass skyscrapers, their mirrored windows reflecting distorted images in their glass. Graduate students discuss their research projects here at this table, he says. The image primes them to be open to different perspectives.

"The striking part is, most of the time we don't know we've been primed," he continues.

"This all seems . . ." I pause, searching for the right word. Thrilling. Crazy. Frightening. ". . . dangerous," I conclude.

Contagious goal pursuit assumes that, through subtle priming, we register an idea and behave as though it has originated from within. Companies invest billions of dollars annually to identify what those cues are, all in an effort to better understand potential customers and engage them. We can use this information to sell widgets as well as influence far more profound social changes. Researchers at Brown University, curious about the evolving nature of racial bias, took data measuring self-reported associations with facial perceptions. Specifically, they were curious about the way white people view faces of black minorities. In 2007 the number of positive associations increased. The timing was during the run-up to the presidential general election, where so much of the imagery around Barack Obama included his face and words such as *hope* and *change*. The study concluded that this level of media exposure conditioned people to invert negative perceptions, successfully reversing pejorative stereotypes.

We are encoding images and objects we see in the world everywhere we go. Nothing is neutral. Each object triggers a judgment, a feeling, a response. It becomes a memory that later, although it may never surface in our conscious minds, informs our decisions. When we see it again, out of context, out of the corner of our eye, it re-invokes visceral memories. This is how marketers and advertisers identify images that can, with very low-level visual properties, speak to us quickly and directly. Once we understand that thoughts, behaviors, and emotions are passed from person to person on an unconscious level, there's very little difference at all between a trend and a contagion.

Like Gollwitzer and his wall art, we often use these primes to cue ourselves, too. We wear a suit to an interview, instilling in ourselves and in potential employers a sense of professionalism on a bodily felt level. We engage in pregame rituals to focus our intent, to stoke our fortitude, to visualize a win.

And yet I can't help but worry that someone wise to these processes might easily manipulate others to engage in pursuits against their better judgment, the way a hypnotist entrances a member of the audience to hand over the contents of his wallet.

"That could happen, except for one thing," says Gollwitzer. The glasses turn in his fingers, and suddenly I'm paranoid that this small but distinct gesture is supposed to make me respond in some way, like a cat chasing string.

"The fail-safe," he says.

"There's a fail-safe?"

"There's always a fail-safe."

Chapter 15

TRIPPING THE FAIL-SAFE

To contract a goal, the goal must already be part of our behavioral vocabulary," Gollwitzer says. The mechanism for
influencing thoughts, behaviors, and emotions in other
people is dependent on certain internal stipulations. This fail-
safe stops us from enacting cues to, say, walk off a cliff or act
upon primes that might convince us to rob a store. It's the very
thing that saves people from catching a social contagion in the
first place. Gollwitzer is talking about a kind of resistance to a
social contagion. "If it's not part of our natural vocabulary, we
call that anti-normative and it won't catch."

Priming the shy to act with aggression only works so long
as they have ever behaved assertively in their lives. For women
to catch the desire to have a baby from the sister of a coworker,
at some point they will have envisioned themselves as mothers.
An unattractive trait like greediness is so universal that even the
most benevolent person is capable of exhibiting it. Therefore,
we're all vulnerable to it.

Returning to the topic of Palo Alto, Gollwitzer says, "You'd
think self-destruction is anti-normative for most of us. Well, if
you were to do an experiment where there's a task to be performed, and you can perform it in a way that is self-destructive,

you can in fact. Because many of us are self-destructive once in a while."

Like other qualities that commonly reside deep within our soul, each of us, in spite of our better judgment, possesses tendencies toward harmful behavior. Usually this stops at irreversible self-harm, but I fret now that this alone isn't enough of a fail-safe to protect people back home.

"All we have to do is identify the problematic cues," I say. If we do that, we can systematically go through and remove them. But even as I say this, I'm aware it's coming off sounding more like a question than a statement of fact.

Gollwitzer sighs doubtfully. The trouble is there are potentially dozens, even hundreds, of cues in our community that could be contributing to the strange contagion event. The iconography of Silicon Valley alone—the self-driving cars, Stanford University, billboards promoting technical products, and career opportunities at the biggest companies—is a prime for achievement, drive, greed, and work ethic. "There are some behaviors that we cannot solve with one or even a series of cues," he says, and I sink a bit.

What about finding primes to slow down the processes? Primes to halt impulsivity? Primes to instill hope in the hopeless? Primes to cue mood changes strong enough to stop mental illnesses? Primes to infuse a desire to think beyond one passing moment where the pain of living burns hotter than anything worth living for?

"In the lab, maybe," he replies. His lab has primed people to be more methodical in their endeavors and more precise in their thinking. The problem is they haven't been very successful in priming everything. Out in the world, he says, even if we slow one or two for some people, this is no match for a widespread cyclone of fear, hysteria, work ethic, greed, and God knows what

else. As much as the Motivation Lab possesses the ability to un-
lock parts of the human experience, the human experience itself
is, for better or worse, far more complicated and nuanced than
any collaboration of bright minds huddled in a research facility
might ever hope to fully decode.

THESE THOUGHTS TRIANGULATE in my head as I walk east, away
from the portico of NYU's psychology department. I turn the
corner onto Broadway and pause at the entrance to the Tisch
School of the Arts. I have a little while before I need to catch
my flight to California. So I tug on the entrance door and step
inside.

The lobby is a cavernous space with polished brick floors and
walls as pallid as teeth. An exhibit of photos features images
of flat desert landscapes, roiling oceans, beaches of smoothed
stone, and arching rock formations. Gollwitzer might say these
pictures prime us for movement or freedom or access to endless
and expansive possibility, activating any number of constructive character traits, exploiting all variety of vulnerabilities, and
launching a cascade of behaviors.

These photographs cull within me a sense of dismal resignation and a ceaseless urgency to keep searching for the coun-
terweight to the self-destructive impulses that speak to us and
move us in our most desperate times.

The Tisch School reminds me of Gunn High student Sonya
Raymakers, who accepted an offer to join this prestigious theater program. A couple of weeks before attending, she became
the second student to die by suicide on the Caltrain tracks. I
also think about home. Holding Gollwitzer's theories up against
this real-world tragedy, I feel at once satisfied and distressed. In
Palo Alto, we can pool our resources, throw up safety nets, and
engage in hard conversations, but without fully understanding

what problematic primes exist, or knowing what primes we might use to stop people from taking their lives, what good are they? My investigation has just become enormously more byzantine now that it involves a search for primes that could literally be anywhere.

I wonder about the cues that set Raymakers and the other four students who died each on their paths and I get stuck on the impossibility of ever truly knowing what those were. Furthermore, if primes are everywhere, manifesting in the form of economics, leaders, even inanimate objects, how do we guard against them? The problem seems monumental, almost hopeless, even.

And yet, in this endeavor to satisfy the journey I'm on and bring it to a plausible end, I can safely say, just as Gollwitzer explained, that the world around us has the capacity to motivate. To keep me moving forward. To provide me with the drive to reach this goal.

For now, however, all I want is to get back home; I want to hold my son again.

It's getting late in the day, so I make one more pass through the gallery and then head outside. Returning to the noise and the crush of people on the sidewalk, I continue down the steps of the Eighth Street Station and move underground to take my place beneath the surface.

Part V

THE INTERRUPTERS

"Aggression unopposed becomes a contagious disease."

—JIMMY CARTER

Chapter 16

FINDING THE MAN
WHO LAUNCHED A RAMPANT
REVOLUTION OF COURAGE

'm driving through a neighborhood of multimillion-dollar homes, each one set behind wrought iron gates, brick walls, or barriers of high bushes. The cars slow ahead, and two valets in matching purple jackets approach mine. One opens and holds my door for me. The other directs me to the house across the street, at the end of an outdoor walkway flanked on one side by a jaw-dropping waterfall spilling down two stories.

A couple of months after returning home from Philadelphia and New York, I received an e-mail from Adam Grant at Wharton. He hoped my fact-gathering trip had gone well and was writing to invite me to come with him to a party when he was in town next. The event was going to be held at the home of a high-powered tech industry executive. There were going to be dozens of big thinkers there who might have some perspective to share about the social contagions in the region.

I've never been invited into a house like this before, the kind that looks like a fancy hotel lobby inside, furnished with postmodern glass chandeliers and banks of video screens that run the entire length of a corridor wall. Grant introduces me to some of his friends and colleagues, each one more self-possessed than the next, dressed in expensive sport coats and blue jeans or little black dresses. At one point I slip away from the party. I find myself wandering the house and admiring its floor-to-ceiling windows and taking in the art installations. This level of abundance, at once overwhelming, grand, and thoroughly awesome, produces a blend of feelings in my chest, including the sense that I've desired something like this my whole life and never known it until right now.

But more than that, there's a thought that I am more than a bit out of my league, drifting among prestigious tech leaders, Silicon Valley celebrities, founders of online platforms, and PhDs in everything from engineering to organizational behavior. An unusual sense of inadequacy displaces any confidence I had at the start of the evening. So I retreat to the kitchen, where I notice a young man standing quietly by himself. His skin is brown. He's cultivated a short length of stubble around his thin mouth and dimpled chin. His shirt is bright red, his slacks sharply pressed. Like many of the faces I recognize tonight, I know him by the mark he's left on the world, which stands out from the other achievements represented here at the party. Unassuming though he is, quietly munching on a plate of sugar cookies he holds in one hand, a couple of years earlier Wael Ghonim, this mild-mannered Google techie, sparked the Egyptian revolution that upended the dictator Hosni Mubarak.

To pass an idea on to others is to spread a kind of truth. To catch it is to acquire a passion to infect others with it. In 2010, Egyptian police arrested and murdered a young man in Wael Ghonim's homeland, and Ghonim, in turn, created a Facebook page denigrating the injustice. Perhaps he felt a kinship to the boy, a connection forged through generational ties and country.

Or maybe turning to social media is just what young people do these days in response to emotions that not even they fully understand. Regardless, the sentiment moved a quarter of a million people to "like" his page. Ghonim then challenged his followers, the working-class Egyptians, silent activists, and disgruntled government employees, to channel their anger at the government into demands for reform through widespread prodemocratic demonstrations. For his efforts, Egyptian officials arrested Ghonim while he visited the country in January 2011. Swift international pressure mounted for his release. Twelve days after his abduction, Ghonim emerged from captivity a hero.

From there, the social contagion of courage he stoked from the portal of his computer spread far and wide. Anti-Mubarak protests cascaded into Tahrir Square with an unparalleled expression of fury and determination. At the Motivation Lab, Peter Gollwitzer told me that everyone has the potential for courage due to the representation of bravery within their character just waiting for a cue to prime them. We catch courage through vicarious prompts, he said, through symbols and stories and by hearing about courageous people.

History is full of soldiers and citizens and artists exploiting primes to steel the masses against fear. The English Romantic poet Percy Bysshe Shelley wrote about courage, epic poems on political attitudes and revolutions, narratives on nonviolence and social justice, cantos as vectors for bravery. After his death, his words spilled over the lips of revolutionaries. Mahatma Gandhi referred to Shelley as the source of his courage, as did Martin Luther King Jr., who suffused the civil rights movement in freedom songs that stirred and roused to, as he said, "give people new courage." Resistant art spreads courage to stand up against power holders. Activist art channels it to influence the political climate and proves to be a contagion as formidable as the sharpest of weapons. Courage remains a virtue in every religion and culture. Carl Rogers calls it the energizing catalyst for choosing growth over safety; Alfred Adler, the core of one's growth; Aristotle, the place in between the extremes of cowardice and foolhardiness; Confucius, bravery beyond the virtue of the noble warrior; Albert Bandura, the prime pronouncement of self-efficacy. No matter how one refers to valor, it is a quality we catch through vicarious modeling, by reading biographies and stories, by hearing about courageous acts, by listening to emboldening music. Even indirect exposure to people who act courageously increases the probability it will inspire the same behavior in others.

I've seen courage in Palo Alto, born out of necessity. Truly, it's an ongoing fight between the social contagions of bravery and fear. We fight to stand together in the face of loss and ask hard questions about ourselves along the way as we face an endless cycle of bad news. Sometimes it feels as though the fear is so much stronger than the courage. The writer William Ian Miller makes the case about the unequal weight of contagious emotions. Bravery is catchable, he writes, but with fear the effects are more lasting and intense.

I suppose, then, that the trick to passing along lasting courage is one of overwhelming the system with examples of it, flooding the environment with models of generosity, authority, demonstrations of personal responsibility, and examples of calm in the heat of battle.

Ghonim has seen wondrous things happen as a result of his example. The social contagion of courage he let loose in Egypt stole across the borderlands. Pro-democratic movements erupted in Libya and led to the first free national elections there in six decades. Demonstrators in Jordan forced King Abdullah to dissolve the parliament and remove the prime minister. The people of Bahrain demanded political freedom. Demonstrations in Saudi Arabia led King Abdullah to impose new economic reforms and granted women the right to vote.

He offers me a cookie from his small blue plate. I'm thinking now, I tell him, that what Silicon Valley needs is heroes, vectors for spreading constructive social contagions like courage and fortitude, social contagions to counter fear and hysteria and bolster resolve in the midst of the kind of uncertainty that arrives after five children take their lives. Luckily, this town comes by heroes easily. Even if you haven't heard of them, you've seen their work. You've integrated their contributions into your life either by function, by lexicon, or both. And when Ghonim returned from Egypt to Silicon Valley, we gained one more.

He puts his plate of cookies down on the counter and rubs a paper napkin across his lips. He then proceeds to tell me just how very wrong I am. Sometimes heroes spread more than just courage.

Chapter 17

WHERE ROLE MODELS ARE
JUST ANOTHER PRIME

Palo Alto is filled with stories of Ivy League achievements, of college dropouts turned billionaires, of geniuses in denim. For his part, Ghonim doesn't believe he merits the banner of hero. His contributions to the Egyptian revolution were relatively small by comparison to others', he says. But he's a representation of the good that role modeling offers, I counter. The problem, he replies, is that young people are trying really hard to emulate their role models and heroes when the reality is they are just buying into a kind of mythology of a person, which may or may not be all or even partially true.

This isn't a new argument. Thus far in my search, I've seen how compelling leaders spread charisma and how business managers inspire a strong work ethic that promotes both cutting-edge innovation and perfectionistic tendencies. The literature proposes that heroes serve a comparable function in arousing enormous ambition, a persistent and generalized striving for success, attainment, and accomplishment. Given this, I question how good role models can possibly be bad.

The truth is they're not. Drawing upon data from a longitudinal research study on high-ability children, organizational psychologists in 2012 published findings in the *Journal of Applied Psychology* that distinguish the ways that "persistent and generalized striving for success, attainment, and accomplishment" has constructive long-term implications. Ambition has acquired something of a bad reputation, as though it's part of a suite of traits that includes a lack of emotional empathy and drive and that supersedes all else. But ambition, according to the study, doesn't constitute a character flaw that leads to dissatisfaction or creates feelings of unquenchable desires for outcomes.

That doesn't mean it can't be, though, writes the Oxford psychiatrist Neel Burton. Highly ambitious people, he suggests, are sensitive to resistance and failure. They experience an almost constant dissatisfaction or frustration. "To live with ambition is to live in fear and anxiety." The level of accomplishment Ghonim brings to Silicon Valley becomes yet another model of unparalleled achievement for children to look up to, and for some to struggle mightily to emulate. Ghonim has returned home to Silicon Valley as just another prime.

And this feeling I've experienced on my way into the house tonight, astounded by a lavishness that stokes a longing in me to own a piece of it, if only for the couple of hours I meander through the party, is exactly the kind of thinking that spreads through Silicon Valley, riding the countenance of role models. A person who falls short, finding himself unable to emulate a kind of achievement in a community rich with success stories, will either become highly ambitious, writes Burton, or "withdraw in the belief that he is fundamentally inadequate," leading him to become "dismissive or even destructive." One has to wonder if our heroes, like the charismatic leaders in our midst—these vectors for social contagions—are doing more damage than good.

GHONIM LAUNCHED HIS campaign on Facebook, and the momentum of the Egyptian uprising ensnared hundreds of thousands of strangers. The funny thing is that fewer than 20 percent of people in Egypt had Internet access. Most demonstrators were entirely unaware of Ghonim's online presence from which he put out his call to action. Rather, they caught an echo contagion so powerful that it overrode competing logic and rational fear to leverage a prevailing desire for change at any cost. This tells me that role models are so influential that oftentimes we don't even know whom we're modeling—or that we're modeling them at all. And that at once enthralls and frightens me. When are our behaviors not our own? I wonder. Even though Gollwitzer said primes cannot cue us to do anything that's not already within our nature, this still leaves a lot of territory to guard.

After the lavish house party Ghonim's story stays with me. I return to the archives and begin digging again. I come across two remarkable scenarios in which primes cued strangers to enact violence. In one of his early behavioral studies, the psychologist Fritz Redl described a spontaneous food fight at a camp for troubled youth. The scene involved dozens of campers and a flurry of flying heavy plastic plates. If I were to follow the substrate of influence back in time, maneuver over tumbling flatware, duck under spinning projectiles, and swerve around half-cocked arms and wide-eyed youngsters, I'd zero in on an instigator whose singular act of bad behavior interrupted the harmony of the mess hall by influencing eighty campers to jump into a fight.

I also find a story in the *New York Post* about an argument that broke out between a few members of a prestigious sports club. Details remained scarce, but according to witnesses the source of discord was a woman. Hearts were involved. Tensions rose. When words no longer sufficed, one member of the club

threw a punch at another. Fist met jaw, and the air crackled. Serotonin levels dropped. Anger moved across the room like a destructive electrical pulse, blowing out prefrontal cortex circuits
that ordinarily controlled their moral judgments. It overloaded
emotion regulation capabilities and activated the clobbering impulse in people not otherwise involved in the dispute. The ensuing barroom brawl pulled dozens into the mix. Police moved in
and arrested three of the club's distinguished members. Ambu-
lances carted others away for medical treatment to repair broken noses and fractured eye sockets.

These two reports, with their cascades of fists and flinging
dishes, speak to the effect of behavioral contagions, a kind of
unconscious communication, a dialect of Mark Micale's proto-
language that takes place between people and that blooms from
social influence. As I read about these scenarios, three things
stand out to me. The first is that Redl observed that people who
introduce these contagions of behavior—the role models—
often don't realize the high-prestige or heroic positions they
hold within the community culture. The sociologist Mark Gra-
novetter suggests that often the holders of these high-prestige
positions are those with the lowest convincing threshold, meaning it takes little to move them to action. Ghonim falls unerr-
ingly into this category. So does the first sports club member to
throw a punch and the camper who Frisbeed his plate across the
mess hall and touched off an epic food fight.

The second thing that strikes me is that, like the instigators
themselves, often the people who catch a social contagion of behavior have no idea who the high-prestige holder is either. While
the holders of high prestige need no convincing from other people to throw a plate or a punch, the next people to join in have
a slightly higher threshold and probably wouldn't have started
the fight without noticing someone else fighting first. The effect

continues, with the last people to jump into the fray having the highest threshold. Unconscious behavioral influence has less to do with the people afforded high prestige and far more to do with the people around them.

Lastly and perhaps most significantly, while holders of high prestige spread courage and ambition, they also have the potential to spread bad behavior. At the tech executive's house party, Ghonim told me that as peaceful as the revolution was, ever since he'd returned to Silicon Valley, he'd watched, heartbroken, as Egypt slid back into hostility. As much as holders of high prestige can prime people for peaceful revolution and courage, they also cue for one of the most contagious things in the register of human behavior: the social contagion of violence.

Which brings me back to my early concern. If our behaviors are not always our own, then holders of high prestige can influence some people to become violent toward others and themselves. It's something I've thought about in recent years, too, particularly as violent episodes like school shootings have seemingly caught across America, often stirring in people the question of just how transmittable something like this actually is. I consider the risk of vulnerable people mirroring toxic thoughts and behaviors transmitted by media, by public discourse, by knowledge seemingly alive in the ether as another school shooting takes place at a rate of one a month in the US. That is, I've begun to recognize this pattern, seeing within it the telltale signs of a strange contagion on a national scale. Following this line of thought, I pull up research by the computational epidemiologist Sherry Towers, whose main area of study involves contagion modeling. Towers mapped incidents of school shootings over time and found that they, like fistfights and food fights, are beholden to the laws of social contagions as well. Towers calculated that 20 to 30 percent of school shootings result from one campus shooter priming the next. Perpetrators have either consciously or unconsciously caught the idea, behaviors, and emotions necessary to pull off such heinous events, not so much from a single holder of high prestige but from high-profile events that tend to get national attention.

And it is here, on this circuitous path from Wharton Business School to New York University to a house party in Silicon Valley and into a research vortex, where I stumble upon my next significant lead for a potential cure to the strange contagion at home.

My reading of Towers's work on gun violence points me toward a little-known area of research involving approaches to eradicating the social contagion of violence. I circle a name in blue pen. If it's true that someone out there is close to creating an effective therapy to end a phenomenon as rampant as violence, this person might bring us closer to ending violence of the self-inflicted kind.

Chapter 18

ON THE TRAIL OF A CURE MODEL

Ever since the deaths of the five children in Palo Alto, I have found myself on at least a half a dozen commuter rails—the Metro-North Railroad, the Long Island Rail Road, the Metra, Amtrak, Caltrain, and, now that I'm back in Chicago, I'm riding the L.

As I travel east of the city I catalog the trains in my head, in particular noting their differences, the way that each system renders unique environments and experiences. There's the distinction between the sound of footsteps inside carpeted cars and those with linoleum floors. There's the thrill of discovering the second level of a double-decker train, and then there's the unanimity, the we're-all-in-this-together-ness, that exists among the people of the single-level trains. There's the forking over of five dollars for a packaged Danish from the café car, and there are trains that don't even serve coffee. There are the cheerful announcers, and there are the announcers who can't be bothered, cutting off the intercom before completing their sentences.

As a kid I loved riding trains, though I didn't take them often. I liked standing and walking in the aisle, trying to hold my balance as the car zipped like a Gimlet rocket. I enjoyed the effortlessness with which the train whisked me from zero to a momentum faster than that of a car's, and the speed with which the landscapes brushed past the windows. The world looks different at these velocities.

You stop seeing the minutiae and start seeing its actual shape. The whole picture comes into greater focus the faster you go.

By now, though, the experience of riding the train has grown to provoke a feeling of melancholy. A man surrounded by the parts of a newspaper sits in the row across from me. In front of him, a guy with a cat T-shirt, torn pants, and dirty sandals is typing on his laptop in the seat. Two little girls a few rows up drink from tall cans of fruit punch. It isn't hard to imagine the effect that stopping short at this speed would have on all of us, what the jolt might feel like, pulling my fellow passengers from the momentum keeping us on the tracks of our ordinary lives. If someone were to stand on the rails just ahead, would we feel the train strike a body? Would we see anything from our windows? Would personnel hide the carnage before allowing us to disembark? Would these images consume us forever?

ALONG WITH CATALOGING the trains, I roll through the components of the strange contagion I've been able to identify over these past two years, the hysteria, the work ethic, the greed, the self-fulfilling prophecy of fear, as well as the ways to counter each of them, and some of the problems inherent in doing so. I've also learned that primes number so many that categorizing them all is virtually impossible. With my trip to Chicago, though, I'm searching for something a little bit different, an all-encompassing solution. I have reason to believe that Sherry Towers's work in gun violence points the way to one, a unique framework for us to model.

And that's where Gary Slutkin factors in.

As a young epidemiologist, Slutkin was fascinated by something he's since come to call *the invisible*—the realm where infectious diseases exist, and where social contagions thrive, all beyond the scope of the human eye. It is in this realm that Slutkin, a specialist in communicable illness control, has learned to exist as well. While he facilitated the containment of a rampant tuberculosis outbreak in San Francisco in the early eighties, he came to understand the invisible. He fought the invisible to stop the spread of cholera among refugee populations in Somalia. He worked to tame the invisible, and when he couldn't tame it, he learned to work with the invisible by creating interconnected systems of local outreach workers that kept his team abreast of symptoms that signaled new occurrences of disease. These networks helped Slutkin persuade resistant populations to accept medication, to change the way they prepared the bodies, to purify their water, to hydrate their children, and to quarantine the sick—the sort of behavioral changes that, in the context of poverty, low resources, traditional thinking, and political corruption, often presented insurmountable boundaries to eradication. These victories were slow and hard-won, and after a decade in the field he felt it was time to return home to the United States.

Slutkin tells me his story as we sit across from each other in his personal office at the University of Illinois at Chicago. I'd taken the L to the school of public health and an elevator to a floor lined with subway tiles and green lockers. It's a friendlier-looking place than Peter Gollwitzer's Motivation Lab, replete with windows and reception areas and well-lit corridors. Slutkin himself strikes me as someone with a low center of gravity, both in looks and disposition. His shoulders are sturdy, his face perpetually offering up a kind of determined regard, even with that softening glint of delight in his eye. At ten in the morning he has already rolled his dark blue shirtsleeves to the bends of his elbows. There is a small United Nations flag mounted on the sill behind his desk, and his window overlooks a brown-gray urban skyline. Outside, the murder rate is higher than it is in New York or Los Angeles. Armed robbery, gang violence, aggravated battery, and rape clock in at rates well above those of most US cities. "When I got back, this problem of violence in Chicago— and all throughout the country, really—was staring me in the face." There was a familiar pattern about it, he says, the way the violence moved from person to person, from one community to the next. "Violence was sharing characteristics of bacterial spread."

Cultures under an electron microscope show individual germs adopting similar morphologies, colors, and chemical character- istics of those around them. Each eats the same way, eliminates the same way, and multiplies the same way. The closer he looked at patterns of violence, the more Slutkin saw that people operate similarly to bacterial cultures when they're exposed to this specific social contagion.

There were other similarities, too. For instance, the biggest barrier to eradicating both infectious diseases and social con- tagions is none other than the contagion itself. Just as cholera leads to more cases of cholera, violence leads to more cases of violence. In both turf wars and civil wars, aggression is the fuel that spreads further acts of brutality. Exposure to violence in the community increases the likelihood that a person will act vi- olently in the home; exposure to violence in the home increases the likelihood that a person will act violently in the commu- nity. "We are not separate from nature. We *are* nature. Behavior catches for the same reason that bacteria does. It's the most effi- cient way to continue its evolution. What has been learned over generations is most easily transferred by modeling, copying, or imitating." He adds, "And hardly any of it is done consciously.

We have an idea that as individuals and as a species we are making decisions about how we behave, but the world is too complex for that. In terms of brain function, we're talking about 100 billion neurons, 100 trillion connections, all firing below our consciousness."

This is the invisible.

It's the method of contraction. It's the process of spreading. It's the pattern that emerges once we modify our perspective, once we speed things up, once we slow them down, once we examine the phenomenon piece by piece as one might explore the complex nature of a strange contagion event.

After chasing the invisible for years across the continent of Africa, Slutkin took his medical model for tracking epidemics of disease and applied it to a growing epidemic of violence in the US. With both disease control and behavioral change methods in mind, Slutkin designed the Cure Violence framework. Where in Africa he relied on networks of local monitors to alert his team to symptoms of cholera or TB, Cure Violence creates hyper-local networks of regional social workers, former gang members, and trusted leaders of the community.

He calls these his *interrupters*. They stop the spread. Kill the progression. Sever the pathway.

I ask Slutkin how you become an interrupter. He says that you explain to people how one incident of violence spreads to others, how to spot the signs of potential spread, and how to de-escalate it before it multiplies.

At the first sign of violence, interrupters fan across the hot zone. Where Slutkin once distributed medication to infected populations, violence interrupters apply immediate social and educational interventions to stop the spread of retaliatory aggression. They show up at the hospitals treating victims and connect with their friends, family members, and any gang affiliations to cool heated emotions, mediating conflicts before they grow more lethal.

Slutkin turns his laptop to me. He's pulled up a screen full of stats. In Baltimore, implementation of the Cure Violence model has reduced killings by 56 percent and shootings by 44 percent. People in program sites are four times more likely to show little or no support for gun use. Saturating the most violent New York neighborhoods, the model has lowered monthly shooting rates by 6 percent; in Puerto Rico's communities, shooting deaths have diminished by 50 percent; and participating communities in the UK have seen a 95 percent reduction in group violence. More than half of the communities that have adopted the model in Chicago experienced a 100 percent reduction in retaliation homicides. In each case, the program has created an infrastructure of police outposts, doctors, social workers, and teachers. Cure Violence has not only trained interrupters to recognize the symptoms leading to outbreaks, it has also taught them to maintain the fortitude to confront them, as well as the presence of mind to pull in the proper resources. Slutkin's premise is a simple but important one. By explaining to people how this social contagion works and why it spreads, the Cure Violence model gives control back to communities. Understanding the way that this social contagion affects our behaviors, our feelings, and our thoughts allows people-as-interrupters to better influence and operate their own destinies.

"We're making the invisible visible," he says.

I take a moment to sort my thoughts. All right, I think, Slutkin figures out that if he builds an infrastructure of highly trained interrupters, educated in how to recognize the signs and treat the symptoms of violence, he can effectively put a stop to a widespread social contagion. Gone are his days of working alongside the invisible. He's now exposing the invisible. Showing people how it works. Explaining why it works. Teaching them ways to stop it from working. Sherry Towers was, in her own way, doing her part to expose the invisible, too. She identified the social contagion; Slutkin identified the cure.

I turn this all over in my head: contagion, cure, exposing the invisible. There's a greedy part of me that wants to buy Slutkin's idea completely, to believe that a cure is within reach, to trust that awareness, that volatile and important ingredient, is ultimately the most effective and influential of weapons against components of a strange contagion. Thus far in my search, Slutkin's approach to awareness is perhaps the most logical of responses I've yet heard. But my reservations rest in what I've thus far learned about social contagions, how they are singularly driven by design to spread. They are dependent on awareness, even on an unconscious level, to thrive. Gerald Russell and Anne. E. Baker highlighted the damaging power of awareness with eating disorders, even as prosocial media campaigns to spread treatment led to other people catching the illness in greater numbers. Yet, there's the argument of awareness as a counterbalance, particularly when we use fact to dampen fear-based contagions like hysteria. Is Slutkin's model strong enough to outsmart the nocebo effect of expectation, where facts fail to supplant superstition, myth, and false beliefs and create a self-fulfilling prophecy?

"Can we talk about Silicon Valley?" I ask. "Can it use your model to treat its symptoms?"

I find myself looking at Slutkin now as though urging him with my gaze to offer up another clue. In response, his eyes flash with confidence.

"Silicon Valley already is."

Chapter 19

IF IT CAN STOP VIOLENCE,
IT CAN STOP THIS

The sister towns of Palo Alto and East Palo Alto are connected by University Avenue and divided by an interstate
that is ostensibly the gateway to Silicon Valley. Despite
proximity and their names, the two communities couldn't be
more different. Palo Alto is one of the wealthiest places in the
country. On the west side of the interstate, University Avenue
is lined with estates, tree-shaded sidewalks, suites occupied by
technology companies, and high-end shops and restaurants.
It's basically a fiber-optic cable shuttling modernity out to the
world. Continue to follow University Avenue in this direction
and it stabs at the heart of Silicon Valley, where ten of the planet's richest people own homes and where the median household
income at the time the suicide cluster began was a staggering
$120,000 a year.

On the opposite side of the interstate, University Avenue
feeds into the unincorporated town of East Palo Alto, a community both surrounded by innovation-driven wealth and
untouched by it. Property values during the dot-com boom
remained dormant. The median household income stagnated
at a little less than $45,000 a year, with more than 22 percent

of families existing below the poverty line. East Palo Alto is known for its high rate of violent crime and gang activity. The town registers more than two hundred assaults annually, while its neighbor, Palo Alto, registers a fifth of that.

Given its proximity, one has to wonder what's preventing the contagion of violence from jumping eight lanes of interstate to infiltrate Palo Alto. It's not as though Palo Alto is impervious to the social contagion of violence. In 1995, police responded to a 911 call reporting gunshots fired amid a group of teens gathered on Channing Avenue. Palo Alto didn't have a gang problem, yet this isolated event worried people that the troubles of East Palo Alto had finally jumped the freeway and were now spreading into this quiet community. Police downgraded the offense from a gang confrontation to a disagreement between two *wannabe* gangs, made up of about a dozen or so students from Palo Alto area schools. One of the kids involved told the *Palo Alto Weekly* that he and his friends wanted to go to Penn State, not the state pen. Even the so-called gang members of Palo Alto aspire to four-year institutions of higher education.

Responding to this singular incident, the Palo Alto city council passed a curfew. A task force on gangs and violence formed in a town where, as one official put it, violent activity often happens by coincidence, not on purpose. East Palo Alto, meanwhile, remained the true center for gang activity with a flourishing drug trade and high murder rate. It's easy to conclude that Palo Alto at best overreacted and at worst fed its reputation in some circles as a rich and entitled community with very little connection to the real world. But a dive into the socioeconomic and cultural data of the region suggests a third explanation. Palo Alto has a very low threshold of tolerance for violence, while East Palo Alto's threshold of tolerance is notably higher.

When she was looking into the spread of gun violence on US

campuses, Sherry Towers noted the effect of this threshold of tolerance. Why, for instance, wasn't gun violence also catching in neighboring Canada, where the rate of mass shooting fatalities remains at a remarkably low 0.01 per hundred thousand? The per capita incidence of mental illness in both countries is relatively similar. Both have broad exposure to the same media. Firearm ownership is the same, although the normative culture associated with them in Canada is overwhelmingly hunters and not self-defense. A culture's threshold of tolerance, Towers concluded, is one of the most important factors regulating the spread of gun violence. Canada's worst mass shooting occurred in 1989 at the Université de Montréal, resulting in the deaths of fourteen students. After a single national catastrophe, Canada underwent a cultural reexamination that led to the passing of stringent gun control laws. Towers concluded that Canada's tolerance threshold for campus shootings was much lower than in America, where gun-related deaths remain far higher than in any other developed country.

Like Canada, the town of Palo Alto has a particularly low threshold of tolerance for violence and therefore moved swiftly to end it the moment it occurred. Decades of exploitation and mistreatment by the region have resulted in East Palo Alto conversely developing a high threshold of tolerance for violence. In the fifties, the county replaced the depressed farming community with cheap housing. The surrounding wealthy suburbs fleeced the East Palo Alto workforce. The expansion of the highway eliminated forty-five major businesses. My town annexed nearly a quarter of East Palo Alto, divesting the community of property tax revenue. At the same time, the county levied significant utility taxes on East Palo Alto. Crime rates rose and the middle class fled. Make no mistake: an area with so few education opportunities and such immense poverty was doomed to cultivate an environment perfect for the spread of this social contagion and a higher threshold of tolerance for violence.

When East Palo Alto adopted the Cure Violence model, it trained violence interrupters to identify and deescalate conflicts. Police and outreach workers infiltrated key points of this vulnerable community. They converted parks and known gangland hangouts into Fitness Improvement Training (FIT) zones, public spaces for power walking classes, mindfulness groups, and aerobic dance to help citizens regain control of their neighborhoods. Within a year of implementation, the campaign led to a 60 percent reduction in shootings.

After finishing his story, Slutkin turns his laptop back around to face him and closes the screen. I look at him again as I consider my next question. I know it's hypothetical, and I know it's beyond the scope of his considerable expertise, but I ask it anyway, because the puzzle piece is in hand, and it has been in hand all this time, working its methods in East Palo Alto without most people's knowledge.

If the Cure Violence model can stop one social contagion, can we retool it and use it to stop several? Building a Cure Violence–style infrastructure to support treatment seems like a viable way to interrupt social contagions beyond aggression and brutality.

Then again, stopping violence is one thing, but using his system to stop a perfect storm of varying social contagions—fear, hysteria, harmful work ethic, greed, and the primes that cue them all—is a task I fear is far grander in scope. Educating people to become interrupters of the strange contagion is to educate them on the signs and symptoms of at least half a dozen components, maybe more. It's an enormous undertaking, and one, I suspect, that's virtually impossible to execute.

"Is it, though?" I ask him.

The question piques his interest; he approaches it with

theoretical aplomb. Is it possible to overlay Palo Alto's strange contagion with an expanded version of his Cure Violence model? His head tilts in consideration, and his mouth flattens as his mind works. The ability to consider hypotheticals is a special skill set, a contradictory mix of truth and yearning, and I find myself deeply appreciative that he's indulging me. His eyes glimmer with empathy.

To build out this theoretical infrastructure, he says, requires creating language to normalize the conversation about contagious thoughts, behaviors, and emotions. Promoting deep emotional talks between families and friends of those at risk. Providing outlets for people to express themselves. Educating the community on all of the mental health resources at its disposal, then scaling the infrastructure by establishing more clinics and hospitals and beds for practitioners to utilize for their patients. Engaging policy makers to mandate adequate insurance reimbursement for outpatient services. Then increasing the number of trained mental health professionals, specifically in suicide risk assessment and treatment.

We will train our teachers, students, and school administrators to be interrupters. They will identify the warning signs of problematic social contagions in play and intercept the chain long before it leads to tragedy. For it to work, literally everyone in these settings must become an interrupter of the invisible. Creating so many interrupters becomes a kind of social contagion in itself. We will educate the holders of high prestige and let them spread the contagion of interrupters through primes, through body language, through fertile memes, "parasiting the mind," turning it, as Richard Dawkins writes, into a vehicle for propagation. Through them, others will contract the social contagion of vigilance. Resilience. Fortitude. They will catch the will to act. Because the more people begin to look out for one another, the more of a chance there is to stop this strange contagion for good.

The fact that the region has already implemented the Cure Violence model to some success suggests to me that it is receptive to this kind of treatment. And now that Slutkin has made the invisible processes visible to me, I now see that expanding the model to encompass the strange contagion is not so much of a hypothetical after all. I recognize the beginnings of that infrastructure already in place. It's here in the way that Gunn High has called in mental health resources, the way Stanford psychologists have encouraged the media to curb their language, the way that the town has held routine symposiums on solutions, the way that the school district has proposed referendums on education practices. And who knows? Maybe that's why we haven't experienced another suicide in more than two years now. The infrastructure, fragile and uncertain, is holding. No, the only hypothetical here is that the interrupters are enough to keep the perfect storm at bay.

Part VI

THE INTERLOPERS

"And not only the pride of intellect, but the stupidity of intellect. And, above all, the dishonesty, yes, the dishonesty of intellect. Yes, indeed, the dishonesty and trickery of intellect."

—LEO TOLSTOY

Chapter 20

THE IMPOSSIBLE REACH

n the summer of 2012, our friends begin to move out of town. The first is a family who has two girls under the age of five. The husband is the principal of a charter elementary school, his wife a nurse at Stanford Health Care. He gets a job at a school in the Central Valley, and they move that fall with little warning.

The next to leave is a couple that has two little children. They buy a little bungalow about twenty miles south of Palo Alto. Another family emigrates to Israel. A family of four we know moves to Arizona. Neighbors three units away from our apartment move with their young kids across the bay to Berkeley. A teacher from the children's center at Google loads her belongings into her flatbed truck and relocates someplace in the Midwest with her fiancé ahead of starting a family.

Each of our acquaintances leaves for different reasons, from job opportunities to the high cost of living that forces them out of town. Yet, down to a person, they admit they are not going to miss worrying about having to raise their children in Silicon Valley. It doesn't seem to matter to any of them that two years have come and gone without another child stepping on the tracks. The memories of the cluster remain fresh. More than memories, though, the fear of another death looms unreasonably high for people in this traumatized town. Life is calm now, but we all know how quickly that calm can crumble into chaos. We all know how little it takes, too, like the tap of a ballpeen hammer against a reconstituted ceramic urn. We assume every inhale leads to an exhale, but the town hasn't released the air in its lungs in thirty months, and at this point neither time nor distance has weakened its resolve. We're waiting for a guarantee it won't happen again, and we'll keep waiting. The five dead have become stand-ins for so many of the troubles of this remarkable place. At the same time, we have come to see the troubles as responsible for taking these children. If I'm honest with myself I'm not yet certain how safe I believe we are, either. It's something we'll only know in hindsight, I suppose.

The truth is I still have so many questions, like what else was going on under the membrane of the strange contagion two years ago. There is more that we do not understand about what's happened. If we don't understand it fully, then we risk it happening again. This investigation doesn't end until it reveals all of its secrets. The strange contagion is the sum of its parts, but it's also bigger than that. If my search has taught me anything, it's that individual social contagions matter in our day-to-day lives. As long as they exist, there also exists potential for another perfect storm forming over our heads. At least, this is what I find myself worrying about as friends leave and we continue to stay behind.

Our talk of absconding from town grows more serious as our group further disperses. My wife and I start to see safety in their decisions to distance themselves. During a recent conversation with Noreen Likins, the principal of Gunn High who retired shortly after the fifth suicide, I learned that she was commuting eighty miles a day from her home in Santa Cruz to work and back. "It was almost a sense of relief," she told me, reflecting on living outside of Silicon Valley. "When you get to the summit on Highway 17 and you start coming down, it's like you leave that behind you. The ability to do that, I think, kept me sane during that time. I could come home. I could try to put it aside."

Yet, for each person we know who has left town, there are many others clamoring to get in, to take advantage of everything it has to offer, and to contribute to making it the community they want it to be. From its natural beauty to a culture rich in aspiring entrepreneurs and flush with money, there's a reason the county is growing faster than any other in California.

The horror embodied in the deaths, typified by the quiet ambition of the maple-shaded streets named after Princeton, Yale, Cornell, Columbia, and Amherst, is really no more frightening than any place otherwise defined, or crushed by, a self-created character. In this case, it is a character so many have tried and failed to mimic.

I've visited Austin's technology incubators and Boston's Route 128 corridor; they've come close. China has invested billions in development spending to galvanize research and innovation with the aim of seeding its own version of Silicon Valley. Policy makers in Australia have done the same. Communities throughout the US are terraforming university towns into new centers of invention. But no one has succeeded in matching the output and advances that are coming out of this fifteen-hundred-square-mile body of land, this dimple in the West Coast, this navel of advancement.

Even if other places do not replicate the magic of Silicon Valley, notes the *MIT Technology Review*, they've taken note of its mind-set. The desire to achieve is as catching as anything so technologically flashy coming out of this place. Still, every attempt to replicate its level of output and achievement has failed to match the spirit of this charmed and overconfident El Dorado. They fumble their attempts to integrate innovation with business strategies. They falter at recreating a community-wide corporate culture that rests on a foundation of openness and idea sharing.

We watch people come and go, and we continue to weigh the elements that constitute the underbelly of Silicon Valley against the beauty and the promise, no better typified than by the event that transpires one fall morning in the skies above us.

I read online that NASA is retiring the space shuttle *Endeavour*. To wish it a bon voyage, the space agency is flying the ship to its final resting place in Los Angeles. Navigationally, its flight path takes it right above our town.

We roll a double stroller with our newborn daughter and now three-year-old son into a brown field across from Google headquarters. We work a bit to find a spot in the gathering throng and then spread our blanket on the ground. We straighten the corners, lay our backs down, and face the sky. Some around us point high-powered cameras to the north. Others are charting the path of the low-level flyover on their smartphones. After about an hour, a dark spec materializes out of the morning haze. As it nears, we can make out that the shuttle is catching a ride on the back of NASA's modified 747 airplane.

I get to my feet, lift my son by the armpits, and seat him on my shoulders. His red tennis shoes swing at my chest. I touch the palms of my hands to his ankles. The craft soars over our heads, so low that we can clearly make out the details of the shuttle and the NASA insignia on the airplane's fin. I feel my son's weight shift. He reaches up to try to grab it.

I notice that a lot of people are reaching for the shuttle, too, as though this marvel of engineering has at once activated something embedded within each of us, an impulse to extend our hands and reach higher than our capacity to achieve. The people we are among pride themselves on refuting these boundaries, having become accustomed to believing that you, too, can learn to reach such heights. Here, you can orbit people, planets, celestial bodies, and even outshine them, leaving everyone else in the dust.

Chapter 21

CONSIDERING THE PIGGYBACK TREATMENT

Autumn in New York brings with it a cooling off of spirit that moves in with the sweep of crispness in the air. The bank of flags across the front of the United Nations Headquarters casts a shadow across the sidewalk of First Avenue as I pass underneath it. Across the street, I move through a heavy glass door and past a United Nations Plaza security station. Neither X-ray machine nor metal detector is strong enough to spot the kind of social contagions I'm after. No amount of security guards, with all the firepower of a small army, possesses the means to stop them, either.

A few days ago I was still at home. The television was switched to the evening news. It featured a clip of the *Endeavour*'s flyover. The camera lens had managed to capture a perspective from a spectacular vantage point that showed the spacecraft in crisp detail, rendering in me a sense that perhaps we hadn't been there at all, or had seen an entirely different event transpire with our own eyes. Watching it on television, that bottomless thrill bloomed in my chest all over again. Such is the power of media, at once capable of revealing and enhancing reality. Watching the space shuttle move across the screen, it occurred to me that if we can catch social contagions like eating disorders and somatic symptoms of hysteria, then we might also use the medium of television to introduce a specific kind of cure. We could allow a foolproof remedy to piggyback on the digitalized, high-definition images just as the *Endeavour* rode on the back of the 747.

To test this theory, today I find myself back in Manhattan, now standing face-to-face with an armed guard who's examining my identification in his big hand with a thoroughness that's a bit excessive. He asks me what exactly brings me here to UN Plaza. I consider telling him that I have reason to believe that the next piece of an impossible puzzle is located on the fifth floor of this building. Or I can tell him that I've come 4,000 miles to ask a man named Sean Southey about how to remedy a strange contagion he's never heard of before.

Instead, I tell him I'm here visiting an organization called PCI Media Impact. The security guard turns my license under a pocket blue light, then looks at me and hands it back with no expression. After checking my name against a roster on the computer, he motions me through a metal detector and into an elevator. He pushes the button for my floor and slips back into the lobby as the doors slide shut. They don't mess around here. I can understand that; I'm not here to mess around, either.

The organization I'm looking for is at the end of a short hallway. I step into a suite full of editing booths and producers toiling quietly at computers. A young guy with short hair and a dark beard closest to the entrance looks up at me, not nearly as skeptical as the lobby guard. Just hang back for a bit, he says. Someone will come to fetch me soon. I sit down on a hard plastic chair. The walls are electric orange. A large poster in a plastic frame reads REACHING THE NEXT BILLION WITH LIFE CONVINCING STORIES.

To my immediate left, my eyes are drawn to, of all things, the vintage wooden case of a century-old Singer sewing machine. I recognize it only because, growing up, my family had an heirloom sewing machine just like it. Similar to the one in the waiting area of this Manhattan media enterprise, mine also served as a table stand. The organization's executive director, Sean Southey, soon appears beside it. He's dressed in a dark sport coat, slacks, and thin-framed glasses.

"Why the sewing machine?" I ask, standing up and shaking his hand over its case.

"You like it?"

"It's beautiful," I say, pressing the flat of my hand against the smooth container. The scuffed wood thirsts for finish. The machine inside is a dull sheen of black and overlaid with gold filigree. Most of its parts are still intact: the balance wheel, the spool pin, the tension disks, and the needle bar. Judging by the look of it, all faded and busted up, no one has worked the sewing machine in a long while. All it might take for the device to come alive again is a simple press of the foot against its cast-iron treadle, cranking its wide band wheel, threading the leather belt up its pulley system, and initiating a symphony of movements, all to pull a single thread into a length of fabric. Such an ordinary motion once seeded a fever that took over all of Latin America. And that, if the security guard must know, is exactly what brings me here.

THE HIGHEST-RATED SOAP opera in broadcast history is a Peruvian-produced telenovela called *Simplemente María*. It aired from 1969 to 1971 and told the story of a rural-urban migrant from the Andes Mountains who came to the big city to find work and fortune. The first dozen or so episodes related her struggles to endure in a poor immigrant neighborhood. To earn a living wage, she cleaned homes and at night attended adult literacy classes led by Maestro Esteban, who was secretly in love with his student. Maestro Esteban's mother was the one to teach María to become a seamstress by running fabric across the needle of a Singer sewing machine—just like the prop that now sits in the lobby of PCI Media Impact. At the end of the four-hundred-episode run, María was no longer a poor maid but the president of an international fashion design empire in Paris.

Though pure entertainment, *Simplemente María* addressed the liberation of migrant women, the treatment of domestic servants, and the conflict between social classes. The series was an instant hit. It garnered higher audience ratings than the World Cup Soccer championship games during all the years it aired.

Interestingly, Singer sewing machine manufacturers during that time also reported a 9 percent increase in sales in all eighteen countries that broadcast the telenovela. This corresponded with household maids there taking up sewing in record numbers. As Southey recounts this story, I'm reminded of the studies of Anne E. Becker and the years she chronicled the people of Fiji catching a slender ideal based on a stable stream of nineties television shows.

Like Becker, far more significant in the eyes of a producer in Mexico named Miguel Sabido was the psychology behind this unexpected correlation. Viewers that strongly identified with the character of María adopted her desire to move up the social ladder, represented by her ability to turn sewing into a symbol of personal empowerment. Later studies were to show that the effect cascaded, reaching people who hadn't even watched the series but who were also taking up sewing. Endeavoring to understand how random elements of the show's larger narrative inadvertently inspired dramatic behavior changes in viewers, Sabido found himself in none other than Palo Alto, California.

Ten years earlier, the Stanford University psychologist Albert Bandura instructed his lab assistants to blow air into inflatable vinyl toys. Fully expanded, each stood roughly the size of a grown adult and was shaped like an upside-down lightbulb. You could buy one of these creepy-looking self-righting punching bags at your local toy store for a few dollars. But Bandura's lab was using them to change the way we understand behavior and how we catch it from one another. One by one, seventy-two children from the university's nursery school entered a playroom filled with toys. Half of the children shared the room with an adult who, during playtime, took a toy mallet and hit the inflatable doll in the face. Later, when left on their own, the children exposed to aggression then punched, kicked, and struck the dolls with hostility, marking the first formal demonstration of social learning theory in action. Until then, psychologists contextualized the source of behavior as one welling from within, impelled by subconscious needs, drives, and impulses. Bandura's ongoing work on social learning now suggested that people "automatically and unconsciously" acquire new patterns of behavior by observing the behavior of others, as well as by witnessing the rewards and consequences that follow. As Southey recounts this for me, I think about Gary Slutkin's story again and his theory of contagious violence, along with the other scenarios in which observation turns to adaptation and a social contagion is born.

Later studies by Bandura went even further than violence and hostility. Through social learning, people also adopt complex competencies, such as languages, mores, customs, and political practices of a culture, either deliberately or inadvertently, by example. And one of the most effective methods for transmitting attitudes, emotional responses, and new behaviors, he writes, is symbolic modeling through television, one of the most important vectors for quickly and efficiently conveying informa-tion, even more so than live demonstrations.

As a producer at Televisa, Miguel Sabido saw exponential opportunity in the prospect of marrying Bandura's theoretical work at Stanford to a practical and purposeful demonstration of a new kind of media project. If a telenovela convinced people to take up sewing, perhaps television was a powerful way to pro-mote and reinforce public health and educational issues as well. After all, with almost daily airings, Latin America's soap operas provided massive messaging exposure.

Sabido tested his theory by producing a telenovela called *Ven Conmigo*. The soap's ratings soared more than 30 percent higher than every other Televisa-produced series ever. What viewers didn't know, however, was that by setting the soap opera in a classroom, Sabido designed the show to promote adult literacy to Mexico's largely illiterate labor market. A follow-up study on the show's impact revealed that, during the broadcast years of 1975 and 1976, nearly a million illiterate people enrolled in adult literacy classes in Mexico, nine times the enrollment from the previous year. Registration doubled the following year, even when the series was no longer on television.

Televisa broadcast nearly two hundred half-hour episodes of Sabido's next series, *Acompáñame*, in 1977. Viewers were wholly unaware that producers designed the soap to address the issue of family planning. After the show aired, despite the fact that Sabido disguised the message in subtext, sales of contraceptives increased 23 percent. More than a million people tuned in per episode, and while not every viewer sought birth control based on the serial drama, peers of those who did were more likely to model this behavior, even if they'd never seriously thought about contraception before.

Sean Southey and organizations like PCI Media Impact

have since used the Bandura-Sabido method to change behavior in populations across the globe. A music video campaign in Nigeria led to a fivefold increase in the number of people seeking contraception every quarter. In parts of India, the radio series *Tinka Tinka Sukh* steered the way toward the discontinuation of child marriages. Sixty percent of Tanzania's population under the age of forty-five tuned into the radio broadcast of *Twende na Wakati*, which fed a 150 percent increase in condom distribution to stop the spread of HIV.

Southey's personal early work with Canada's department of the environment and climate change and the United Nations led him to conclude that if you really want to change the world, you don't engage the government or social programs. You've got to interact with everyday people responsible for making wise decisions in their own lives. "It's the only way to get individuals thinking and changing what they do, and taking ownership for their social well-being, mental well-being, physical well-being, and all of these attributes that make up life," Southey tells me. PCI Media Impact has produced 5,000 episodes of entertainment education television and radio for social change using the Bandura-Sabido method, broadcasting from Peru to Guinea, Mexico, and Uganda, in total numbering forty-five countries.

"And none of them know that you're weaving educational cues into the stories?"

"We've found that if you're transparently educational in any way, then you've failed," Southey says.

"For the viewers it's purely entertainment."

"Exactly. To work, you've got to be understated, delicate, and strategic in how you plant your messages."

It occurs to me that I've run into yet another contradiction that rattles my comprehension of the strange contagion. I bring up the Cure Violence model and Gary Slutkin's construct for changing people's behavior by making the invisible visible. He believes, I explain, that he can stop the spread of undesirable conduct, and the thoughts and emotions that lead to them, by teaching people about the invisible, by making people aware of the contagion and its pattern of spread. The more people who know about the contagiousness of violence, the more interrupters he creates.

Sean Southey's theory is exactly the opposite of Slutkin's. Changing people's behaviors requires change agents to *be* invisible. Southey's work relies on his ability to keep the processes in the realm of the invisible and forever concealed beyond conscious detection. Preach and you perish. "Our shows are 100 percent entertainment and 30 percent education," Southey says. "The 30 percent is hidden." Instead, what Southey needs in order to change behavior on a massive scale is a blockbuster hit. For contagious behavior and ideas to catch, his producers carefully bury the takeaway messages within a compelling story to such a degree that no one is ever the wiser. Like the space shuttle riding on the back of a 747, the learned behavior change piggybacks on the story drama and moves into the psyche, an interloper to the mind.

"You have a toddler back at home," Southey says, and I nod. "Just wait until he starts doing the opposite of everything you say." I remember urging my son to drink cherry-flavored medicine to ease his fever once, and the fight he put up that ended in Children's Tylenol dripping down the front of my white shirt. I understand the difficulty of encouraging a foreign country to change deeply ingrained behaviors to benefit public health when doing so pushes against strongly held cultural norms and values. Sometimes, I suppose, it's just easier to slip the medicine into chocolate milk.

"The power of narrative is change," he says. "Story is a way to define and understand the world. Story is a sense-making tool. And the beauty of media is that your rate of return on modeling is beyond measure. You can never communicate every behavior we need to make the world a better place. But if you fall in love with the vision of who you could be, through the eyes and actions of a character you fall in love with on a show, that changes things."

And from there, he says, viewers develop into role models for other people. You don't have to see the soap opera to adopt a new way of thinking and behaving. At some point the meme takes over a community; at some point you catch an echo contagion; at some point you adopt the culture of change around you, having scarily noticed that you, too, have become a role model for others.

I'm thinking about Peter Gollwitzer at the Motivation Lab again, and how he'd spoken with me about hidden cues, subtle and sometimes deeply concealed primes that activate and modulate people's behaviors, thoughts, and emotions without their knowledge. Am I looking at the same thing now, I wonder, only on a much larger scale? Where Gollwitzer planted photos on his walls to prime his creativity or sharpen his focus, here at PCI Media Impact, producers plant subtle messages in stories to prime for extensive changes.

To be honest, it makes me nervous, this slippery slope. The inherent moral ambiguity, however humble and true the mission, remains dubious. In their findings, the researchers William J. Brown and Arvind Singhal present social intervention as a series of unwinnable dilemmas. Producers face decisions over which problems and social groups to address and which to ignore. Tools of social intervention destroy values as often as they create them. Anyone who believes in self-reliance has to accept that this faith disappears under the auspices of priming people for the greater good. As a tool for engineering specific changes "in knowledge, attitudes, or practices," prosocial media is inseparable from the notion of "what ought to be done" to attain a certain goal. Deciphering goals, however, becomes difficult when cultures rarely share moral and ethical values. "At the heart of the prosocial content dilemma is determining who will decide for whom, what is prosocial and what is not," Brown and Singhal write. In the best cases, these manipulations save lives. In the worst, they result in horrendous government abuses and unintentional consequences. Even television shows that espouse positive social messages can, in some people, reinforce their problematic beliefs.

Where there is a disagreement about rightness and wrongness of social beliefs and behaviors, producers make a case that, in matters of epidemics and pandemics, the conversation no longer belongs in the realm of subjective right and wrong. Saving lives is—objectively—the objective.

As hesitant as I am to accept this rationale, I truly do sympathize with it. The politics of saving lives is the politics of parental responsibility, and to a larger extent the responsibility of anyone upholding a standard for which no standard exists. This is tantamount to secretly adding medicine to my child's drink. We do it because we want what's best, because we know what *worse* can look like.

MAYBE THE TRICK to making sure the suicide cluster in my town is gone for good comes down to taking what we know about social contagions and using it to our advantage. In Palo Alto, we can add something curative to the mix by way of subterfuge.

Southey thinks it's an interesting idea. "But I'm not sure what the Sabido method might look like if we applied it to Palo Alto," he comments.

We're seated now at a small vinyl booth in a sushi restaurant on East Forty-Fourth Street. The place is crowded and cramped. The air smells like tempura. He carefully brings a bite of pink tuna to his mouth with a pair of chopsticks. "The Sabido method works. We have the studies to prove it," he says, chewing. "But we've run into a problem. Not every behavior we introduce catches."

This isn't entirely a surprise to me. At the Motivation Lab, Gollwitzer pointed out that in order to prime someone for a certain behavior, the behavior change already has to be a part of a person's makeup. But all things being equal, until now I've suspected that in matters of what might be considered fairly universal characteristics, we're all equally susceptible to common primes. However, later I'll find a 1995 collection of national data on age showing that fear spreads most readily among the middle-aged and eighteen- to twenty-four-year-olds, suggesting age is a boundary for certain social contagions. I'll also read studies by Elaine Hatfield theorizing that women are more susceptible to emotional contagions than men; they read facial expressions with far greater accuracy, establish eye contact with others faster, and process, store, and retrieve social stimuli better. Another study by Hatfield reveals that, beyond gender boundaries, occupations are limiting factors, too. Physicians, for instance, are more susceptible to the social contagions of anger and sadness than Marines.

Inasmuch as television producers have gotten the Sabido method down to a fairly precise equation, some issues remain incredibly difficult to crack, partly because some are just so big that there's no one specific behavior to isolate within a problem, Southey explains. Other times, limiting factors make it so that curative behavior contagions don't catch like he's hoped they might.

But when they do catch, the benefits are vast. So, after our meal and over small porcelain cups of hot tea, Southey and I engage in a speculative exercise, something I'm becoming good at initiating. I ask him what a curative entertainment education program might look like if he were to bring the Bandura-Sabido model to Palo Alto.

The process, he says, always begins with formative research and local coalition building with people in business, education, local government, and health care. Southey's producers pull in key policy makers. Locate NGOs deeply involved in the issue. Drill down to key enabling factors, including all of the psychological, emotional, and behavioral social contagions they can identify. They then gather their findings, hauling their knowledge to the writers' room. There they spread a silk parachute cloth along a wall and add pushpins to its corners. In felt-tip marker on green note cards they create character profiles. With 3M adhesive, they stick the cards to the cloth to form a sprawling narrative map.

Instead of creating a telenovela, not nearly as popular in the US as they are in Latin America, we'd produce a radio drama. Or, better yet, a Web-based series. Or, better still, an enhanced video game with social features. In our hypothetical, the team creates the gameplay settings and plot points, perhaps set within the high-pressure, high-stakes world of a simulated Silicon Valley start-up.

And, someplace within the immense weave, Southey will plant a single narrative thread engineered to instill a behavior change: perhaps to view one's self-worth beyond letter grades, or to accept failure as growth, or to seek help, or to become an interrupter—a story line as fine, in fact, as the thread spooling through a Singer sewing machine.

Chapter 22

CATCHING THE IVY LEAGUES

've never met my neighbors in the apartment across the landing from us. They live out of state, and most of the time their unit is empty. They haven't so much purchased an apartment as they have an address for their grandkids. Despite its more recent history of student suicide, the school district of Palo Alto remains one of the highest rated in the country. Sometimes people hold on to properties to fool the district and get their children or grandchildren into the education system. The risk, if you're caught, is a child's expulsion. But it's worth it, isn't it? To get your children into the best school, what wouldn't a parent do? On some level we believe, or hope, that intentional proximity to good education and intelligent people rubs off on our kids, giving them the best shot at a good life, maybe even a great one.

To that point, I once read a feature in *Fast Company* about a nineteen-year-old university interloper named Guillaume Dumas. In 2008 he slipped into a large lecture hall at McGill University to take a political science class in which he was not enrolled. At Concordia University, he snuck into literature and philosophy classes. As spring quarter wrapped up, he had drinks with students from the Université de Montréal. If anyone asked him, he was auditing classes, or was a liberal arts major just scoping out his options. The thing was most times people didn't ask. They assumed he was a student. Once he was in a class long enough, he faded into the fabric of everyone else's reality. When he grew bored, he moved on to another city, to another campus he had no business being at. He held his own at Yale, performed well, even made some astute comments in lectures, although he appeared on no class roster. He gate-crashed Brown University, contributed to debates with students who'd legitimately earned their way into the school—unlike Dumas, who, through casual bravado and impish charm, attached himself through the art of the soft con. At UC Berkeley, a professor came close to reporting him, a bon vivant stimulated by art, philosophy, and science who was stealing knowledge as one might siphon a Wi-Fi connection. From there he booked it an hour south to Palo Alto and without much trouble he infiltrated Stanford University. Dumas claimed that attending these universities without actually graduating from any of them was a kind of experiment to figure out what, exactly, a university degree can get you in life. The cynic in me believes it's just a story of another lost young soul.

In the end he didn't come away with an Ivy League degree, but that's not to say this impersonator among the educated wasn't catching intelligence. Beyond sitting through lectures and taking in information, his proximity to smart people also likely made Dumas smarter.

At NYU, Peter Gollwitzer told me that in academia people unconsciously pass and catch ideas from others all the time, regardless of IQ, personal proficiencies, or intellectual deficits. We might catch intelligence in the same way we catch ambition or greed. Bucking forty years of research supporting the idea that students in smaller classes excel more than students in larger ones, Harvard University finds that students in large classes are better able to unconsciously develop skills that aid in learning and retention. The larger the class, the more opportunities an individual has to hear others challenge assumptions. That is, they catch new ways of thinking and questioning. They imitate study techniques. They pick up cues that aid in the development of stronger communication skills. The bigger the class, the larger the pool of knowledge from which to drink.

I discover studies on cooperative learning from both Johns Hopkins and the University of Texas showing that individual gain correlates with group gain, just as cooperative learning increases individual learning in kids as early as kindergarten. From the classroom to the boardroom, group grades and team rewards stoke personal motivation. Existing within a group environment affects the brain's synaptic plasticity. When one cell excites another repeatedly, a change takes place in one or both. In an experiment in the sixties, researchers placed lab mice into an enriched environment within large groups of other mice, allowing the animals the opportunity for more complex social interactions. Such enrichment enhanced memory function in the mice. They performed better than isolated mice on the water maze task and a running wheel task. The brains of the rodents also gained weight and size.

For people, too, group learning is essential for adaptation. In his book *The Wisdom of Crowds*, the writer James Surowiecki highlights the importance of taking our cues from everyone else's behavior. "Instead of having to undertake complicated calculations before every action, we let others guide us," he writes, ". . . piggybacking as it were on the wisdom of others.

"In a sense, imitation is a kind of rational response to our own cognitive limits. Each person can't know everything. With imitation, people can specialize and the benefits of their investment in uncovering information can be spread widely when others mimic them."

The brain then becomes a muscle that responds to the group environment around it. By dropping himself into a setting full of highly intelligent people, Dumas forced his mind to rise to the occasion. To keep up at Yale, at Brown, at Stanford, Dumas had to think quicker. With increasing probability that a professor was going to call upon him to answer a question about a subject matter he was supposed to know, he needed to absorb information differently from the way he had before. He surrounded himself with students who used more sophisticated language, and his mind responded in kind, the way a traveler's language center picks up words in a foreign country.

In this way, I reason it's good that we've found ourselves in this town with its magnificent school district. As long as we remain in Palo Alto, our kids will get the gold standard in education. This cache of highly intelligent students and teachers will influence the way my children think and learn by virtue of who they surround themselves with. There's a good chance they will adopt a good work ethic, too, and healthy ambition.

We take our chances if we leave town. When we follow this line of thought, as we find ourselves doing more often these days, my wife reminds me she didn't go to a top-rated high school. She attended a public school in Maryland ranked somewhere near the middle of a good district. Despite this, perhaps because of it, she was able to get into Tufts University and later Harvard Business School. She worries today because the cost of living in Palo Alto is too high, and yet the cost of staying might be even higher.

There is no getting around the fact that Gunn High, and the town that populates it, has become a cautionary tale. While the rate of completed suicide in Palo Alto over the past three years has now slowed, people still regard the district with suspicion. The lingering memory of the suicides continues to highlight the worst parts of an otherwise gleaming system. We are just as blameworthy for buying into this story, for having revisited a familiar uncertainty too many times to count: By staying, are we putting our children in harm's way? We are experiencing the fallout of an event that has nothing to do with us. We didn't know the five deceased children, yet we have entered these horrible acts into evidence as we build our case for either staying or leaving.

Another couple, the Thadanis, in the condo underneath us, sometimes invites us to share traditional Indian meals in their home. The husband is a good, neat, and thoughtful man named Sanjeet, who, in the years we have grown to know each other, I've come to like very much. I've gathered through his vague stories that he's started a couple of failed companies in India. He's had better luck in Silicon Valley as a consultant. In seven months the surrogate he and his wife, Poonam, are using will be delivering a son for them. In terms of what the future holds for their young family, they tell us that they are planning to stay in their condo, even though they also own a big house in the next town over that he rents to a vice president of Hewlett Packard. They're keeping the small condo so that their child will get into the Palo Alto school system and receive a Palo Alto–level education.

"We could move into that bigger house, but the schools here are wonderful," Sanjeet Thadani says as we share slices of apple off a dish together in his living room one evening. I ask him if they're at all concerned about the kind of intelligence the system is passing along to its children, the kind that places significant weight on excelling. "Who is *the system?* What *system?* It's *we,*" he asserts. "*We* push kids too far. *We* place importance on outshining others, believing that it's the best path to the top." Indeed, we all want our children to be successful. Each of us believes we can and should try to engineer outcomes for our kids. We feel better when our children are achieving. We want them to aim high. But Thadani also believes that when we measure people by their grades, their achievements, their test scores, and their abilities, only bad things happen.

The real problem is in the *we*, he says. The *us*. The interlopers.

At some point we all become part of the fabric of a place, contributing the social and behavioral contagions simply by virtue of being here. We catch and become carriers of standards, buy into the culture, perpetuate cascades of ideas and behaviors. I'm no different. My family and I have lived in Silicon Valley for more than four years at this point. I'm chasing bigger writing contracts and a livelihood devoted to rousing people by shining a spotlight on innovation and big thinkers taking on enormous problems with radical solutions. Then there's my wife, an executive for a company that famously hires graduates mostly from Ivy League universities. Her job in human resources is, in so many words, to add to the region's deep pool of highly educated and motivated people. We've bought into the mythology of this town. We've contributed to Silicon Valley's impossibly high standards. We are among those who claim the dream is easy, that it is attainable, and that it is expected of us.

In terms of the strange contagion, this perfect storm of infectious ideas, behaviors, and emotions, we are complicit in creating and nurturing it. We've contributed to this nocebo effect. Our overblown responses to the deaths that happened here years ago have made us culpable in the promotion of hysteria and in pushing the social contagion of irrational fear that the specter of some immutable influence might guide our children into harm's way. We are as culpable as anyone is for creating an environment that supports achievement, and for the actions of five teenagers who walked on the tracks, just as we are for protecting the children of this town. We've poisoned the well with contrarian positions, that unassailable sense of hopelessness even as we look to the future with promise and the belief that we are going to achieve more and do better, earning promotions, raises, and bigger book contracts.

If people catch knowledge by proximity, it seems to me that perhaps we have an opportunity to redefine intelligence and what it is our children are learning by proximity.

We can add primes for new behaviors that promote resilience. We can introduce the knowledge to seek help when we're struggling and begin to break the stigma around mental health. We can redefine the belief systems around success: that it's not just about the right scores, the best accolades, the shiniest awards. We can insert prosocial story lines, weave in examples of those who have responded to failure and met hardships and yet continue to live and to live well.

Thadani finishes his slice of apple and leans forward on the sofa. "I've started more failed start-ups than I can count," he says joyfully. "That's what I love about this country. Here you get second chances." He suggests that, like the maxim of Silicon Valley, in life there is always time for course correcting and iterating until we get it right. But, of course, not all of us get second chances. Five children are gone. Families remain irrevocably harmed. A community is forever changed by the weight of these irreversible losses.

When my son faced exposure to a herpes virus at his child care center, we calculated his chances of catching it and debated the value of removing him from the classroom, always painfully aware that our puzzling over this dilemma carried no assurances one way or the other. Before removing him from the program, our psychological processes provoked interminable debates, each argument between my wife and me a prelude to mornings spent second-guessing every treaty we'd come to the previous night, until each conclusion was one we reversed a dozen times.

But this situation is different. The odds are smaller but the stakes are so much higher. By staying, we have the opportunity to make changes to the culture, the classroom, and the community. Like Dumas, we'll infiltrate systems. Like Sean Southey, we'll introduce behavior changes that others might catch by proximity. Like Peter Gollwitzer, we'll utilize primes to activate behaviors that pull toward psychological well-being. Like Gary Slutkin, we'll teach people to become interrupters, reinforcing the knowledge until it becomes memory ingrained deeply in the muscle. We'll do this, I believe, even if we have to reach one person at a time.

A couple of days after my meal with Sanjeet Thadani, my iPhone pings with a text message from my friend, the economics teacher Roni Habib. My daughter woke up earlier that evening crying in her crib. She fell back asleep on my shoulder as I paced the hallway in my gym shorts and socks, her cheek warm against my bare shoulder, the top of her head smelling of baby shampoo.

I carefully reach for the phone and tilt the screen toward me, careful not to wake her.

It reads: "There's been another one."

The hopefulness I've been carrying since my conversation with Thadani instantly dims, the familiar questions immediately returning, along with a familiar lack of understanding. We still have so much further to go to find the answers, and what we've found isn't enough. Will it ever be?

Part VII

THE CONVERSATION

"I am not what you see and hear."
—DAVID FOSTER WALLACE

Chapter 23

ARRIVAL, PART II

The train sees things that most people do not, like the purlieu of cities and bluish tree groves hidden from the highways. Aesthetically, Caltrain is industrial and functional; there's nothing luxurious about its mottled cloth and pleather double seats or the sluggish interior light it offers passengers.

Yet, as a metaphor for connection, really there's none better than a train. Coupler heads join its cars. Its commuters are fixed to one another, even in their isolating silences. Its construct merges new technology with one of the world's oldest modes of transportation. Its very function marries departures with arrivals.

As a metaphor for severing, a train also does the trick. The construct is engineered to put space between people. It maintains distinct gaps amongst seats, rows, upper and lower levels, as well as the cars themselves. It cuts the land and the sky by way of a distinct horizon.

And in the near dark of a late-October day in 2014, a nineteen-year-old boy named Quinn Gens, a recent graduate of Gunn High standing on the tracks, was there and then he was gone. This unique moment joined every other moment, both before it and after it, although it was also a moment distinct and separate from time. The train stopped briefly as the tracks were cleared. Soon it would start up again.

A COUPLE OF weeks after receiving Roni Habib's distressing text message about the sixth teen from town to die by train, he forwards me an early morning e-mail the school superintendent has sent to teachers: authorities have now also recovered the body of a seventh Gunn High student on the rails, a boy named Cameron Lee. Then, four weeks later, an obituary appears in papers for a Gunn High student named Harry Hann-yi Lee, unrelated to Cameron Lee except by hometown and school. The teen jumped off a rooftop.

The eighth suicide takes the form of widespread wretched shock. There's pain and heartache residing within the quiet homes that make up the pretty little neighborhoods, but there's also anger raging in there like never before. Its ferociousness reveals itself in the public outcry, in the op-eds and posts that appear online, in the community forums where parents shout at teachers and the district deflects and the students feel they must stand up to defend their schools against an onslaught of criticism. But mostly there's just sadness. A broken, aimless kind.

And we know the reason that this sadness feels different from the sort we felt before. For a couple of months after any place experiences a suicide cluster, it exists in a kind of danger zone, with a higher-than-average risk for echo clusters. After Brian Bennion Taylor's death in January 2010, things quieted down, and we were hopeful that the calm might last, and then when it did we gradually came to believe that the cluster was over. Now, in the winter of 2014, with this gift of hindsight we now know that we were likely right. Epidemiologists and psychologists do not articulate metrics to determine the end of a cluster any more than they have defined the condition itself beyond instances of *multiple* suicidal behaviors within an imprecise accelerated time frame and area. After so much time passes between one and the next, we begin to view these instances as unique pockets of activity. Frequency between concentrated episodes allows us the space to wrap our heads around experiences that will never add up logically. In such scenarios, I suppose time is the best definition we really have.

What we are experiencing today isn't a resurgence so much as the manifestation of a second cluster. The sadness feels more profound than before because we now have evidence there's something specific about this place, this community, this town, that cultivates strange contagions. We're broken by both the knowledge and the ignorance of our fated makeup.

After Henry Lee's passing, grief counseling services and Stanford University psychiatrists visit Gunn High with the same frequency they did at the peak of the first cluster. Crisis response teams deploy to area schools. The mayor issues a statement pledging to dedicate resources, support more public conversations about mental health, and extend the hours for track guards at crossings. At public forums, psychologists talk about the need to destigmatize mental health issues, build new mental health facilities, make resources more readily available to kids in school and in the community, and expand them to accommodate more kids.

Roni Habib tells me he's worried this might be 2009 and 2010 all over again. Around town it certainly feels like it did four years ago, with emotions tender and bleeding and the fear sharp in our guts. The stakes remain the same but the picture has changed. We've done everything right to fix what's broken, employed safety measures and taken into account the ways social contagions matter in our lives, appointing interrupters and considering the primes in our midst. These measures prove not to be strong enough to address our particular type of strange contagion. Or maybe we simply haven't uncovered all of the dimensions of it yet.

So we arrive at new conclusions. One of the dominant theories about the two suicide clusters is that the deaths are specifically tied to a problem of unacknowledged depression, anxiety, and stress cascading through the school. The sheer scale that such a possibility suggests is massive. I e-mail Adam Grant. I wonder if he's ever encountered an emotional contagion of this scope in organizational psychology before, and, most important, if we can somehow use this knowledge to our advantage.

Grant replies within the hour. There's someone's work I need to know.

Chapter 24

FINDING HOPE WITHIN
THE BARSADE CASCADE

Early in her career, the management professor Sigal Barsade was working for an innovative photo processing technology start-up saddled with an unpleasant colleague. When the coworker went away on business, Barsade experienced a palpable difference in the office. She and her coworkers were happier, chattier, and overall more amiable than usual. Of course, when the unpleasant coworker returned, the environment tensed up once again. Later, in graduate school, Barsade developed this casual observation into a theory of emotional contagions in groups, the way in which they persist, and what this effect means within the world of emotional organizational culture. Later she continued this work, in part, by studying the degree of caring, compassion, and tenderness that employees showed one another, an effect known as companionate love.

Over the course of seven years, Barsade and her colleagues conducted a study at a long-term health care facility. There they mapped the new idea of emotional culture among two hundred employees operating within thirteen treatment units. Monitoring facial expressions, body language, and vocal tones, Barsade measured the frequency that group home employees expressed companionate love to each other, gauging flow and reverse flow of positive and negative emotions within work groups. By unconsciously mimicking facial expressions, tone, and body language, the facility's social workers, psychologists, nurses, and even food service personnel caught companionate love. Along with better cooperation, its spread led directly to less employee absenteeism, conflict, and burnout.

Even more remarkable, Barsade watched the positive culture ripple outward to influence the center's patients. The correlation tracked perfectly to the units with higher companionate love scores among staff. These residential units in turn housed people with greater reported quality of life, greater observed positive moods, and fewer unnecessary emergency room transfers. The residents surrounded by care teams with higher companionate love scores likely found themselves experiencing the emotional states of their caregivers.

Barsade went on to track the phenomenon of a culture of companionate love through workplace populations in biopharmaceutical companies, technology firms, financial services, higher-education facilities, real estate businesses, travel companies, and public utility plants. Regardless of the differences in environment or population size, the results remained consistent.

I continue to move through the research and find that while good influences present in companionate love impact collective energy and create a competitive advantage for companies, the opposite is also true. Negative emotions percolate through group culture as well.

Positive or negative, Barsade found that most of the time, we have no idea that we've caught an emotion at all. In one experiment she divided students into groups and assigned each with the theoretical task of distributing bonuses to employees. A confederate she secretly planted in each group acted out a preassigned emotion. When the confederate was enthusiastic, he "smiled often, looked intently into people's eyes, and spoke rapidly." When the confederate simulated depression, he "spoke slowly, avoided eye contact, and slouched in his seat." A measure of baseline moods before and after the experiment concluded that students caught the actor's positive or negative emotions but they attributed these emotions to their own processes, with no clue that another was influencing them. The methods for catching this social contagion, that amalgam of behavioral mimicry and facial guesswork, audio cues, or word triggers, lead associated memory networks to fire and convince people who are "contaged" that these emotions are their own, when in reality they've caught them from the people in their environment.

And just because transferring an emotion to another person requires direct visual contact, anyone sufficiently empathetic to others is susceptible to vicarious contamination, too. We can be in contact with people we have neither met nor had direct interaction with, except *in the mind's eye*. When people ruminate, they are in essence continuing to infect themselves.

DEFENSE ADVANCED RESEARCH Projects Agency (DARPA) researcher J. C. R. Licklider first envisioned interconnected computers back in 1962. Mostly remembered today for his contributions to computer science, he was, however, first and foremost a psychologist. His big idea was to create what he called a galactic network from which to send and retrieve data through a community of linked processors. Three years later Stanford Research Institute (SRI) was among the original host computers to link to an early version of the Internet, a nexus called ARPANET. In 1965, SRI received the first host-to-host message. It wasn't long before it was connected to computers at UCLA, UC Santa Barbara, and the University of Utah. Today, online networks unite more than 3 billion people and connect them to 2 million terabytes of data.

And forty years later we learned that the Internet also transfers emotions.

Five miles away from the world's first interconnected computer node, Facebook used sophisticated linguistic software to analyze text. The program took a word like *proud* and categorized it as a positive emotion, or a word like *furious* and sorted it as a negative emotion. Facebook then manipulated the algorithm by which the social media service pushes posts into personal newsfeeds. When Facebook reduced the number of positive expressions in users' newsfeeds, users produced more negative posts themselves. And when the company pruned feeds to display only positive expressions, Facebook users posted more positive messages.

The 2009 study I come across in the *Proceedings of the National Academy of Sciences* speculates that Facebook's results constituted evidence for massive-scale emotional contagion through social networks. While researchers like Sigal Barsade were underscoring the importance of direct contact for transmission, Facebook was able to provide empirical data that physical proximity was no longer a restriction for the social contagion. Shortly after Facebook released the results of its study, Indiana University conducted a follow-up experiment that measured emotional contagions on Twitter. Users tweeted positively or negatively depending on how much contact they previously had with other positive or negative tweets. Exposure to roughly 4 percent more positive or negative content tipped the scale one way or the other.

The more I read, the more I fully grasp the sweeping implications of this discovery. They stretch far beyond the effects of our own rather trivial online lives. No issue in politics or public interest is spared from the savviest of operatives stoking emotions through words and images online, intent on curating empathy and anger as a means to move others to act. The Department of Defense has taken such an interest in the infectiousness of emotions online that it's dedicated significant time and resources to a project called the Minerva Research Initiative, a Pentagon-led endeavor to model civil unrest and learn how to control, facilitate, and combat contagions through emotional manipulation via social media.

Experts in suicide prevention worry that public memorials for those who have died glamorize suicide. Vigils, they worry, invite vulnerable people to emulate these acts of self-destruction. The truth is, in terms of stopping kids from assembling memorials for their friends, the town criers sounding alarms in Palo Alto never had a chance: The twenty-first-century versions flourish in that online troposphere that hangs just above their reach. In the land that's perfected Instagram, Twitter, YouTube, and Facebook, if anyone is using social media, it's these kids. UCLA researchers highlight a decline in children's face-to-face social skills due to their growing use of digital media, yet the same children are also far more comfortable sharing personal expressions in this faceless void than within the realm of the tactile and the corporeal. The Palo Alto incidents, now numbering eight, spur an outpouring of online responses. To the extent that the Annenberg Public Policy Center of the University of Pennsylvania has any sway on how people report suicide, there is no such oversight on social media. Here, where classmates meet, online platforms become a kind of a de facto town square. Conversations bourgeon with questions and rampant speculation about the emotional motives of their friends. For many of the students I speak to, it doesn't feel like it's a bad thing to participate. In fact, it feels pretty good.

I pull up findings from the Centers for Disease Control and Prevention. In 2012 it verified the dangers that online forums such as these can create, where the sentiments of good people can eventually cast an unintended pall. By now I've come to expect that the sources of contagious influence are rarely so obvious as the words and images themselves. The mind is left to translate pictures and text, to interpret tone, to distinguish meaning. I reflect on how we become complicit in spreading emotions online, guileless and unaware of the kind of effect a comment, a repost, an uploaded photo, a thought in 140 characters, can unconsciously have on others. In an effort to show support and solidarity, what are we propagating by clicking the "like" button on a friend's post? When is an emoji not just a shorthand emotional expression but a vessel carrying active ingredients of a virulent strange contagion?

Along with the dangers of social media as a vector for emotional spread, I also see its promise. At some point the tool of exposure becomes a vehicle transporting a viable emotional cure and not simply a mouthpiece for the strange contagion. We can use its unlimited reach to administer our healing balm.

I consider the flow of helpful emotions and the impact that something as powerful as companionate love has on people participating online. I want to know if a cascade of empathy and support can buttress people from problematic emotional runoff. Might we employ Gary Slutkin's Cure Violence model and create interrupters and responders out of the most casual of online participants? I'm curious about what it will take to galvanize the strongest of emotions online the way that Wael Ghonim spread courage and outrage, inspiring people to channel their vigilance into a kind of antidote for something rotten and corrupt. As a network of highly interconnected minds, there is no limit to the reach of emotional contagions and no person they cannot touch.

Chapter 25

STRESS IS A GATEWAY

'm standing at my desk, my fingers laced together behind my head. I've printed out studies by Sigal Barsade, those by Facebook, reports by the Department of Defense, and others by researchers at the Max Planck Institute for Human Cognitive and Brain Sciences. I've laid the sheets of paper in front of me. It's midday, and I've been staring at these two-dimensional cases for a long while, rereading their highlighted portions, assembling their conclusions in my head, and thinking, in light of everything that's happened these past few weeks in Palo Alto, Where do we go from here?

At a quarter past one I sort the pages into a green cardboard filing box system that I've created to organize myself. I replace the lid and then add the file box to the stacks of others I've arranged against the wall of my home study. Every box in the barricade of green cartons represents a different element of the two strange contagion events. Some contain evidence on the spread of hysteria, work ethic, greed, and unbridled emotions. Others hold information on vectors for spread like mirroring, charismatic leadership, and primes like economics, heroes, and role models. Still others contain the treatments, from heightened awareness, to prosocial suggestion, to the work of interrupters.

Taking it all in, I'm struck by how tidy the first and the second strange contagion events look when I have them contained in small boxes. The latest developments remind me just how unwieldy this phenomenon really is. Its ungainly nature is one of constant change. Every new component that adds power to the storm makes it that much harder to classify. I used to believe that coming up with a definition would somehow make it simpler for us to find a solution, but the definition is difficult to peg. I'm standing here, looking at this puzzle of boxes, taking into consideration that there are now eight dead young people.

I have to know what it is that makes Palo Alto so good at creating strange contagion events. The obvious cause is one that people have pointed to from the beginning, one that many believe to be an incontrovertible fact about this place. Stress, a biological response to demanding circumstances in our lives, remains a crucial factor. If true, what is it about Palo Alto that makes stress so dangerous?

To examine the validity of this theory, I drive north on El Camino Real toward Menlo Park. I pass Palo Alto High, a Spanish mission–style group of buildings surrounded by oak trees that also serves as Gunn High's rival school. The crest of Hoover Tower on Stanford University's campus passes on my left above a skyline of palm trees. There's a high-end shopping mall, and the blink-and-you'll-miss-it turnoff for Sand Hill Road and Tesla Motors' first showroom. I pull into a small restaurant situated just steps away from the Caltrain tracks. The writer Julie Lythcott-Haims is dressed in a light-colored T-shirt and jeans, her hair curled tight, as though each strand is wrapped around an invisible dime. As we wait for our food, she tells me a bit about her two children, both students at Gunn High, and their experiences within the school system, with all of its cumbersome and sparkling virtues and its manifestation of an achingly determined generation of youth.

Lythcott-Haims has witnessed the effects of stress among the young of Palo Alto firsthand, both as a mother and as the dean of freshmen at Stanford University for ten years. She has since become a kind of spokesperson advocating the end of highly orchestrated parenting that steers children forcefully toward a small number of colleges and careers, and something she sees as a direct path for passing stress onto children. Yet overparenting is but one of many sources of stress rampant in this town, she says. "After so long you have to step back and look at all of the people and institutions putting pressure on these students," she tells me. For instance, a school system that's invested in maintaining its top position in both the state and the nation. A culture that nurtures compulsively ambitious people who've mastered the art of delayed gratification, willing to put in eighty-hour workweeks for the promise of some potential future wealth. Jump on a plane to Silicon Valley, she says, and you'll find yourself among an accumulation of people who harbor over-the-top expectations and set unreasonably high bars for others and themselves. All of a sudden you're part of a community that prides itself on setting outrageous standards and lives under the sort of conditions Apple's Bud Tribble famously called a reality distortion field, a purposeful bending of one's perception of what is possible. It's this very thing, this focused warping of one's sense of proportion and scale of difficulty, that leads people to incredible innovation and achievements. It also places a great amount of stress on them.

We see the reality distortion field in a now-familiar refrain about a school and some parents that demand too much of their students, Lythcott-Haims says. We hear it as well in the way young people require too much of themselves, feverishly working to impress college admissions officers by stacking their records with AP courses to get into the right classes, to earn the highest scores, to rack up the best accolades, to win the shiniest awards, to enroll in enough sports and activities, to join the best clubs, and to volunteer for community service programs. "The authors of this stress have led young people to believe they will literally have no future unless they meet outrageous benchmarks of success."

As she says this, I think back to something else Peter Gollwitzer told me in New York. Personal ambition, he said, is largely dependent on community norms and how we view ourselves measuring up to them. Motivation becomes a tug-of-war between the mastery one needs for achievement and the fear of failure. Lythcott-Haims tells me now about the common pressure for children to reach a high and arbitrary standard that has become the status quo in communities of privilege all over the country, a social contagion of Western ideals, a bastardization of the American dream, or perhaps just a twisted interpretation of it that has gone viral. It's not difficult to imagine a school filled with students caught up in this madness, hungry for accomplishment, and regarding its lofty bar as perfectly reasonable given the community values into which they were born and raised. In any endeavor where one's self-worth is at stake, never misjudge the lengths one will go to in order to succeed. Those who find themselves fearing failure, or achieving less, will succumb. And a community that prides itself on bottling, scrutinizing, pressurizing, idealizing, and lording over its children with the assiduousness one offers rare and precious stones will inevitably polish some and inadvertently crush others.

Americans, meanwhile, continue to experience more stress than ever, with one study I read citing an increase of more than 1,000 percent in the past three decades. Student burnout as the result of "stress as they try to get into some of the most competitive colleges in the country" finds young people in a "cycle of school, homework, extracurricular activities, sleep, repeat," writes the New York University researcher Noelle Leonard. "Students in these selective, high-pressure high schools can get burned out even before they reach college." At Stanford, Lythcott-Haims saw it happen, the expression of this toxic disorder, this all-encompassing sense of diminishing, this lassitude among students. Contracting stress-related burnout is no more complicated than seeing, experiencing, or sensing someone else's symptoms. Ninety percent of those who experience it are members of peer groups having at least 50 percent of all members suffering from it.

"But why Palo Alto? There have to be dozens of places more stressful."

"Right," she says. "Why Palo Alto?" When I lift my eyes to hers, I see her face set, earnest and sad. Look around, she suggests. Consider what the application of just a little bit of pressure can lead to. Not just advances in technology, a great education system, and prosperity, but the things beneath all of that, the underbelly of this town. Take the elements I've collected in my green file boxes at home and then add this: if stress is a biological response to pressures, then it is also a gateway that produces a deluge of emotions.

Stress can be problematic, but it's not nearly as problematic as the emotions it creates. Stress opens the portal to experiencing feelings of defeat, inferiority, humiliation, frustration, sorrow, anguish, and even shame, emotions that are not only highly contagious but will also, as Sigal Barsade noted, cascade through closed environments. Even a high school.

Those who are not naturally affected by stress are still susceptible to catching the emotions it produces in others. And now this is where Palo Alto finds itself, catching and spreading a plague of problematic emotions.

As both a mother and a thought leader in this space, Lythcott-Haims maintains her faith in this town. She tells me she loves it and she continues to pull for it, because she has not given up on the idea that there's a way to reduce this pain, that there's a pathway to making things better and right again. About this she's certain. People say Gunn High needs to get rid of class rankings and grades, two of the most important criteria that colleges use to determine who they let in, and one of the biggest contributors to student stress. Signs point to a growing willingness among parents, educators, and students alike to acknowledge the problem of stress and the storm of negative contagious emotions it produces.

To that end, as the second cluster unfolds, the superintendent authorizes a new district policy to stop the practice of homework stacking. Gunn High students fill out time-management grids with counselors to map their schedules and even set aside blocks of time for sleeping. The district expedites the construction of a student wellness center at Gunn High, a full-service hub for physical, emotional, social, psychological, and spiritual health. Given these measures, she wants to be able to tell me that things have been getting better here. Instead, all she can really say is that her own children seem to be doing fine, all things considered. They're popular and have strong groups of friends. One will be graduating from Gunn High next year.

She asks me about my son and daughter. I scoot my chair around the table to her side, where we compare pictures of our kids on our iPhones. The images skate by with a touch of my finger. As we roll through the photo timeline, I remember struggling to assemble my son's crib in his room all those years ago, right when the original strange contagion was first manifesting.

I also remember my lack of faith in my skills as a father-to-be, which was why I enrolled in that parenting class. Would I know how to raise him and care for him and avoid the kinds of mistakes Lythcott-Haims is talking about, the kinds that ply our kids with too much pressure?

Here I am now. Five years have come and gone. It's a strange world that I find myself constantly trying to organize and define, as though setting out to put a name to this terrifying phenomenon would in turn guide me to be the better father, far more than those baby swaddling lessons ever did. Instead, I think I wanted to wrap his world in protective cotton, to identify and then to shield him from the dangers as seen in the forces of rampant social contagions. But emotions in particular are impossible to avoid catching. That fact alone is enough to subdue my own overparenting instincts and supplant them with a more constructive desire for both of my children.

More than anything, I just want them to grow up happy, no matter what form that happiness takes.

On some level I feel that happiness supersedes any benchmark of success and our own lofty dreams for our children. And, here in Palo Alto, happiness might just be the ointment that makes everything better again. It occurs to me that where Sigal Barsade recorded the effects of companionate love as it cascaded across a hospital, noting the accumulative effects of caring, compassion, and tenderness changing lives and even saving some of them, perhaps Palo Alto can employ a similar tactic. If the Pentagon can manipulate social movements and political discord with keystrokes, words, and subtext, I have to believe that we can counter alienation, loneliness, regret, hopelessness, numbness, rejection, and bitterness. The thing that all of the experiments in emotional contagiousness conclude is that positive emotions like joy spread rapidly. The USC Viterbi School of Engineering, authors of the Twitter study, determined that, regardless of personal susceptibility, those least likely to be affected by emotional contagions are still roughly twice as likely to be influenced by positive tweets as negative ones. Even more promising, the social contagion of happiness prevents and helps people recover from the contagion of depression.

What might it take to purposefully launch a social contagion, a cascade of companionate love and of happiness, across the entire breadth of this town? Even as I close in on the one person who I believe may hold the key to pulling off such a monumental feat, I have to wonder if happiness will be enough to counter all the others.

Chapter 26

HOW TO CATCH HAPPINESS

Each year, Gunn High's theater department alternates between a Shakespeare production and a musical. It's coming off of *Macbeth*, a brutal and blood-filled production of a truly Grand Guignol story of ambition and death. James Shelby, the department's director, has chosen far lighter fare this season. When we talk, Shelby tells me about the fondness he's nurtured in his heart for Cole Porter's tunes: the joyful buzz of "There's No Cure Like Travel/Bon Voyage," the sizzling elation of "I Want to Row on the Crew," the wallop of the alliteration of "It's De-lovely." Given the events of this past autumn and early winter, Shelby believes an exhilarating production of *Anything Goes* is the right fit for a community hindered by renewed despair. I feel it, too—we all do—the stress compounding, the need to depressurize, an overture to bring the community together.

Rehearsals take place after school for nine weeks in the winter of 2015. The students tighten, block, and perfect their performances. As the premiere nears, it becomes more obvious to Shelby that something quite lofty rests on the shoulders of this production. Before starting its weeklong run, the school's open throat of a theater sells out every show, making it the most anticipated musical Shelby has ever produced in his thirty years at Gunn High.

"What does something like this say to you?"

"It makes me think that the community really, really needs to feel something good," he says. "After everything we've been through, what's wrong with spreading a bit of happiness?"

AS THE THEATER department runs through rehearsals, the United Nations Secretary General Ban Ki-moon cultivates the world's happiest music playlist. It includes "If This World Were Mine" by Luther Vandross, "Signed, Sealed, Delivered I'm Yours" by Stevie Wonder, "Kiss" by Prince, "We Are Young" by fun., "Zip-a-Dee-Doo-Dah" by James Baskett, "I Got You (I Feel Good)" by James Brown, and the prelude to Bach's Suite No. 1 conducted by Pablo Casals. There are lots of official lists cataloging the happiest songs in the world, but this one launches an international campaign called #HappinessSoundsLike, and it becomes the soundtrack to the International Day of Happiness.

Inspired by Ban Ki-moon, I decide to conduct my own straw poll among friends on Facebook for the music that makes them the happiest. Responses are all over the map. "Oblivious" by Aztec Camera; "Brown Eyed Girl" by Van Morrison; "Rapper's Delight" by The Sugar Hill Gang; "Big Rock Candy Mountain" by Harry McClintock; Sam Cooke's "Wonderful World"; and "anything by Queen." Tastes span the spectrum and defy a single genre, yet each carries with it the exact same physiological effect in the spread of happiness.

As for my contribution, inspired by Shelby, I add "I Get a Kick out of You" by Cole Porter, which made its debut in the musical *Anything Goes*. After the show's original Broadway bow in 1934, the *New York Times* boasted, "Take it from me, the

Depression is over!" The Depression wasn't over, of course. The country was in for another seven years of economic turmoil. But here, within the environment of pure narrative and whimsy, for a while each night it must have looked to Broadway audiences as though something significant and terribly sad had ended.

Musical theater is rooted in drama reduced to musical beats. Like the transformative medium of any artistic endeavor, it seamlessly blends reality and fantasy within the quickening thrum of musical cues, flashes of color, spinning bodies. If there's something fictitious about the concept of musical theater, it's the fabrication of sudden and instantaneous song and dance that requires that we suspend doubt. Music casts a spell that switches off our logical brain and lulls us in into the hypnosis of pure belief, an ointment that eases the discomfort.

"Music stimulates primitive, evolutionarily ancient and deep brain structures," writes the psychologist Ruth Herbert. It stokes emotion, reaches into the guts, and coordinates the body's systems, the head, the pulse, the muscles, and the bones. Brain cells work together to decipher melody, rhythm, pitch, and lyrics. Music lights up the visual cortex, fires up the motor cortex, creates a contagious nodding of the head, stokes the reward centers of the brain, and exposes our mind's eye to flashes of memory. It's a cipher for emotions and emotional reactions. Tones activate endorphins, regulating mood, affecting every person within earshot on a nonconscious level. Moreover, it becomes an epoxy for moments and memories and community-forged camaraderie.

Music is also perhaps the most effective vector for the spread of contagious emotion. "When you're in a choir you literally 'catch' certain feelings from one another," continues Herbert. Music cues physiological changes. Our bodies pick up the thrum of a thickly jubilant tempo cast in a bright major key that fills our chests with bravura. Music therapy has a common benefit above and beyond most types of treatments for depression. Hospitalized children are happier during music therapy, more so than in play therapy. Sad music reduces the internal beat of one's heart, but it also boosts immunity, dampens stress, and decreases blood pressure.

While there is no common taste in music, there is a common link between cultures, as though the archetype of music is less a form we fill with meaning and more a collectively acknowledged trope.

Next to chocolate and true north, music is the closest thing to universal agreement we have.

The plague of happiness is an elusive scourge to pin down in part because the way we generally define emotions is subjective. Some refer to happiness in terms of pleasant sensations, as optimism, or as pure indulgence. In biological terms, happiness is nothing more than signals from the brain's limbic system, our emotional core. In *The Republic*, Plato wrote that happiness spreads among those who are moral, who harness their power responsibly, and who shoulder the burden of social justice. That is, happiness is earned, a quality that one aspires to and is contingent upon qualities of one's personality. More contemporary views like those of the neurologist and psychiatrist Victor Frankl put forth that the spread of happiness requires a person to look inward and host a desire to be beholden to something greater than oneself. In all cases, susceptibility to happiness relies on contingencies.

When I met with Nicholas Christakis, he spoke about his work with James Fowler at UC San Diego and their findings on the collective phenomenon of happiness, based on their twenty-year longitudinal study published in 2008. Emotions, they learned, move across social networks, and happiness is its own vivacious affliction. Happiness is more easily understood than any of the 6,000 spoken languages around the world. A happy next-door neighbor increases our chances of being happy ourselves by 34 percent. Every happy individual in one's social network increases a person's chances of catching happiness by 9 percent.

Happiness by proximity is also a panacea for depression. The biggest difference between the contagions of depression and happiness is that this hovering and deep feeling of sadness comes with its own built-in mechanism that limits spread. Unlike happiness, depression tends to make people isolate themselves and disengage from social networks. If you're not around others, you're less likely to spread your temperament. The National Longitudinal Study of Adolescent to Adult Health looked at 2,000 US high school students and determined that having five or more friends with a healthy and happy mood can halve the probability of developing depression and double the probability of recovering from depression over a six- to twelve-month period. Having depressed friends puts people at risk for catching clinical depression, while having happy friends is apparently "both protective and curative."

But what I find most fascinating is that happiness spreads by up to three degrees of separation. Like goals and greed, we can catch happiness from people without even realizing it and from sources we have yet to come face-to-face with. A happy Patient Zero has a 25 percent chance of passing happiness to the person next to her; she has a roughly 10 percent chance of passing happiness to her friend; and from there, her friend has nearly a 6 percent increased chance of passing happiness to another.

AT A QUARTER to seven on an evening in March 2015, Gunn High is a campus filled with shadows. The classroom windows are black. The sunken outdoor eating area colloquially known as the Bat Cave is abandoned. The empty grounds still contain traces of student life. Battle of the Bands posters stapled to walls. Notices from the student executive council taped to pin boards. Staff golf carts parked under an awning.

Lights orange as brass ceiling tins illuminate the parking lot. It begins to fill with cars. Campus walkways grow loud with foot traffic. Guests gather outside the closed doors of Spangenberg Theatre. Inside, students work feverishly backstage. They slip into costumes and apply makeup to their faces. The orchestra tunes instruments. When the doors open, the theater quickly grows warm with bodies. People in every seat. Voices popping in this commodious pavilion.

Walking in, there's a sense that we are welcome strangers here, that the teenage occupiers who oversee this campus have invited us onto their turf, allowing us a glimpse at their lives behind these walls. We are here so that they can say to us: *See us! Look at us! We are so much more than the stories you've heard about us. We are more than our academics. We have interests in break dancing, automotive technology, robotics, and art. Don't pity us. Don't call us purely depressed, angry, fearful, or panic-stricken. We are kind and warm and excitable. We have the ability to be resilient and the capacity for hopefulness. If we can smile and sing, then you can, too. We give you permission to be happy, and to be happy for us.*

Later, James Shelby will tell me that while he's backstage, waiting for the show to start, he feels the significance of this moment deeply. As the house lights dim he realizes he isn't breathing. It's only as the overture begins that he slowly exhales.

As the character of Reno Sweeney moves into the bright melody of "I Get a Kick out of You" and the stage swims in faux sequin dresses, chiffon skirts, tams, white sailor uniforms, and linen jumpers, I imagine what the audience around me is feeling in these moments. A sense of letting go. A sense of giving in. For a couple of hours Gunn High will be a gateway to something good and something healing. When we arrive at the song "There's No Cure Like Travel/Bon Voyage," our minds turn to the notion of *cure* and *escape*. Joy wells within my lungs. I forget I'm watching a high school performance. The silhouetted members of the audience in front and beside me are enraptured, caught up in this bright buoyancy, too. We are all synchronized to it. By the time we reach "You're the Top," our collective feeling has emulsified. It's a good feeling. A perfect feeling.

Shelby senses it, too, as the beats and rhythms connect the audience members to the show and to each other. He feels a warmth dispersing quickly and completely through the room, as it will with each performance this week, during which parents, students, administrators, and community members will come together to create a kind of celebration of life.

At the entr'acte, the theater becomes a jumble of voices again. There are beaming faces. Rich conversations. Students huddling outside with their friends. People check their phones for messages that have come in during the show. It's just the real world trying to edge back into their lives. We are saved at the last minute by act two. The ensemble pushes the theatrics of joy back in front of us. We take our medicine, and it goes down sweet and good, the way Miguel Sabido and Sean Southey administer their linctus to populations in Latin America, in India, in the Caribbean. These are targeted treatments for the masses. Tonight we'll go home. The hope is that we'll carry something of this back with us and that it will stay with us for a little while. Tomorrow we'll feel a bit happier than usual. We may not even know why.

Gunn High's unique depression era is not over, and I don't

think anyone in the theater tonight is fooled into believing the respite is anything more than what the ticket promises: a pageant of music, ensemble glee, a bit of spectacle, and a drop of humor that the town so desperately needs. Shelby will feel it happen with every encore, a sense of gratitude and release. When the show wraps and the crew goes to strike the set, Shelby is left wondering if this feeling hovering tenderly in his chest might carry into the town and exist here, and at least for a while remain a resource to tap as easily as one might hum the bars of a song.

Chapter 27

APPLYING THE SALVE
OF EMOTIONAL ATTUNEMENT

W e're fighting a hurricane with umbrellas.

James Shelby, pitting one social contagion against many others. Julie Lythcott-Haims, crusading to end a component of stress. These are small victories against a far more powerful enemy. There must be a way to merge these practices and present a concentrated front.

So after Gunn High's spring musical, I call Sigal Barsade at the Wharton School. I ask her if she has ever come across a better tool in her studies on companionate love that stops problematic social contagions from spreading. Is it a matter of overwhelming the system with examples of positive emotions, I ask, or is it about systematically putting up boundaries against the emotions that tear people apart?

"It's not about spreading companionate love, or being a moral leader," she says. "When I teach about emotional contagions, one of the points I make is the value of being emotionally intelligent."

I frown. Emotional intelligence rests on the assumption that we know how to read our own emotions as well as recognize them in others. Not long after the strange contagion of 2009 began, I'd asked Roni Habib at Printers Cafe how he thought the students at the school were doing. Habib said they were frightened and depressed, but that the students were also guarded in how they expressed themselves. Sure, there were displays of grief and rallies of support, but over the course of our subsequent meetings and conversations throughout the years, Habib also pointed out that this stoicism he saw had revealed itself to be far more systemic. At some point he realized it wasn't fortitude or resignation he was seeing in his students but a flat affect that revealed, in his estimation, a lack of the basic tools of knowledge about emotion. How are people supposed to express how they feel if they're not particularly good at recognizing how they feel in the first place?

"I'm working on a new technique," Habib told me once in reference to something rather unorthodox he was attempting with his classes. For some time, in fact, Habib has suspected that a long-term fix requires not simply teaching people about the processes of emotional contagions but teaching students an entirely new language.

The dialect of emotion.

I TEXT HABIB later that night about visiting the campus again next week to see what he's been up to.

I've come to enjoy our time together, Habib with dark eyes that in happier times burn with affection. Over the past few years we've met in his classroom during his office hours or after school. We talk about his children, a son and a daughter who are the same ages as my own. I've met his wife, a psychotherapist who was actually fulfilling her training hours through a psychotherapy internship at Gunn High when the first cluster came together in 2009. Today we're barreling toward the end of another school year, racing perilously fast toward finals, AP

test week, and the period during which college admissions no-
tify seniors of acceptances and rejections. It is what some here
refer to as the start of *suicide season*. This time of year naturally
makes Habib nervous.

I arrive just as the school's electric bell sounds. His classroom empties except for a couple of students who stay behind
to take a makeup test. Habib gets them set up and then comes
over, embracing me hard. When he lets go, he catches himself
on the edge of a desk with two fingers. His knees buckle. He
slowly lowers himself to the floor, crawls on all fours, and lies
outstretched on his back, squeezing his eyes shut.

He recently pulled a muscle in his back, he tells me. He's not
exactly sure how; it's stress, he figures. And it takes all of his
strength to stand on his feet throughout the day and lecture.

Eight students gone. He taught many of them. Habib finds
himself alone at the end of his days here, facing empty desks
and the fact that we're still no closer to experiencing closure. He
likes his job, but a constant feeling of losing has wicked some of
that joy away. Maybe this is why Habib's invitations to visit him
after school have grown more frequent lately. It's difficult to be
here alone.

It is easy to imagine Habib as a student at Gunn High in
the nineties, a young kid, tall and lean and with a little more
hair on the top of his head. Back then he somehow managed to
sidestep the cultural snare of competitiveness and full-throttle
ambition the school's culture exposed him to. And, in the end,
maybe that kind of bit him in the ass. His friends got into top
schools and edged closer to that dream of making it big in the
tech industry. Instead, Habib went to UC Santa Cruz and later
became a teacher.

Between the third and fourth suicide by one of his students,
Habib found himself returning to some of the coursework he'd

taken in college on personal empowerment, the classes that focused on techniques to break negative patterns of thinking and
behaving through a grounded awareness of our emotions. Habib
had come away with a fundamental understanding that emotions are not a luxury but a necessity, as essential as any survival
instinct. "Paying attention to how I feel is the compass I need
to go through this maze that is life," he tells me. Just beyond
the windows of his classroom, 2,000 students cross between the
buildings and through the causeways. They seem happy and
engaged with each other. Yet, beneath the surface, the high-
achievement mind-set is still as much a part of Gunn High's
makeup as it was when Habib was a student here. Back then
kids weren't killing themselves in uncoordinated and seemingly
random acts. But, looking back, he says there were warnings
indicating trouble ahead. Habib points to a community-wide
plague of mental illness—major depression and generalized
anxiety among them—that has historically gone unacknowledged and unrecognized by students and faculty alike.

Where emotion takes a backseat to ambition, social contagions reign with absolute impunity. The best you can do in
such a scenario is to cultivate happiness and create a kind of
counterbalance to the effects of negative emotions, although
to Habib that seems rather shortsighted. You might convince
the school to pipe upbeat music through the public-address
system and manually infect people with joy, or ask teachers
to increase their smile quotient in the classrooms. Even a
bogus expression of delight triggers a dopamine effect in our
minds, unsophisticated in their ability to tell a fake smile from
a real one.

But coming up with a tangible solution to this plague has
been more complicated. To impose some kind of rule of law on
the free-for-all of contagious emotions, Habib has decided that,

rather than trying to teach students to wipe out problematic feelings, he'll endeavor to pull every emotion forward.

What Sigal Barsade says about emotional awareness is true, Habib comments, but it ignores one big problem. "Silicon Valley has never been good at being emotionally attuned." One arm is latched around my neck as Habib braces himself with his other arm against a chair. He puts his weight against me and stands upright. "It's part of our culture."

Similar to Gary Slutkin's Cure Violence model, Habib recognizes that if students have a low threshold for depression and anxiety, the answer is to train everyone in the school to identify the warning signs and become interrupters to stop the cascade that leads from thoughts of self-harm to completing suicide. The problem is students have no idea what those signs are. Hindsight may be twenty-twenty, but if you don't know what it is you're looking at, you have no chance of finding what it is you're looking for.

As a son of Silicon Valley, well aware of its emphasis on education, Habib has found his students to be dangerously ignorant of the emotional processes taking place within and around them. Catching emotions is inevitable. With no way to stop people from contracting them, Habib has started teaching his students the language tools they lack.

"My students can't regulate and manage strong emotions if they don't have the words to identify the feelings in the first place," he explains.

Teaching this skill set seems easy enough, except that there's a difference between teaching to the common core and teaching to the invisible. The reason for this is as much biological as it is philosophical. Concrete learning takes place in the brain's neocortex, the conductor of all abilities analytical and technical, conceptual and logical. The language of empathy, however, requires a far different dialect. It engages the neurotransmitters of the limbic system, the emotional center of the mind.

Beginning with the first cluster, Habib suspected that if he were able to teach his students how to identify the emotional processes taking place within them, then they might be able to understand and regulate these emotions the moment they catch them.

As we talk, his efforts recall for me the tale of the Oracle of Delphi, an ancient Greek story about interpretation. The myth tells of a priestess who sees the future by inhaling trance-inducing vapors. The rub is that, in her manic state, her words come out as gibberish, so it is up to the priests and poets to translate her prattle into coherent prophecies. Like interpreting gibberish, teaching emotional intelligence is about interpreting unintelligible and impulsive reactions, putting words to what was once unrecognizable, and learning the language to decipher meaning from the unknown.

Emotional intelligence programs began to catch in the United States in the 1990s under the leadership of chief architects like psychologists Peter Salovey, John D. Mayer, Martin Seligman, and Daniel Goleman. While people and organizations succeed through intellectual and technical skills, an awareness of emotions and our ability to adjust and best control them, they suggest, is as much, if not more important, than many other skill sets. Understanding and managing emotions, Goleman writes, is also a protective factor against both suicidal thoughts and actual attempts.

Without an awareness of emotion, there is a perception of death without true consequence. Discouraging suicide hinges on the ability one has to fully imagine the immeasurable grief that such a tremendous loss will generate in the loved ones left behind. If only we knew what to say when someone asks us,

How are you doing? How are you feeling? How's life? What's on your mind? Without awareness of emotion, there's no honest way to answer. Where Silicon Valley eschews emotional intelligence for intellectual brilliance, social and emotional learning becomes an instruction manual for people who do not know how to operate the very system that controls them.

Thus, in 2011, Habib launched a pilot emotional contagion awareness program in earnest. He opened his economics classes with a five-minute silent meditation to make his students conscious of their mental chatter. What began as an awkward experiment became a self-sustaining student-initiated practice. "I noticed that, within twelve weeks, self-reported anxiety in the classroom significantly declined," he tells me. "I could see it, too. It was a visceral change. My students were able to concentrate better. They smiled more. Their grades were stronger. They just seemed healthier." With results like this, he asked permission to offer the country's first positive psychology class ever taught at an American high school. Usually, electives at Gunn High reach capacity at twenty-five students. The moment he opened enrollment, more than a hundred people applied. "They were hungry for something like this. Look, academics are important, but so is understanding how to be more aware of our inner thoughts, sensations, and emotions, and using that information to self-regulate, even save each other's lives."

Habib encourages his students to talk about their frustrations out loud and to acknowledge whether they feel heard, and in so doing identify, among other emotions, their sadness, happiness, despair, and unease. They come away recognizing symptoms, too, what it means when they experience an accelerated heartbeat, the sweat on their skin, a shortness of breath, a tightening in the chest. The Collaborative for Academic, Social, and Emotional Learning has since found that schools that heavily invest in social and emotional learning programs show systemic change. Habib sees kids helping each other manage their anxiety and treat themselves much more kindly than ever before.

Trained to have a nuanced understanding of emotions, for the first time ever his students show a deeper desire for happiness. That goes for educators as well. Because burnout dulls sharpness of perception, it becomes harder for teachers to recognize the signs of emotional and psychological distress in their students. Since emotional intelligence programs have gone into effect at Gunn High, students and teachers have recognized and flagged more than fifty students a year for suicidal thinking and have sent many of them on for professional emotional support. "If we imagine the action of a vaccine not just in terms of how it affects a single body, but also in terms of how it affects the collective body of a community, it is fair to think of vaccination as a kind of banking of immunity. Contributions to this bank are donations to those who cannot or will not be protected by their own immunity," writes Eula Biss. ". . . [M]ass vaccination becomes far more effective than individual vaccination." At Gunn High, emotional intelligence is as much a collective vaccination as it is an individual one, reliant on the community's capacity to recognize and to act.

Habib tells me that once his students gain such awareness, he has something he can work with. "You can say to a student, 'All right, you feel inferior relative to others, and you feel anxious when you're about to have a test. Okay, great. Let's actually tackle that. Let's give you some concrete skills that you can use before a test to relieve anxiety. Or let's give you concrete skills that you can use in order to deal with this question of inferiority.' At this point, we're having an entirely different conversation than we've ever been able to have in the past here."

Yet inherent in this calculation is another paradox. The best salve for negative emotional contagions continues to be the purposeful sharpening of one's emotional awareness and the acquisition of coping tools. But the consistency of social contagions is second only to the absurdity of their rubric; the Max Planck Institute for Human Cognitive and Brain Sciences points out that, while emotional attunement and empathy fight symptoms, social contagions of emotion spread faster among people who are themselves aware of the emotions of others. To be emotionally attuned to people is also to be emotionally vulnerable and therefore susceptible to them. Empathy becomes both our redeemer and the orchestrator of our undoing.

Perhaps the trick, submits Habib, is to create an army of what might be called interrupters. Habib trains school educators and students in the use of tools of emotion recognition and what to do when they encounter people edging toward a dangerous breaking point. But there's no reason for this training to end with the people closest to these students. A problem of this magnitude requires a solution that does not stop with the schools. We must train Uber drivers, restaurant staff, hairstylists, massage therapists, gardeners, baristas, and guitar buskers, each stranger on the street, every neighbor on the block. They need to know the signs and symptoms and public services available when people ensnared in the elements of this strange contagion show up in their shops, in the backseats of their cars, in the last rows of their classrooms.

In the end, literally everyone in this town becomes an interrupter.

Part VIII

THE COMMUNITY

"Four things annul the decree that seals a person's fate; namely alms, prayer, change of name, and change of deeds."
—THE TALMUD

"Strange things blow in through my window on the wings of the night wind and I don't worry about my destiny."
—CARL SANDBURG

Chapter 28

ALL THE ANSWERS
LEAD BACK HOME

'm not sure how I've missed it before. I've made a dozen visits to Gunn High since my first appointment six years ago with Roni Habib; yet, turning into the school on a spring afternoon in 2016, I notice for the first time that directly across the street from the entrance is Alta Mesa Memorial Park. A cemetery.

The train tracks are two miles to the east of Gunn High, but directly south of campus, at the doorway of the school, sits the graveyard's low perimeter wall. The path leads beyond a steel gate and into vivid green lawns. Sprinkler streams cross overtrimmed hedges and trees and sun-drenched meadows and stately mausoleums as white as sunlight beating against Jerusalem stone. Steve Jobs is buried in here someplace. David Packard and William Shockley are as well. So is Frederick Terman, the Stanford provost who cultivated the relationship between the university and tech companies that formed the bedrock of this town. Each grave site within the oceanic swell of headstones is connected to a person and a legacy prompting ideas, emotions, and behaviors, even in their passive conditions. For us, this is the place where the line ends, but for a strange contagion it's so far from the end of the line.

I pull into Gunn High's visitors' lot and as I cross the drive to the awning the cemetery is on my left. I have to question what a cemetery at the gateway to the school might prime in the most vulnerable. Gollwitzer spoke to me about the everyday things in the environment that we register unconsciously, these objects and images we don't think twice about that somehow influence, move, inspire, and prompt us. And damned if that cemetery isn't *right there*, like a canvasser handing out leaflets to the students streaming in and out of the campus. Beyond the tall electronic marquee, TITANS ROCK boastfully flashing across its screen, it's the first thing that students see.

Everything about Silicon Valley is centered in this cemetery: its founders and tech celebrities and Stanford academics, all buried here along with the fear that the end of the line represents. Maybe I'm reading too much into this. But given all that's happened over the past six years—eight deaths and the aftermath—it's hard not to see the parallels or to consider the correlations. And consider them I have, each and every one of them, the primes and the cascades, the social contagions both deleterious and advantageous.

The visitor parking is unusually full today, making me circle back around to find a spot in the student lot. Walking toward the main office, I join up with a group of women carrying portable massage chairs into the school, a service for students during finals week. I groan. It's the conundrum of the self-fulfilling prophecy: Like the presence of hazmat suites or visitors from infectious disease control in places that warrant neither, expectation promotes manifestation like a sugar pill. If the students see that people expect them to be so stressed over finals that they need a massage chair, they will stress themselves out enough that they actually *do* need one.

There's something everlastingly humbling at any age about

waiting to meet with a school principal. It is just before the end of the school day and I'm one of a half dozen people in the waiting area of the main office. To be honest, I've been hesitant to meet Denise Herrmann. Until now, every teacher, every student, and every parent I've reached out to about the suicide clusters has shown a guarded willingness to tell me their stories, to have their perspective become a part of the record. I've worried about talking to Herrmann because, if anybody in town has a reason to remain quiet or tow a party line, if there is such a line, it is the principal, the face of a school that's gone to great lengths to put on a show of calm, de-amplify tension, and avoid undesirable publicity.

A little less than a year ago, the *Atlantic* published a cover story about the Silicon Valley suicide clusters. Obviously it wasn't the typical tech-related Silicon Valley coverage people around here are used to reading about themselves. The spotlight fell on the broken parts of the region and, more specifically, the town of Palo Alto. The story picked up after the 2014 resurgence of the cluster phenomenon at Gunn High. It included scenes of the immediate aftermath of Cameron Lee's death, of teachers comforting people in their classrooms and in the school hallways, of Gunn High hosting suicide prevention experts from Stanford University, of a parent reading a child's suicide note aloud at a house gathering. By my second reading of the article, the names, faces, school buildings, and questions about the clusters rose up in me like brackish bay water. None of the pieces of the puzzle it presented was new to us here. By now we were all well aware of Gunn High's top national ranking, and we'd considered the contrast between that title and its more regionally known designation among some as the suicide high school. I wondered how many times we needed to hear that the ten-year suicide rate for high schools here is roughly five times the national average, or that 12 percent of high school students in this town have seriously contemplated suicide over the past year. We'd all heard the charges people made against parents who impose a high standard of excellence upon their kids to the point that it drives some to feel isolated from their families, and others to learn how to hide their failures well. We'd questioned the influence of so-called tiger mothers raising their children according to strict traditional Chinese ways. More than 40 percent of this town is made up of Asians, and, yes, right or wrong, we've deliberated, as the article pointed out, over how the culture shift might be "poisoning the culture of the entire school."

We already understood all of this. Where had all of these facts gotten us? And now these ugly and obvious truths were laid bare for the rest of the world to read. Our little secret had begun to slip beyond the confines of the community. As Gerald Russell said, once information is out in the world, no one can put it back in the bottle.

Given this, I wouldn't have been at all surprised if Denise Herrmann had received orders from above to stop talking to writers. Setting up the meeting had been easy enough, though. That she'd accepted my request for a meeting meant one of two things: she was either going to hew closely to talking points, or cancel the interview once she thought more about it. But she hadn't canceled the interview. So I'm prepared for her to hide behind a veil of denial, which would not only be easy but perfectly logical, given everything.

Before arriving this afternoon, I learned that Herrmann and her husband come from, of all places, DeKalb County, Illinois. They still own six hundred acres of corn and soybeans back home, and fifty windmills spin shadows adjacent to their property. I find myself marveling at serendipitous connections, at life's unexpected symmetry, even amid its tendency to tip toward disorder. Herrmann taught chemistry for a while, became an assistant principal, and then was a principal at a high school in Middleton, Wisconsin, for close to eight years before Gunn High hired her.

Coming to gather me in the waiting area, Herrmann approaches with an open expression, eyes swimming in warmth. She's apologizing to me for starting our meeting a little bit late; her meeting with the assistant superintendent ran long. I hadn't noticed the time. It's been an unexpectedly busy day around here, she continues, but she's glad that we can find some space to talk.

She points me to a table in her personal office, and as I take a seat I look around a room that's big and clean. I get the sense that she hasn't quite finished moving into this space, even though she's occupied it since the school recruited her back in 2014. "Did you know about Gunn High's story?" I ask.

"A little," she says. The school didn't keep its troubling history a secret from her. But at the time there hadn't been an incident at Gunn High in more than four years. Driving around with a real estate agent, looking for homes to rent, she noticed the track monitors at the railroad crossings. Above their sun tarps hung a simple white-on-black sign with the number for the national suicide prevention hotline, and another warning pedestrians to stay away from the crossing. In rural Illinois, Herrmann grew up around trains, but she'd never seen any safety measures like those here. "That's when I started to get an idea of what this place had gone through." Eight weeks into her first year at Gunn High, when a train struck and killed the student Quinn Gens, Herrmann says the pretense of distance—both in terms of the safety that time creates between problems of the past and today, as well as her own arm's-length association with the story of Palo Alto—dematerialized.

Now she was in charge of dusting off the old machinery from the era of 2009 and 2010, the array of countermeasures and proactive risk reduction methods. Herrmann reactivated partnerships that the school district established with Stanford University, mental health agencies, and the county. There were days when Herrmann hosted more than twenty different mental health providers on the campus at a time. The components of the prevention system worked together smoothly. Gunn High had become tragically efficient at responding to calamity.

As the second cluster persisted through 2015, the psychological, behavioral, and emotional social contagions swirled and interacted with one another in this microcosm. More than any other social contagion, Herrmann saw the effects of fear spread. "There was a lot of fear from students that, if it could happen to a person who seemed so happy and positive, maybe it could happen to them, too. That same fear spread among parents, about what may or may not be contributing to student health and well-being, and feelings of stress, and not feeling they could manage that for their child. The staff worried that students were dying because they were assigning too much homework, or that they didn't have good relationships with these kids."

But eventually, Herrmann noticed the story of social contagions changing from one of fear and hysteria to a story of community. There is now, more than ever, she tells me, a catchable sense that everyone is in this together. For six years Palo Alto has questioned what's wrong with its community. But what if the community is, in fact, a major reason why we've been able to combat the two strange contagions in the first place? We cannot determine the effect of a strange contagion without identifying the parameters of the community that contains it. The hot zone is not a person but a location on a map. Without borders, social contagions defy categorization. A cluster is so defined by behaviors that fall within an accelerated time frame and a geo-graphical area. When a social contagion jumps its boundaries, be it those of a work group, a classroom, or an entire town, these parameters are the measures by which we define the leap. Com-munities are the vessels that contain social contagions, and the vessels that social contagions escape from.

But community is also the closest thing we have to a viable treatment. Community answers social contagions with well-informed rational discourse over overblown rejoinders. Com-munity primes people for bravery and grounds them against irrational fear. A community attuned to the telltale signs of its emotions will respond to even the most subtle of warning signs. And, in the end, communities will choose to leverage social con-tagions or fall victim to them.

When they strike, a community's effort to defend itself de-fines the narrative of the strange contagion. Each must ask: Will this be a story of irrational fear, hysteria, greed, burnout, and unrestrained anger? Or will this be a story of hope, rationality, bravery, and unification?

Herrmann questions what to do with a population that has suffered as greatly as this town. As a transmitter of informa-tion, resources, and knowledge, the community's fighting pop-ulace remains on the front lines of the battle against student suicide. We've positioned ourselves on committees, developed systems to offer outreach, and created programs to take care of the grieving, to monitor kids, and to graft emotional intelligence onto their psyches. Yes, Herrmann has seen social contagions do their damage, but she's also discovered a community that's learned to leverage them to its advantage.

"We've had some luck spreading bravery. Once we experi-enced loss, there was a great external force to do things differ-ently, to take responsibility. If we were gonna do this, we were gonna have the courage to listen and to visit problems," she says. Courage trickled down from teachers to students, from students to parents, from parents to kids. "I've watched that courage spread. Kids are taking on the mentality of mandated reporters. Peers who know that a friend is in a bad space, but were once reluctant to tell an adult because they feared that it would be jeopardizing a friendship, now know firsthand that worse things can happen from not helping them get help. That takes a lot of courage, and we're seeing it more frequently. Our students are more vocal than they ever were before. They want to be active participants in school-wide decisions and push for even stronger voices than we've had in the past."

These social contagions, she says, aren't simply mixing and interacting within the community to be used as helping tools or weapons against the problem. This perfect storm of social phenomena *is* the community. My neighbor, Sanjeet Thadani, said that at some point the interlopers become part of the fabric of a place, contributing the social contagions simply by virtue of being here. The same is also true for social contagions, interlopers that take over a place to the point that the two are indistinguishable from each other.

Taking a wide view of the past six years, I believe that Herrmann is right. This town is circumscribed by the social contagions it harbors, by the dangerous and the destructive outcomes, as well as by the benign and the beneficial consequences. This is our strange contagion, and our strange contagion defines this place.

Herrmann shares her perspective with me about the ways in which the school's focus has shifted over her two years here to bring awareness of social contagions to the forefront. We talk about the importance of being deliberate in what we say and do, given how catchable thoughts, behaviors, and emotions are, and how Gunn High has worked hard to spark a positive mood, courage, and a cohesive sense of school pride. She's approved the formation of a student wellness committee that recently launched a campaign to reduce stigma around help-seeking activities. She tells me about Gunn High's efforts to work in tandem with families to support their students through emotional crises. In that time, a year has come and gone without the death of another Gunn High student, statistics that seem to justify the employment of such tremendous efforts. Meanwhile, time has healed the community as best it can.

When the phone rings, Herrmann glances across the room at her desk and decides to let it go to voice mail. The interview continues for a couple of minutes, but the phone rings again. Herrmann gets up to check the incoming number. "It's the superintendent's office," she says. She takes the call and turns her back to me.

When she finishes the conversation, she returns to the table and, fearing she's coming across as a bit distracted this afternoon, apologizes to me again. If I was ever at all concerned Herrmann might be guarded during our meeting today, all worry has long since vanished. She continues to come across as open, honest, and disarmingly unguarded.

"You've probably noticed a lot of things going on around here," she continues.

It's only as she mentions it that the innocuous details of the day unexpectedly begin to tilt a little in my mind. The overcrowded parking lot becomes a sign of urgency. And the chair massage specialists I observed setting up stations like an amenity at a start-up appear less like a Silicon Valley–style perk and more like something jarringly out of place. The main office was so busy that the assistant to the principal neglected to issue me a parking permit when I signed in, a highly unusual oversight.

Herrmann draws in a long sip from her water bottle. "It's going to be reported, so I guess I can share it with you."

Her voice is thin. I catch a quiver in her face. After a moment I realize the air has stalled in my lungs. The moment arrives with the force of sudden ice-water immersion; cold shock grasps at my body and I gasp even as Herrmann's gaze softens. The county coroner conveyed the news to her that responders recovered the body of a nineteen-year-old Gunn High alum named Sarah Marie Longyear. She was struck by the northbound number 155 train.

Chapter 29

A PLAGUE OF YELLOW JACKS

This interview, everything we're talking about, is real right
now."

I don't know quite what to say to her. My mouth is dry.
I lean away from Herrmann and slide my hands along the table
between us.

"I'm so sorry."

The words sound flat and insincere. I want to turn off the
digital voice recorder under my fingers. She says we should continue the interview.

"Throughout this whole school year we've been working really hard to find that balance between remembering and honor-
ing what's happened, but trying to move past it and focus on all
of the great things that are also happening at Gunn High," she
says. She tries to remind herself every day that these students
only have four years here, and she wants those years to be good
for them. Last year the school had a lot of tragedy. This year
they strived to make it a positive and special experience for the
students. "And we succeeded at that for a really long time."

"Can I ask how you're doing?"

Herrmann exhales slowly. A little tremor flutters through
this simple action. I'm sitting here helpless to do anything. She

is peering back at me, looking into me clearly, without reservation, hard and cool.

"This shouldn't be something that we've done so many times that we're good at it. It feels unhealthy. I think that's the thing that's stuck with me the most, just knowing that for me this is the fourth Gunn student who's died under my principalship, but for many of my staff it's their ninth in the last six years. That's what I'm really feeling. We're going back into autopilot."

The school and the town are good at dealing with this. Denise Herrmann and I know what will happen next. The local high schools will be calling assemblies. Grief support programs will deploy their prevention tool kits, with scripts to read to the media, public service announcements, and crisis plans. In the days and weeks to come, we will repeat a familiar cycle of responses as one applies an ointment to an open wound. We will come at this the way we always do, using our treatment models and wanting so desperately to make things better. The mind-set is always the same. The strange contagion *must* stop and therefore it's *going* to stop. But, sitting in Herrmann's office, still reeling from the news, I'm unsure if it ever will.

We have the means to address elements of the strange contagion, but we still have no tangible way to fully stop it. Six years have passed since I first set out to uncover the components of this perfect storm with the hope that in doing so we might learn how to end it. What I'm left with is a series of insights and contradictions: Media limits dispersion but also perpetuates it. Emotional intelligence counters the effects of emotional contagions even while it does little to stop their spread. Behavioral primes foster bravery and yet they also promote impossible standards. Support groups slow contagions but they also spread them. Responding to hysteria reduces contamination but it also increases it. Cuing people to catch positive behaviors can backfire and trigger our innate propensity for self-harm. The search for a surefire cure, that most vital of grails, only brings me back to Palo Alto empty-handed.

WHEN THE STRANGE contagion began and I first spoke with Nicholas Christakis, my question to him was a simple one: Is it possible to cultivate a cure to Palo Alto's strange contagion? Throughout my search, I've been operating under the assumption that there is the potential for a remedy, but I may have had the wrong goal all along. In the end, maybe containing the suicide cluster wasn't the right objective. The question I should have been asking him, and myself, was: What are we going to do about it now that it's here and part of the fabric of our reality?

The best we can do, I suppose, is to treat it as we would any other illness. Harmful and helpful social contagions exist everywhere. There's really no avoiding them. We have ways to address the ones that create negative consequences and promote the ones that produce positive consequences. But in terms of finding that single thing that's going to finish this strange contagion for good, the fact is the underlying social contagions and regional vulnerabilities will persist. As one does during an outbreak of a virulent disease, we treat the symptoms, avoid the triggers, and maintain unyielding vigilance. And we are left to support one another through our sickness and grief in a way that yields goodness.

It's not going to stop. The six-year search has amounted to this intolerable fact.

Of course, this really shouldn't surprise me. Every person I've visited and each scenario I've met over the years has implicitly imparted such wisdom. Gerald Russell spoke of entropy, one's inability to put back what has since escaped. Kern County harbors uncertainty and irrational fear to this day, despite fully trusting the undeniable facts that otherwise discount regional hysteria. Wael Ghonim, in his story of post-revolution Egypt, referred to it as the inevitable decline into old behaviors. When I asked Gary Slutkin at the University of Illinois if he believed that violence is truly curable, he responded carefully. "Well, with diseases, rather than make pronouncements of cure, we talk about them in terms of the likelihood of relapse. There's no real reason why we shouldn't be able to stop a social contagion the same way we stop other infectious processes like smallpox, polio, tuberculosis, leprosy, or plague when the right strategies are put into place within the right infrastructures." But he didn't really answer my question, and I realize now, as the strange contagion claims another life, that it is in this absence where his true answer remains.

With contagious illnesses, both physical and psychological, eradication requires some combination of exposure and resistance. The math of infectious processes is the math of transmission and the susceptibility of a community. "Once a contagion starts to propagate," Slutkin told me, "stopping it is a matter of bending the curve enough that fewer people are exposed to it. Then you have resistance. But never eradication."

The answers I've found on this search have pointed to the hard reality of something pervasive and unyielding and incurable. I've come away with a clear understanding as to the sources feeding a big problem: the pathogens of cultural influence, frenzies, hysteria, a nocebo effect, ambition, and greed; of goal contagions; of elevated thresholds of acceptance; of stress and depression; of the dangers of conformity and pressure. But within these answers I'm beginning to see a common thread. I notice that every resource I've visited and response I've collected speaks to our responsibility to one another as individual members of a collective. The teacher Roni Habib and the writer Julie

Lythcott-Haims both spoke of applying emotional awareness to the community, the way that each of us must watch out for one another, especially when we do not have the language to express our pain. Gary Slutkin at Cure Violence took this further. When all members of the community—from taxi drivers to baristas—become knowledgeable interrupters of problematic social contagions, watching for signs and knowing the resources available to them, only good things can happen. Peter Gollwitzer at the Motivation Lab spoke of changing primes in the community, of teaching people to become mindful of the cues we inadvertently parade and how each can affect moods and behaviors of others around us. Sanjeet Thadani, my neighbor, spoke of modifying the character of the community's collective intelligence and the remarkable changes one can expect when we alter what we teach our children. At PCI Media Impact, Sean Southey spoke of relying on the community to spread curative memes and behaviors through story. Without a responsive community, the message becomes lost, the positive change rendered inert.

In the beginning of my investigation, I found myself in the middle of two strange contagion events, and I've come away now with a more holistic understanding of the necessity of individuals to care for one another, to watch out for one another, to take on an awareness of what it is we are capable of communicating as well as our powers of influence. Somewhere along the way my purpose became one of trying to understand how the community can best face its crisis and sustain itself amid the natural phenomena of social contagions, which are as inevitable and untamable as a cyclone.

HERRMANN ACCOMPANIES ME out of her office. From the outside looking in, Gunn High might as well be any high school in the country today. You'd never know what's transpired here. But then you look closer—it practically invites you to—and details come into focus. Together, Herrmann and I walk past the Bat Cave, inset with long picnic tables, orange patterns of brick, and a sign on a post with a large black arrow pointed to the sky. It's there reminding students to keep their heads up. On another building, someone has tacked up a hand-drawn sign that reads WE CARE. Along the side of a classroom is a wall reserved for personal rejection letters from universities, a reminder that failure is not the exception. In other locations around campus there hang signs with phone numbers to suicide and crisis centers.

Herrmann smiles at me, an act of courage more eloquent, comforting, and tender than any I have found at Gunn High during these past six years. "Our students are amazingly resilient, strong, caring, everyday kids," she says. Today they look one another in the eyes, Herrmann tells me. When they ask how you're doing, this is not some empty pleasantry but a penetrating, deeply meaningful exchange. In one another they monitor for vocal inflections, sloping affect, the dulling of light in other people's faces. And if they see a sign they recognize and it sets off in them something electric and awful, they will sound the warning. They prime courage in one another, as well as hope and resilience.

My focus momentarily shifts to a point just beyond Herrmann's shoulder. In the center of one of the courtyards rises the school's flagpole. The white and red California state flag, emblazoned with a brown bear on a green grass plat, moves in the breeze.

Maybe it's time to add another flag to it, I think. A bright yellow flag, a yellow jack, a visual reminder of the psychological, emotional, and the behavioral contagions we all spread and contract and resist. Perhaps we should all raise yellow jacks. They'd ride atop of office cubicles, cars, mall entrances, coffee shops, crowded movie theaters, and the entrances of crammed subway terminals and bus stations. The color guard would protect the yellow jack, not out of a sense of militaristic honor, but out of personal duty and responsibility to others who make up the collective regiments. From office parks to community parks across the planet, they'd wash cities in number-two-pencil yellow, flags effortlessly blowing past boundaries of all designation, in line with endemic anxiety, odious behaviors, the corruption of rational thinking, but no more or less than laughter, happiness, courage, the flash of mirror neurons that align heart rates, the transmissible wealth of knowledge, and, above all else, the infection of hope. I picture them all, and I feel comforted by a sense of connection to the world.

In the coming months my family and I will leave the community of Palo Alto for good. We'll dismantle the apartment. Haul our moving boxes from the storage room and fill them with our things. Wrap packing paper over our dishes, fold our clothes, take down the art from the walls. We won't have to go far to leave Silicon Valley; we'll move into a house twenty miles north. Unlike our old community, mostly made up of technology industry professionals, our new neighborhood, somewhat off the grid, will be more of a hodgepodge of aging hippies, teachers, social workers, blue-collar folks, and retired military. Instead of Stanford University, we'll have a community college and a boys' reformatory down the hill. We'll swap boutique markets for a Safeway with linoleum the color of day-old orange rinds. Instead of start-ups, we'll have a mini-mall and two gas stations. My wife will resign from Google and join a nonprofit organization, which friends will regard as financially foolish. Our choice to leave will be based, in part, on an irrational fear that we'll dress in reasons of practicality. But let's be clear, we've bought into the hysteria. The fear. The "just in case."

Standing in my new home office, surrounded by moving boxes full of my notes, I'll grow more disenfranchised from the belief that we might outrun everything we saw and experienced in Palo Alto. Leaving the town matters little, because, really, where is there to hide? Social contagions influence businesses, health care, education, government policy, politics, and international relations everywhere. Beneath the surface we are all connected.

Then again, why do we need to hide? In spite of crippling tragedy, Palo Alto is nothing if not an example of how to fight, how to live, how to be happy, and how to remain strong. Oddly enough, this place is one to mirror. It is a shining example of how to care for one another in the darkest of times. A vital reminder of our responsibility to one another. In the end, this lesson is something good, something clean, something like redemption.

ACKNOWLEDGMENTS

To the people who endlessly display their courage: faculty, students, and parents affiliated with Gunn High School, with specific thanks to Roni Habib, Dr. Denise Herrmann, Noreen Likins, Paul Dunlap, James Shelby, and Joyce Lui.

To the people who continue to have faith in me: Richard Pine, Alexis Hurley, Eliza Rothstein, and everyone at Inkwell Management; Karen Rinaldi, Hannah Robinson, Victoria Comella, Brian Perrin, the house of Harper Wave, and the banner of HarperCollins.

To the writers and thinkers on whose shoulders I continue to prop myself on top of: Adam Grant, Sheryl Sandberg, Julie Lythcott-Haims, Dan Ariely, Po Bronson, Ethan Watters, Scott James, Shana Mahaffey, Janis Cooke Newman, Susanne Pari, Ethel Rohan, Cameron Tuttle, TJ Stiles, Fred Vogelstein, Yukari Kane, and Mona Kerby.

To the researchers who pointed me on the right paths, and gently corrected me when I was on the wrong ones: Dr. Nicholas Christakis at the Human Nature Lab at Yale University; Dr. Sigal Barsade at the Wharton School at the University of Pennsylvania; Dr. Peter Gollwitzer at New York University; Dr. Shashank V. Joshi, Dr. Albert Bandura, Dr. James Lock at Stanford University; Dr. Gary Slutkin at the University of

Illinois; Dr. Sherry Towers at Arizona State University; Jim Santucci, Shelly Gillan, and the Kara organization; Dr. Ramsey Khasho, Dr. Rosalie Witlock, and Lori McGilpin at the Children's Health Council; Dr. Eric Kuhn at the National Center for PTSD and the VA Palo Alto Health Care System; the Cecil H. Green Library at Stanford University; Patrick Cook Deegan and the research of the "d.school": the Hasso Plattner Institute of Design at Stanford; the additional support of Sunisa Manning; Brandon Martin, Cindy Tidwell and Kern Talks; Sean Southey at PCI Media Impact; and EQ Schools.

To Silicon Valley and the innovators of Northern California, including Gary Briggs at Facebook and Sophie Lebrecht and Nicole Halmi at Neon Lab.

To my early readers and idea generators: Tomer Altman, Joanna Samuels, Allison Shotwell, Jenna Scatena, Melissa Dodd, Roger Studley, Cheryl Dolinger Brown, Terri and James Kravetz, Carin and Paul Feldman, Matthew DeCoster, Travis Peterson, Amy Marcott, Juliette Kelley, and Nick Geisler.

To the people I do this for: Mimi, Alec, and Chloe.

To the people who put a roof over my head and supplied me with a table and a light: this book was written in part at the Castro Writers' Cooperative; the San Francisco Writers' Grotto; the Lit Camp Writer's Conference; the Jackson Family Retreat at Big Sur; and Jupiter taproom in Berkeley, California.

Thank you all for collectively sharing with me your contagious spirit of giving, your kindness, and, above all else, your wisdom.

This is a book of nonfiction and based on the accounts of teachers, students, parents, researchers, and my personal observations. It does not attempt to be an all-encompassing book on suicide prevention. If you are concerned about your mental health or that of someone you know, resources like these are beneficial and save lives:

The National Suicide Prevention Hotline

The National Suicide Prevention Lifeline is a national network of local crisis centers that provides free and confidential emotional support to people in suicidal crisis or emotional distress 24 hours a day, 7 days a week. We're committed to improving crisis services and advancing suicide prevention by empowering individuals, advancing professional best practices, and building awareness.

1-800-273-8255

Crisis Text Line

Your best friend. Your dad. That lady down the street. That quiet kid in school. That loud kid in school. That dude in accounting.

Your cousin in Alaska. That hipster in flannel in Brooklyn. That "rando" who might lurk online. Crisis Text Line is for everyone. Crisis Text Line is free, 24/7 support for those in crisis. Text 741741 from anywhere in the USA to text with a trained Crisis Counselor. Crisis Text Line trains volunteers (like you!) to support people in crisis.

Text HELLO to 741741 for free, 24/7 crisis support.

Mental Health America

Mental Health America (MHA)—founded in 1909—is the nation's leading community-based nonprofit dedicated to helping Americans achieve wellness by living mentally healthier lives. Their work is driven by a commitment to promote mental health as a critical part of overall wellness, including prevention for all, early identification and intervention for those at risk, integrated health, behavioral health and other services for those who need them, and recovery as a goal. Their mental health screening program (www.mhascreening.org) provides individuals with tools to help address their mental health before a point of crisis.

www.mentalhealthamerica.net

The American Foundation for Suicide Prevention

The AFSP's mission is to save lives and bring hope to those affected by suicide.

To fully achieve its mission, the AFSP engages in the following Five Core Strategies: funds scientific research, offers educational programs for professionals, educates the public about mood disorders and suicide prevention, promotes policies and legislation that impact suicide and prevention, and provides programs and resources for survivors of suicide loss and people at risk, and involves them in the work of the Foundation.

https://afsp.org

International Association for Suicide Prevention

The International Association for Suicide Prevention (IASP) is dedicated to preventing suicidal behavior, alleviating its effects, and providing a forum for academics, mental health professionals, crisis workers, volunteers, and suicide survivors. Founded by the late Professor Erwin Ringel and Dr. Norman Farberow in 1960, IASP now includes professionals and volunteers from more than fifty different countries. IASP is a Non-Governmental Organization in official relationship with the World Health Organization (WHO) concerned with suicide prevention.

www.iasp.info

American Association of Suicidology

AAS is a nonprofit organization that promotes research, public awareness programs, public education, and training for professionals and volunteers. It serves as a national clearinghouse for information on suicide, publishing and disseminating statistics and suicide prevention resources. AAS also hosts national annual conferences for professionals and survivors.

www.suicideology.org

Suicide Awareness Voices of Education (SAVE)

SAVE is a nonprofit organization whose mission is to prevent suicide through public awareness and education, reduce stigma, and serve as a resource to people affected by suicide. Its prevention and education programs are designed to increase knowledge about depression, suicide, and accessing community resources and to increase understanding and use of intervention skills to help prevent suicide.

www.save.org

Children's Safety Network

CSN is a national resource center for injury and violence prevention, including suicide prevention. CSN provides technical assistance on injury prevention planning, programs, and best practices; analyzes and interprets injury data; partners with national organizations and federal agencies to promote child and adolescent health and safety; disseminates injury prevention research; conducts trainings and presentations; and produces publications.

www.childrenssafetynetwork.org

SELECTED SOURCES

Aarts, Henk, Peter M. Gollwitzer, and Ran R. Hassin. "Goal Contagion: Perceiving Is for Pursuing." *Journal of Personality and Social Psychology* 87, no. 1 (2004), 23–37.

Abbott, Megan. "When Social Media Makes Something Go Viral in Real Life." Huffington Post. September 2, 2015. http://www.huffington post.com/megan-abbott-/dont-look-now-social-medi_b_5534200 .html

Adams, Jill U. "Tracking the 'Contagion' in Suicide Clusters." *Los Angeles Times.* November 9, 2009.

Akagi, H., and A. House. "The Clinical Epidemiology of Hysteria: Vanishingly Rare, or Just Vanishing?" *Psychological Medicine* 32, no. 2. (2002), 191–94.

Alderman, Lesley. "Treating Eating Disorders and Paying for It." *New York Times.* December 3, 2010.

Aleccia, Jonel. "Teens More Stressed-out Than Adults, Survey Shows." nbc.com. February 11, 2014. http://www.nbcnews.com/health/kids -health/teens-more-stressed-out-adults-survey-shows-n26921

American Psychiatric Association. *Diagnostic and Statistical Manual of Mental Disorders,* 3rd ed. Washington, DC: APA, 1980.

Amin, Kareem, Hoda Heidari, and Michael Kearns. "Learning from Contagion (Without Timestamps)." *Proceedings of the 31st International Conference on Machine Learning* 32 (2014), 1845–53.

Amstad, F. T. and N. K. Semmer, "Spillover and Crossover of Work and Family-Related Negative Emotions in Couples." *Journal Psychologie des Alltagshandelns / Psychology of Everyday Activity* 4, no. 1 (2011).

Ariely, Dan. *Predictably Irrational: The Hidden Forces That Shape Our Decisions* (New York: HarperCollins, 2009).

———. *The Upside of Irrationality: The Unexpected Benefits of Defying Logic* (New York: Harper Perennial, 2010).

Associated Press. "Mass Hysteria Rare, but More Often Seen in Girls." Fox News Health. February 3, 2012. http://www.foxnews.com /health/2012/02/03/mass-hysteria-rare-but-usually-seen-in-girls.html

———. "A Nation Challenged: The False Alarms; Postal Service Is Kept Busy Tracking Down Anthrax Scares." *New York Times.* December 22, 2001.

———. "Video Helps Clear Convict of Abuse After 21 Years." www.msnbc .com. August 9, 2009. http://www.msnbc.msn.com/id/32341725/ns /us_newscrime_and_courts/Associated Press/MSNBC

Atkinson, Donald R. *Counseling American Minorities*, 6th edition (New York: McGraw-Hill, 2004).

Bachner-Melman, Rachel, and Pesach Lichtenberg. "Freud's Relevance to Hypnosis: A Reevaluation." *American Journal of Clinical Hypnosis* 44, no. 1 (2001), 37–50.

Bacigalupe, Gonzalo. "Teen Suicides in Privileged Suburb: We Have to Keep Talking." WBUR 90.9. February 21, 2014. http://www.wbur .org/commonhealth/2014/02/21/teen-suicide-suburb

Bailey, R. "Is Crime Contagious? Experiments Vindicate the Broken Windows Theory of How Disorder Spreads." www.reason.com. November 25, 2008. http://reason.com/archives/2008/11/25/is-crime -contagious

Baker, Anne E. "Television, Disordered Eating, and Young Women in Fiji: Negotiating Body Image and Identity During Rapid Social Change." *Culture, Medicine and Psychiatry* 28 (2004), 533–59.

Bakker, Arnold B., and Pascale M. Le Blanc. "Burnout Contagion Among Intensive Care Nurses." *Journal of Advanced Nursing* 51, no. 3 (2005), 276–87.

Bakker, Arnold B., and Wilmar B. Schaufeli. "Burnout Contagion Processes Among Teachers." *Journal of Applied Social Psychology* 30, no. 1 (2000), 2289–308.

Balis, Theodora, and Theodor T. Postolache. "Ethnic Differences in Adolescent Suicide in the United States" *International Journal Child Health Human Development* 1, no. 3 (2008), 281–96.

Bandura, Albert. "Social Cognitive Theory of Mass Communication." *Mediapsychology* 3 (2001), 265–99.

———. *Social Foundations of Thought and Action: A Social-Cognitive Theory* (Englewood Cliffs, NJ: Prentice-Hall, 1986).

———. *Social Learning Theory* (New York: General Learning Press, 1971).

Barsade, Sigal. "Faster Than a Speeding Text: 'Emotional Contagion' at Work." *Psychology Today.* October 15, 2014. https://www.psychol ogytoday.com/blog/the-science-work/201410/faster-speeding-text -emotional-contagion-work

Barsade, Sigal, and Joseph Frank Bernstein. "For Better Results, Emotional Contagion Matters." Wharton @ Work. Executive Education. February 2011. http://executiveeducation.wharton.upenn.edu/thought -leadership/wharton-at-work/2011/02/emotional-contagion

Barsade, Sigal G. "The Ripple Effect: Emotional Contagion and Its Influence on Group Behavior." *Administrative Science Quarterly* 47 (2002), 644–675.

Barsade, Sigal G., and Andrew P. Knight. "Group Affect." *Annual Review of Organizational Psychology and Organizational Behavior* 2 (2015), 21–46.

Barsade, Sigal G., and Donald E. Gibson. "Why Does Affect Matter in Organizations?" *Academy of Management Perspectives.* February 2007.

Barsade, Sigal G., Lakshmi and Olivia A. O'Neill. "What's Love Got to Do with It? A Longitudinal Study of the Culture of Companionate Love and Employee and Client Outcomes in a Long-term Care Setting." *Administrative Science Quarterly* 59, no. 551 (2014).

Barsade, Sigal G., Lakshmi Ramarajan, and Drew Westen. "Implicit Affect in Organizations." *Research in Organizational Behavior* 29 (2009), 135–62.

Bartholomew, Robert E., and Simon Wessely. "Protean Nature of Mass Sociogenic Illness from Possessed Nuns to Chemical and Biological Terrorism Fears." *British Journal of Psychiatry* 180, no. 4 (2002), 300–306.

Basten, Stuart. "Mass Media and Reproductive Behaviour: Serial Narratives, Soap Operas and Telenovelas." The Future of Human Reproduction: Working Paper #7. St John's College, Oxford, and Vienna Institute of Demography. June 2009. https://www.spi.ox.ac.uk/filead min/documents/PDF/Soaps_-_Number_7.pdf

Beck, Julie. "How Friendship Fights Depression: A New Study Shows That a Healthy Mood Can Spread Through Friend Groups." *Atlantic.* August 19, 2015.

Becker, Anne E., Rebecca A. Burwell, David B. Herzog, Paul Hamburg, and Stephen E. Gilman. "Eating Behaviours and Attitudes Following Prolonged Exposure to Television Among Ethnic Fijian Adolescent Girls." *British Journal of Psychiatry* 180, no. 6 (2002), 509–514.

Becker, Eva S., Melanie M. Keller, Thomas Goetz, Anne C. Frenzel, and Jamie L. Taxer. "Antecedents of Teachers' Emotions in the Classroom: An Intra-Individual Approach." *Frontiers in Psychology* 6, no. 635 (2015).

Belk, Russell W., and Gülnur Tumbat. "The Cult of Macintosh." *Consumption, Markets and Culture* 8, no. 3 (2005), 205–217.

Bellock, Sian. "Is Depression Contagious?" *Psychology Today.* January 15, 2014. https://www.psychologytoday.com/blog/choke/201401/is-depression -contagious

Benedetti, F., M. Lanotte, L. Lopiano, and L. Colloca. "When Words Are Painful: Unraveling the Mechanisms of the Nocebo Effect." *Neuroscience* 147, no. 2 (2007), 260–71.

Berger, Jonah. *Contagious: Why Things Catch On* (New York: Simon & Schuster, 2013).

Bernstein, David. "From Pesthouses to AIDS Hospices: Neighbors' Irrational Fears of Treatment Facilities for Contagious Diseases." *Columbia Human Rights Law Review* 22, no. 1 (1990), 1–20.

Bies, Robert, J. Bies, Thomas M. Tripp, Roderick M. Kramer, Robert A. Giacalone, and Jerald Greenberg. "At the Breaking Point: Cognitive and Social Dynamics of Revenge in Organizations." *Antisocial Behavior in Organizations* (Thousand Oaks, CA: Sage Publications, 1997), 18–36.

Birch, Hayley. "Where Is the World's Most Stressful City?" *Guardian.* October 8, 2015.

Bishop, George D., Albert L. Alva, Lionel Cantu, and Telecia K. Rittiman. "Responses to Persons with AIDS: Fear of Contagion or Stigma?" *Journal of Applied Social Psychology* 21, no. 23 (1991), 1877–88.

Biss, Eula. *On Immunity: An Inoculation* (Minneapolis: Graywolf, 2014).

Blake, Joseph P., and Gloria Campisi. "A Step Ahead of the Sheriff, AIDS Group Avoids Eviction, Exits W. Mount Airy Home." *Philadelphia Daily News.* February 28, 1991.

Blake, Matt. "Goldman Sachs Memo Insists Its Employees Not Work on Weekends—Except for Sundays (and, of Course, Some Saturdays)." *Daily Mail.* November 8, 2013.

Blakeslee, Sandra. "Cells That Read Minds." *New York Times.* January 10, 2006.

Blasco-Fontecilla, Hilario. "On Suicide Clusters: More Than Contagion." *Australian & New Zealand Journal of Psychiatry* 47, no. 5 (2015), 490–91.

Bloch, Hannah. "An ISIS School Teaches Jihad to Children at Age 3." NPR. November 19, 2015. http://www.npr.org/sections/parallels/2015/11/19/456508362/an-isis-school-that-teaches-jihad-to -children-at-age-3

Bloomberg News. "Subprime Star Josh Birnbaum Leaves Goldman." *Telegraph.* April 17, 2008.

Blössner, Norbert. *The City-Soul Analogy: The Cambridge Companion to Plato's Republic* (Cambridge, UK: Cambridge University Press, 2007).

Booth, David. "Some Words of Comfort, and Advice, After an Apparent Suicide." *J-Weekly.* June 11, 2009.

Bosman, Julie. "Pine Ridge Indian Reservation Struggles with Suicides Among Its Young." *New York Times.* May 1, 2015.

Boss, Leslie P. "Epidemic Hysteria: A Review of the Published Literature." *Epidemiologic Reviews* 19, no. 2 (1997), 233–34.

Bowers, K. J., and S. D. Johnson. "Who Commits Near Repeats? A Test of the Boost Explanation." *Western Criminology Review* 5, no. 3 (2004), 12–24.

Boyd, Danah. "What Does the Facebook Experiment Teach Us?" *Medium.* July 1, 2014. https://medium.com/message/what-does-the-facebook -experiment-teach-us-c858c08e287f#.ala4978me

Boyd, Robert, Peter J. Richerson, and Joseph Henrich. "The Cultural Niche: Why Social Learning Is Essential for Human Adaptation." *Proceedings of the National Academy of Sciences* 108, no. 2 (2011).

Brady, Charles. "Presentation: How to Build and Sustain the Courage Needed for Recovery." Lindner Center of Hope.

Bremmer, Jan. *The Early Greek Concept of the Soul* (Princeton, NJ: Princeton University Press, 1983).

Brody, Jane E. "An Eating Disorder of Binging and Purging Reported." *New York Times.* October 20, 1981.

———. "Personal Health." *New York Times.* March 30, 1983.

Brogan, Jan. "Teens' Brains Make Them More Vulnerable to Suicide." *Boston Globe.* March 10, 2014.

Brouwers, André, and Welko Tomic. "A Longitudinal Study of Teacher Burnout and Perceived Self-Efficacy in Classroom Management." *Teaching and Teacher Education* 16 (2000), 239–53.

Brown, Scott. "What Really Happened to the Girls in Le Roy?" NBC/ WGRZ.com. February 21, 2013. http://archive.wgrz.com/news/arti cle/201715/37/What-Really-Happened-To-The-Girls-In-Le-Roy

Brown, William W. *The Anti-Slavery Harp: A Collection of Songs for Anti-Slavery Meetings* (Boston: Bela Marsh, 1848).

Brunstein, J. C., and G. W. Maier. "Implicit and Self-Attributed Motives to Achieve: Two Separate but Interacting Needs." *Journal of Personality and Social Psychology* 89 (2005), 205–222.

Buchanan, Leigh. "Zumba Fitness: Company of the Year." *Inc.* December 4, 2012.

Buhaug, Halvard, and Kristian Skrede Gleditsch. "Contagion or Confusion?

Why Conflicts Cluster in Space." *International Studies Quarterly* 52, no. 2 (2008), 215–33.

Burnett, Dean. "Phobias: The Rationale Behind Irrational Fears." *Guardian.* June 28, 2013.

Butler, R. "Information Seeking and Achievement Motivation in Middle Childhood and Adolescence: The Role of Conceptions of Ability." *Developmental Psychology* 35, no. 1 (1999), 146–63.

Cabanatuan, Michael, and Jill Tucker. "Tragedy Strikes Twice at Palo Alto School: Teen Suicide." *San Francisco Chronicle.* June 4, 2009. http://www.sfgate.com/bayarea/article/Tragedy-strikes-twice-at-Palo-Alto-school-3296390.php

Cain, Susan. *Quiet: The Power of Introverts in a World That Can't Stop Talking* (New York: Broadway Books, 2012).

Calomiris, Charles W., and Joseph R. Mason. "Contagion and Bank Failures During the Great Depression: The June 1932 Chicago Banking Panic." *American Economic Review* 87, no. 5 (1997), 863–83.

Campisi, Gloria. "$ Woes Peril AIDS Hospice." *Philadelphia Daily News.* April 1, 1993.

Cardon, Melissa S., and Michael Glauser. "Entrepreneurial Passion: Sources and Sustenance." Wilson Center for Social Entrepreneurship. Paper 3. 2011. http://digitalcommons.pace.edu/wilson/3

Carey, Benedict. "Experts Offer Steps for Avoiding Public Hysteria, a Different Contagious Threat." *New York Times.* October 15, 2014.

Carod-Artal, Francisco Javier, and Carolina Vázquez-Cabrera. "Burnout Syndrome in an International Setting." In *Burnout for Experts: Prevention in the Context of Living and Working,* edited by Sabine Bährer-Kohler (New York: Springer Science & Business Media, 2012).

Carte, Sherrie Bourg. "Emotions Are Contagious—Choose Your Company Wisely." *Psychology Today.* October 20, 2012. https://www.psychologytoday.com/blog/high-octane-women/201210/emotions-are-contagious-choose-your-company-wisely

Cassidy, Kimberly Wright, Deborah Shaw Fineberg, Kimberly Brown, and Alexis Perkins. "Theory of Mind May Be Contagious, but You Don't Catch It from Your Twin." *Child Development* 76, no. 1 (2005), 97–106.

Cerel, Julie, John R. Jordan, and Paul R. Duberstein. "The Impact of Suicide on the Family." *Crisis* 29, no. 1 (2008), 38–44.

Cerretani, Jessica. "The Contagion of Happiness: Harvard Researchers Are Discovering How We Can All Get Happy." Harvard Medical School

Online. https://hms.harvard.edu/news/harvard-medicine/contagion
-happiness

Cha, Christine B., and Marin K. Nowak. "Emotional Intelligence Is a Protective Factor for Suicidal Behavior." *Journal of the American Academy
of Child and Adolescent Psychiatry* 48 (2009), 422–30.

Chang, Bettina. "The Problem with a Culture of Excellence." *Pacific Standard.* June 18, 2014.

Chaykowski, Kathleen. "Students Cope with Gunn High Suicides." *Stanford Daily.* November 12, 2009.

Cherulnik, Paul D., Kristina A. Donley, Tay Sha R. Wiewel, and Susan
R. Miller. "Charisma Is Contagious: The Effect of Leaders' Charisma
on Observers' Affect." *Journal of Applied Social Psychology* 31, no. 10
(2001), 2149–59.

Christakis, Nicholas A., and James H. Fowler. *Connected: The Surprising
Power of Our Social Networks and How They Shape Our Lives—How
Your Friends' Friends' Friends Affect Everything You Feel, Think, and
Do* (New York: Back Bay Books, 2011).

———. "Social Contagion Theory: Examining Dynamic Social Networks
and Human Behavior." *Statistics in Medicine* 32, no. 4 (2013), 556–77.

———. "The Spread of Obesity in a Large Social Network over 32 Years."
New England Journal of Medicine 357 (2007), 370–79.

Clark, Andrew. "How the Collapse of Lehman Brothers Pushed Capitalism
to the Brink: The Wall Street Titan's Bankruptcy Triggered a System-
Wide Crisis of Confidence in Banks Across the Globe." *Guardian.*
September 4, 2009.

———. "Success Shines Unwelcome Spotlight on to Goldman Sachs."
Guardian. December 21, 2007.

Clay, Alexa, and Kyra Maya Phillips. "Violence Is Contagious: Stopping
Its Transmission Became the Mission of the Man Who'd Fought TB
and Cholera in Somalia." Salon.com. June 27, 2015. http://www.salon
.com/2015/06/27/violence_is_contagious_stopping_its_transmis
sion_became_the_mission_of_the_man_whod_fought_tb_and
_cholera_in_somalia/

Codrea-Rado, Anna, "Using Social Media to Prevent Suicide." *Atlantic.*
April 18, 2012.

Coe, Andrew, and Amanda Garrett. "Is Civil War Really Contagious?" Paper
prepared as a Gov 2001 final project, Harvard University. March 5, 2008.

Cohen, Geoffrey L., and Mitchell J. Prinstein. "Peer Contagion of Aggression
and Health Risk Behavior Among Adolescent Males: An Experimental

Investigation of Effects on Public Conduct and Private Attitudes." *Child Development* 77, no. 4 (2006), 967–83.

Collier, D. A., and J. L. Treasure. "The Aetiology of Eating Disorders." *British Journal of Psychology* 185, no. 5 (2004), 363–65.

Colon, Israel, and Brett Marston. "Resistance to a Residential AIDS Home: An Empirical Test of NIMBY." *Journal of Homosexuality* 37, no. 3 (1999). 135–45.

Connolly, Terry, and Lars Åberg. "Some Contagion Models of Speeding." *Accident Analysis and Prevention* 25, no. 1 (1993), 57–66.

Cools, Sara, and Rannveig V. Kaldager. "Does an Additional Nephew Increase Fertility? Identifying Fertility Contagion Using Random Fertility Shocks." Prepared for the Population Association of America, 2015 Annual Meeting, San Diego, California, April 30, 2015.

Cordon, Melissa S. "Is Passion Contagious? The Transference of Entrepreneurial Passion to Employees." *Human Resource Management Review* 18, no. 2 (2008), 77–86.

Cortina, Matthew. "Are Parents, Officials to Blame in Suicides of Teen Girls?" Christian Post. November 16, 2011.

Cougle, Jesse R., and Kirsten H. Dillon. "Priming of Courageous Behavior: Contrast Effects in Spider Fearful Women." *Journal of Clinical Psychology* 69, no. 9 (September 2013), 1–7.

Cowan, Samantha. "Fear Thy Neighbor? This Community Wants to Evict a Hospice Housing HIV Patients." Takepart.com. January 23, 2015.

Crandall, Christian S. "Social Contagion of Binge Eating." *Journal of Personality and Social Psychology* 55, no. 4 (1988), 588–98.

Crosby, Alex E., Beth Han, LaVonne A. G. Ortega, Sharyn E. Parks, and Joseph Gfroerer. "Suicidal Thoughts and Behaviors Among Adults Aged ≥18 Years—United States, 2008–2009." Centers for Disease Control and Prevention: Morbidity and Mortality Weekly Report (October 21, 2011), 1-22. https://www.cdc.gov/mmwr/preview/mmwrhtml/ss6013a1.htm

Cross, Bernadette, and Anthony Travaglione, "The Untold Story: Is the Entrepreneur of the 21st Century Defined by Emotional Intelligence?" *International Journal of Organizational Psychology* 11, no. 3 (2003), 221-28.

Crovitz, L. Gordon. "Why Terrorists Love Silicon Valley." *Wall Street Journal.* July 5, 2015.

CTVNews Staff. "Eating Disorders on the Rise in Canada, as Sufferers Wait for Treatment." CTVNews. February 10, 2013. http://www.ctvnews.ca/health/lets-talk/eating-disorders-on-the-rise-in-canada-as-sufferers-wait-for-treatment-1.1151323

Currin, Laura, Ulrike Schmidt, Janet Treasure, and Hershel Jick. "Time Trends in Eating Disorder Incidence." *British Journal of Psychiatry* 186, no. 2 (2005), 132–35.

Cutler, David M., Edward L. Glaeser, and Karen E. Norberg. "Explaining the Rise in Youth Suicide." *Risky Behavior Among Youths: An Economic Analysis* (Chicago: University of Chicago Press, 2001).

Dahl, Melissa. "Ebola Fears Are Triggering Mass Hypochondria." *New York*. October 7, 2014.

———. "Your Happiness Could Be Contagious." NBCnews.com. December 4. 2008. http://www.nbcnews.com/id/28058552/ns/health-behavior/t/your-happiness-could-be-contagious/#.VtfDCpMrKu4

Danneman, Nathan, and Emily Hencken Ritter. "Contagious Rebellion and Preemptive Repression." *Journal of Conflict Resolution*. January 20, 2013.

Darling, Elizabeth. "Gangs in Palo Alto?" Palo Alto Online. Wednesday, April 19, 1995.

Dawkins, Richard. *The Selfish Gene* (Cary, NC: Oxford University Press, 1989).

Dearborn, Katie. "Studies in Emotional Intelligence Redefine Our Approach to Leadership Development." *Public Personnel Management* 31, no. 4 (2002), 523–30.

Decety, Jean, and Meghan Meyer. "From Emotion Resonance to Empathic Understanding: A Social Developmental Neuroscience Account." *Development and Psychopathology* 20, no. 4 (2008), 1053–80.

De Gelder, Beatrice, Josh Snyder, Doug Greve, George Gerard, and Nouchine Hadjikhani. "Fear Fosters Flight: A Mechanism for Fear Contagion When Perceiving Emotion Expressed by a Whole Body." *Proceedings of the National Academy of Sciences* 101, no. 47 (2004), 16701–6.

De Groot, Jasper H. B., Monique A. M. Smeets, Annemarie Kaldewaij, Maarten J. A. Duijndam, and Gün R. Semin. "Chemosignals Communicate Human Emotions." *Psychological Science*. November 13, 2012.

De Maio, Jennifer L. "Is War Contagious? The Trans-nationalization of Conflict in Darfur." *African Studies Quarterly* 11, no. 4 (2010), 25–44.

Dervik, Kanita, Madelyn S. Gould, Gerhard Lenz, Marjorie Kleinman, Tuerkan Akkaya-Kalayci, Drew Velting, Geenot Sonnece, and Max H. Friedrich. "Youth Suicide Risk Factors and Attitudes in New York and Vienna: A Cross-Cultural Comparison." *Suicide & Life-Threatening Behavior* 36, no. 5 (October 2006), 539–52.

DiDonato, Theresa E. "Are Pregnancy, Marriage, and Divorce Contagious?" *Kidspace*. March 5, 2015.

Dietz, Graham, and Nicole Gillespie. "The Recovery of Trust: Case Studies of Organizational Failures and Trust Repair." Occasional Paper 5. Institute of Business Ethics, London (February 2012). http://www.ibe.org.uk/userfiles/op_trustcasestudies.pdf

Dishion, Thomas J., and Jessica M. Tipsord. "Peer Contagion in Child and Adolescent Social and Emotional Development." *Annual Review of Psychology* 62 (2011), 189–214.

Dishion, Thomas J., and Kenneth A. Dodge. "Peer Contagion in Interventions for Children and Adolescents: Moving Towards an Understanding of the Ecology and Dynamics of Change." *Journal of Abnormal Child Psychology* 33, no. 3 (2005), 395–400.

Dodds, P. S., and D. J. Watts. "A Generalized Model of Social and Biological Contagion." *Journal of Theoretical Biology* 232 (2005), 587–604.

Doherty, R. William. "The Emotional Contagion Scale: A Measure of Individual Differences." *Journal of Nonverbal Behavior* 21, no. 2 (June 1997), 131-54.

Dokoupil, Tony. "Why Suicide Has Become an Epidemic—and What We Can Do to Help." *Newsweek*. May 23, 2013.

Dolan, Maura. "4th Teen from Same Palo Alto High School Commits Suicide." L.A. Now. *Los Angeles Times*. October 23, 2009.

Dominus, Susan. "What Happened to the Girls in Le Roy." *New York Times*. March 7, 2012.

Donaldson-Evans, Catherine. "Small-Town Police Forces Struggle to Meet Demands of Anthrax Scare." FoxNews.com. October 18, 2001. http://www.foxnews.com/story/2001/10/18/small-town-police-forces-struggle-to-meet-demands-anthrax-scare.html

Dotson, Jeanie M. "Cooperative Learning Structures Can Increase Student Achievement." Kagan Online Magazine. Winter 2001. http://www.kaganonline.com/free_articles/research_and_rationale/increase_achievement.php

Dove, Rachael. "Anxiety: The Epidemic Sweeping Through Generation Y." *Telegraph*. April 20, 2015.

Dovey, Dana. "Feeling Cold Is Contagious: How Emotional Contagions Play an Important Role in Human Interaction." *Medical Daily*. January 5, 2015. http://www.medicaldaily.com/feeling-cold-contagious-how-emotional-contagions-play-important-role-human-316288

Dremann, Sue. "Coroner Releases Identity of Man Killed on Train Tracks:

Family of 19 Year Old Palo Alto Man Issues a Statement." *Palo Alto Weekly*. October 20, 2014.

Druckerman, Pamela. "A Cure for Hyper-Parenting." *New York Times*. October 12, 2014.

Drum, Kevin. "Is Broken Windows a Broken Theory of Crime?" *Mother Jones*. December 31, 2014.

Durden, Tyler. "Prozac World: These Are the Most Stressed Out Countries." *Zero Hedge*. July 17, 2013.

Dvorak, Petula. "Teen Suicide: Adults Need to Listen to Kids, and It's Time to Talk About the Issue." *Washington Post*. April 14, 2014.

Eagle, Nathan. "Hawaii Youth Suicide Rate Doubles in 5 Years." *Honolulu Civil Beat*. October 26, 2012. http://www.civilbeat.com/2012/10/17476 -hawaii-youth-suicide-rate-doubles-in-5-years/

Eagleman, David. *Incognito: The Secret Lives of the Brain* (New York: Vintage, 2012).

ECRI. "Can Bulimia Nervosa Be Cured?" *ECRI's Bulimia Nervosa Resource Guide*. 2015.

Editorial Board. "Editorial: An Appreciation of Teacher Support at Paly." *Paly Voice*. February 1, 2015. http://palyvoice.com/2015/02/01 /editorial-an-appreciation-of-teacher-support-at-paly/

Eggen, Dan, and Eric Planin. "Anthrax Cases in Three Cities Share Strain." *Washington Post*. October 20, 2001.

Eley, Thalia C., Tom A. McAdams, Fruhling V. Rijsdijk, Paul Lichtenstein, Jurgita Narusyte, David Reiss, Erica L. Spotts, Jody M. Garban, and Jenae M. Neiderhiser. "The Intergenerational Transmission of Anxiety: A Children of Twins Study." *American Journal of Psychiatry* 172, no. 7 (2015), 630–37.

Eley, T. C., K. Sugden, A. Corsico, A. M. Gregory, P. Sham, P. McGuffin, R. Plomin, and I. W. Craig. "Gene-Environment Interaction Analysis of Serotonin System Markers with Adolescent Depression." *Molecular Psychiatry* 9, no. 10 (October 2004), 908–15.

Elinson, Zusha. "For the Engineer, a Death on the Tracks Means Horrifying Memories." Bay Citizen. *New York Times*. December 10, 2011.

Elliot, A. J., and H. A. McGregor. "Test Anxiety and the Hierarchical Model of Approach and Avoidance Achievement Motivation." *Journal of Personality and Social Psychology* 76 (1999), 628–44.

Elksnin, Linda K., and Nick Elksnin. "Fostering Social-Emotional Learning in the Classroom." *Education* 124, no. 1 (Fall 2003), 63.

Elliot, Andrew J., and Judith M. Harackiewicz. "Approach and Avoidance

Achievement Goals and Intrinsic Motivation: A Mediational Analysis." *Journal of Personality and Social Psychology* 70, no. 3 (1996), 461–75.

Elliot, A. J., and K. M. Sheldon. "Avoidance Achievement Motivation: A Personal Goals analysis." *Journal of Personality and Social Psychology* 73, no. 1 (1997), 171–85.

Elliot, A. J., and M. A. Church. "A Hierarchical Model of Approach and Avoidance Achievement Motivation." *Journal of Personality and Social Psychology* 72, no. 1 (1997), 218–32.

Emmons, Mark. "Caltrain: Lasting Effects of Suicides on Railway." *San Jose Mercury News*. March 20, 2015.

Emslie, Alex. "Caltrain, South Bay Communities Work to Reduce Suicides on Train Tracks." KQED News. March 10, 2015. http://www .kqed.org/news/2015/03/10/caltrain-south-bay-communities-work-to -reduce-suicides-on-train-tracks

Enck, Paul, F. Benedetti, and M. Schedlowski."New Insights into the Placebo and Nocebo Responses." *Neuron* 52, no. 2 (July 2008), 195–206.

Engel, Bridget, Natalie Staats Reiss, and Mark Dombeck. "Historical Understandings." Mentalhelp.net. February 2, 2007. https://www.men talhelp.net/articles/historical-understandings

Engel, Pamela. "Why 3 of America's Most Dangerous Cities Are in Wealthy Connecticut." *Business Insider*. June 14, 2013.

Engelking, Carl. "Asian Americans Are High Achievers Because They Work Harder." Discover.com. May 4, 2015. http://blogs.discoverma gazine.com/d-brief/2014/05/05/asian-americans-are-high-achievers -because-they-work-harder/#.VtUj5pMrLUoB

Engert, V., F. Plessow, R. Miller, C. Kirschbaum, and T. Singer. "Cortisol Increase in Empathic Stress Is Modulated by Social Closeness and Observation Modality." *Psychoneuroendocrinology* 45 (July 2014), 192–201.

Erwert, Anna Marie. "$2M for 180 Square Foot Home in Palo Alto Exemplifies Insanity of Peninsula Real Estate." *San Francisco Chronicle*. November 5, 2015. http://blog.sfgate.com/ontheblock/2015/11/05/2m -for-180-square-foot-home-in-palo-alto-exemplifies-insanity-of-penins ula-real-estate/

———. "New Study Shows Profound Impact of Tech Industry on Bay Area Real Estate." *San Francisco Chronicle*. November 2, 2015. http:// blog.sfgate.com/ontheblock/2015/11/02/new-study-shows-profound -impact-of-tech-industry-on-bay-area-real-estate/

Eskenazi, Joe. "Again? Gunn High School Students' Moth-Like Attraction to Caltrain Tracks Has Grown Surreal." SF Weekly. June 5, 2009.

Etzersdorfer, Elmer, Gernot Sonneck. "Preventing Suicide by Influencing Mass-Media Reporting: The Viennese Experience, 1980–1996." Journal Archives of Suicide Research 4, no. 1 (1988), 67–74.

Even, Dan. "New Israeli Study Finds Signs of Trauma in Grandchildren of Holocaust Survivors." Haaretz. April 16, 2012.

Fairburn, C. G., and S. J. Beglin. "Studies of the Epidemiology of Bulimia Nervosa." American Journal Psychiatry 147, no. 4 (1990), 401–408.

Farr, Christina. "After Five Suicides, Palo Alto High School Students Change Culture Through Peer Support." Peninsula Press. January 4, 2011.

Felps, Will, Terence R. Mitchell, David R. Hekman, Thomas W. Lee, Brooks C. Holtom, and Wendy S. Harman. "Turnover Contagion: How Coworkers' Job Embeddedness and Job Search Behaviors Influence Quitting." Academy of Management Journal 52, no. 3 (2009), 545–61.

Fernandez, Lisa, and Sandra Gonzales. "Palo Alto Mom Stops Son's Suicide on Tracks Where Gunn Teens Died." San Jose Mercury News. June 5, 2009.

Fisher, Max. "Chart: The U.S. Has Far More Gun-Related Killings Than Any Other Developed Country." Washington Post. December 14, 2012.

Flor-Henry, P., D. Fromm-Auch, M. Tapper, and D. Schopflocher. "A Neuropsychological Study of the Stable Syndrome of Hysteria." Biological Psychiatry 16, no. 7 (1981), 601–626.

Forestieri, Kevin. "Panel: No Easy Fixes for Teen Depression/Suicide; Peer-Support Groups Touted at Roundtable Discussion in Mountain View." Palo Alto Online. April 13, 2015. http://www.almanacnews.com/news/2015/04/11/panel-no-easy-fixes-for-teen-depression-suicide

Frank, Robert H., Thomas Gilovich, and Dennis T. Regan. "Does Studying Economics Inhibit Cooperation?" Journal of Economic Perspectives 7, no. 2 (1993), 159–71.

Frankl, Daniel. "Taming the Beast: Excessive Parental Involvement in Youth Sports." kidsfirstsoccer.com. February 2004.

Freud, Sigmund. The Aetiology of Hysteria, Standard Edition, vol. 3 (London: Hogarth Press, 1962).

Gallagher, Mary Elizabeth. Contagious Capitalism: Globalization and the Politics of Labor in China (Princeton, NJ: Princeton University Press, 2007).

Gandel, Stephen. "Goldman Sachs' Earnings Plunge, as Looming

Mortgage Settlement Dents." Fortune.com. July 16, 2015. http://fortune
.com/2015/07/16/goldmans-second-quarter-earnings/

Garner, D. M., and P. E. Garfinkel. "Sociocultural Factors in the Development of Anorexia Nervosa." *Psychological Medicine* 10, no. 4 (1980), 647–56.

Garside, Juliette, and Jill Treanor. "Goldman Sachs Director Quits 'Morally Bankrupt' Wall Street Bank." *Guardian*. March 14, 2012.

Gehlen, F. L. "Toward a Revised Theory of Hysterical Contagion." *Journal of Health and Social Behavior* 18, no. 1 (1977), 27–35.

Gelles, Jeff. "A Reprieve for AIDS Facility: The Nursing Home Was Told It Must Give 30 Days' Notice of Closing; Its Future Is Still in Doubt." *Philadelphia Daily News.* June 6, 1994.

Gerrard, Michael B. "The Victims of NIMBY." *Fordham Urban Law Journal* 21, no. 3 (1993), Article 4.

Ghose, Tia. "Humans Smell Fear, and It's Contagious." *Science.* November 6, 2012.

Gino, Francesca, Shahar Ayal, and Dan Ariely. "Contagion and Differentiation in Unethical Behavior: The Effect of One Bad Apple on the Barrel." *Psychological Science* 20, no. 3 (2009), 393–98.

Gladwell, Malcolm. "Thresholds of Violence." *New Yorker.* October 19, 2015.

———. *The Tipping Point* (New York: Little Brown, 2000).

Godsey, Michael. "Why Introverted Teachers Are Burning Out." *Atlantic.* January 25, 2016.

Goleman, Daniel. "Emotional Intelligence: Leadership That Gets Results." *Harvard Business Review.* March–April 2000.

———. "Happy or Sad, a Mood Can Prove Contagious." *New York Times.* October 15, 1991.

———. *Social Intelligence: The Revolutionary New Science of Human Relationships.* (New York: Bantam, 2006).

———. "What Makes a Leader?" *HBR's 10 Must Reads: On Emotional Intelligence.* (Cambridge, MA: Harvard Business School Publishing, 2015).

Goleman, Daniel, Richard Boyatzis, and Annie McKee. "Primal Leadership: The Hidden Driver of Great Performance." *Harvard Business Review* (December 2001), 42–51.

Gollowitzer, Peter. *The Psychology of Action: Linking Cognition and Motivation to Behavior* (New York: Guilford, 1996).

Gomez, Mark. "Palo Alto: Caltrain Hits, Kills 15-Year-Old High School Student in Apparent Suicide." *San Jose Mercury News.* March 9, 2015.

Goode, Erica. "Study Finds TV Alters Fiji Girls' View of Body." *New York Times*. May 20, 1999.

Gosline, Anna. "Do Women Who Live Together Menstruate Together? Does Sisterhood Among Women Extend to the Monthly Period?" *Scientific American*. December 7, 2007.

Goud, Nelson H. "Courage: Its Nature and Development." *American Counseling Association* 44, no. 1 (2005), 102–116.

Gould, Madelyn, Patrick Jamieson, and Daniel Romer. "Media Contagion and Suicide Among the Young." *American Behavioral Scientist* 46, no. 9 (2003), 1269–84.

Goyal, Nikhil. "After a String of Suicides, Students in Palo Alto Are Demanding a Part in Reforming Their School's Culture." *VICE*. September 8, 2015.

Grady, William. "Town Sued over AIDS Hospice." *Chicago Tribune*. June 14, 1989.

Graham, Ruth. "Mass Hysteria in Upstate New York: Why More Than a Dozen Teenage Girls Are Exhibiting Tourette's-Like Symptoms." *Doublex*. January 31, 2012.

Grant, Adam. "Does Studying Economics Breed Greed? Even Thinking About Economics Can Make Us Less Compassionate." *Psychology Today*. October 22, 2013. https://www.psychologytoday.com/blog/give-and-take/201310/does-studying-economics-breed-greed

———. *Originals: How Non-Conformists Move the World* (New York: Viking, 2016).

Green, Jason. "Palo Alto: Community Searches for Answers in Wake of Student Suicides." *San Jose Mercury News*. January 28, 2010.

Greenberg, David F. "Studying New York City's Crime Decline: Methodological Issues Preview." *Justice Quarterly* 31, no. 1 (2013), 154–88.

Gregoire, Carolyn. "The Science of Conquering Your Fears and Living a More Courageous Life." Huffington Post. September 15, 2013. http://www.huffingtonpost.com/2013/09/15/conquering-fear_n_3909020.html

Grodin, Michael A. "Holocaust Trauma: Psychological Effects and Treatment." *Journal of the American Medical Association* 304, no. 5 (2010), 580–84.

Gruzd, Anatoliy, Sophie Doiron, and Philip Mai. "Is Happiness Contagious Online? A Case of Twitter and the 2010 Winter Olympics." 44th Hawaii International Conference on System Sciences. January 4–7, 2011. http://anatoliygruzd.com/wp-content/uploads/2009/04/HICSS44_Gruzd_Twitter_Happiness.pdf

Guerra, Kristine. "Social Media Raises Fear of Teen Suicide Contagion." *Indianapolis Star.* May 3, 2014.

Gunnars, Kris. "12 Graphs That Show Why People Get Fat." *Authority Nutrition.* July 2015. http://authoritynutrition.com/12-graphs-that -show-why-people-get-fat/

Haeffel, Gerald J., and Jennifer L. Hames. "Cognitive Vulnerability to Depression Can Be Contagious." *Clinical Psychological Science.* April 16, 2013.

Hahn, Robert A. "The Nocebo Phenomenon: Concept, Evidence, and Implications for Public Health." *Preventive Medicine* 26, article no. PM960124 (1997), 607–611.

Han, Beth, Richard McKeon, and Joe Gfroerer. "Suicidal Ideation Among Community-Dwelling Adults in the United States." *American Journal of Public Health* 104, no. 3 (2014), 488–97.

Hannessens, Leonore. "Suicide Echo Clusters." *Aboriginal & Islander Health Worker Journal* 35, no. 1 (2011), 14–23.

Harackiewicz, J. M., K. E. Barron, S. M. Carter, A. T. Lehto, and A. J. Elliot. "Predictors and Consequences of Achievement Goals in the College Classroom: Maintaining Interest and Making the Grade." *Journal of Personality and Social Psychology* 73 (1997), 1284–95.

Harmon, Lawrence. "Teen Suicide's Tragic Lure." *Boston Globe.* February 15, 2014.

Harvard Medical School. "Special Health Report: Why People Become Overweight." *Weigh Less, Live Longer: Strategies for Successful Weight Loss.* Harvard Health Publications. June 2009. http://www.health .harvard.edu/staying-healthy/why-people-become-overweight

Hennig-Thurau, Thorsten, Markus Groth, Michael Paul, and Dwayne D. Gremler. "Are All Smiles Created Equal? How Emotional Contagion and Emotional Labor Affect Service Relationships." *Journal of Marketing* 70 (July 2006), 58–73.

Hensvik, Lena, and Peter Nilsson. "Businesses, Buddies, and Babies: Social Ties and Fertility at Work." No. 9 in Working Paper Series from IFAU: Institution for Evaluation of Labour Market and Education Police. June 30, 2010.

Herman, Judith. *Trauma and Recovery: The Aftermath of Violence; From Domestic Abuse to Political Terror* (New York: Basic Books, 1992).

Hersey, John. *Creating Contagious Leadership* (Leaders Publishing Group, 2003).

Hessa, Ursula, and Sylvie Blairy. "Facial Mimicry and Emotional Contagion to Dynamic Emotional Facial Expressions and Their Influence on Decoding Accuracy." *International Journal of Psychophysiology* 40 (2001), 129–41.

Holodny, Elena. "Tulipmania: How a Country Went Totally Nuts for Flower Bulbs." *Business Insider*. September 16, 2014.

Horn, Colonel Brend. "The Worm Revisited: An Examination of Fear and Courage in Combat." *Canadian Military Journal* (Summer 2004), 5–16.

Hsee, Christopher K., Elaine Hatfield, and John G. Carlson. "The Effect of Power on Susceptibility to Emotional Contagion." *Contagion and Emotion* 4, no. 4 (1990), 327–40.

Hu, Elise. "Even the Planes Stop Flying for South Korea's National Exam Day." NPR. November 12, 2015.

Hubner, Sylvia, and Matthias Baum. "Passion Contagion in Entrepreneurial Firms." Greater Region PhD Workshop on Entrepreneurship and Innovation. TU Kaiserslautern memo. March 26, 2015.

Hughes, Mark. "Bar-Room Brawl in Prestigious New York Sports Club." *Telegraph*. April 25, 2012.

Huntsinger, Carol S., Paul E. Jose, and Shari L. Larson. "Do Parent Practices to Encourage Academic Competence Influence the Social Adjustment of Young European American and Chinese American children?" *Developmental Psychology* 34, no. 4 (1998), 747–56.

Iacoboni, Marco. *Mirroring People: The Science of Empathy and How We Connect with Others* (New York: Picador, 2008).

Ichino, Andrea, and Giovanni Maggi. "Work Environment and Individual Background: Explaining Regional Shirking Differentials in a Large Italian Firm." National Bureau of Economic Research Working Paper No. 7415 (November 1999). http://www.nber.org/papers/w7415.pdf

Idov, Michael. "Are Wall Street Suicide Epidemics Real? *New York*. January 11, 2009.

Iliades, Chris. "The Binge-Purge Cycle of Bulimia." *Everyday Health*. May 10, 2010.

Ireland, Corydon. "Fijian Girls Succumb to Western Dysmorphia." *Harvard Gazette*. March 19, 2009.

James, Emily. "Days Before Graduation, Gunn Students Grieve: Sonya Raymakers, 17, Remembered for Her Creativity." Palo Alto Online. June 3, 2009. http://www.paloaltoonline.com/print/story/2009/06/05/days-before-graduation-gunn-students-grieve

Jayson, Sharon. "Stress Levels Increased Since 1983, New Analysis Shows." *USA Today*. June 13, 2012.

Johansson, Lars, Per Lindqvist, and Anders Eriksson. "Teenage Suicide

Cluster Formation and Contagion: Implications for Primary Care." *BMC Family Practice* 7, no. 32 (2006).

Johnson, Camille S. "Unethical Behavior Can Become Contagious." *Psychology Today*. June 29, 2012. https://www.psychologytoday .com/blog/its-all-relative/201206/unethical-behavior-can-become -contagious

Johnson, Margaret Wheeler. "Burnout Is Everywhere—Here's What Countries Are Doing to Fix It." *World Post*. August 5, 2013.

Johnston, David, and Douglas Jehl. "C.I.A. Sends Terror Experts to Tell Small Towns of Risk." *New York Times*. July 18, 2004.

Joiner, Thomas E., Jr., and Jennifer Katz. "Contagion of Depressive Symptoms and Mood: Meta-analytic Review and Explanations from Cognitive, Behavioral, and Interpersonal Viewpoints." *Clinical Psychology: Science and Practice* 6, no. 2 (1999), 149–64.

Joiner, Jr., Thomas E. "The Clustering and Contagion of Suicide." *Current Directions in Psychological Science* 8, no. 3 (1999), 89–92.

Jolfaei, Atefeh Ghanbari, Mehdi Nasr Isfahani, and Reza Bidaki. "Folie à deux and Delusional Disorder by Proxy in a Family." *Journal of Research in Medical Sciences* (2011), S453–S455.

Jones, Mary Cover. "A Laboratory Study of Fear: The Case of Peter." *Pedagogical Seminary* 31 (1924), 308–315.

Joshi, Kaustubh G., Richard L. Frierson, and Tracy D. Gunter. "Shared Psychotic Disorder and Criminal Responsibility: A Review and Case Report of Folie à Trois." *Journal of American Academy Psychiatry Law* 34, no. 4 (2006), 511–17.

Judkis, Maura. "Berlin Laughter Project Gets Entire Subway Car Giggling; What's So Funny?" *Washington Post*. December 16, 2011. https://www .washingtonpost.com/blogs/arts-post/post/berlin-laughter-project -gets-entire-subway-car-giggling-whats-so-funny/2011/12/16/gIQAy hDbyO_blog.html

Jung, Alex. "The United Nations Released a Playlist of the World's Happiest Songs." *Vulture*. March 21, 2015.

Kadvany, Elena. "Caltrain Fatality Identified as Palo Alto Teen; School District Superintendent Encourages Parents to Talk with Their Children." *Palo Alto Weekly*. March 10, 2015.

———. "Community Writes 'Love Notes' to Palo Alto Youth: Three Mothers Organize Small-Scale Way to Express Support." *Palo Alto Weekly*. March 17, 2015.

———. "Palo Alto High Schools Take Action to Ease Student Stress: District Superintendent Directs Immediate Implementation of

Homework Policy." *Palo Alto Online.* February 6, 2015. http://www
.paloaltoonline.com/news/2015/02/06/high-schools-take-action-to
-ease-student-stress

———. "Palo Alto Teen Killed on Tracks Tuesday: Early Morning Fatality
Involved Day's Last Southbound Train." *Palo Alto Weekly.* November
8, 2014.

Kane, Carla. "Stanford Program Takes Aim at Eating Disorders: Researchers Adjust Their Thinking About the Causes and Treatment of Eating
Disorders." *Palo Alto Weekly.* June 24, 2011.

Kantor, Jodi, and David Streitfeld. "Inside Amazon: Wrestling Big Ideas in
a Bruising Workplace." *New York Times.* August 15, 2015.

Kapp, Diana. "Why Are Palo Alto's Kids Killing Themselves? A Panicked
Town Struggles with a Wave of Suicides." *San Francisco.* May 22, 2015.
http://www.sfgate.com/bayarea/article/Why-are-Palo-Alto-s-kids
-killing-themselves-6270854.php

Kassai, S. C., and R. W. Motta. "An Investigation of Potential Holocaust-
Related Secondary Traumatization in the Third Generation." *International Journal of Emergency Mental Health* 8, no. 1 (2006), 35–47.

Katzman, M. A., and S. Lee. "Beyond Body Image: The Integration of
Feminist and Transcultural Theories in the Understanding of Self
Starvation." *International Journal of Eating Disorders* 22, no. 4 (1997),
385–94.

Keim, Brandon. "Happiness and Sadness Spread Just Like a Disease."
Wired. July 14, 2010.

Keizer, Kees, Siegwart Lindenberg, and Linda Steg. "The Spreading of Disorder." *Science* 322, no. 1681 (2008), 1681–85.

Kelling, George L., and James Q. Wilson. "Broken Windows: The Police
and Neighborhood Safety." *Atlantic.* March 1982.

Kelly, Kate. "Goldman's Take-No-Prisoners Attitude: Mortgage Division
Cast Bets Boldly; Awaiting 'Big One.'" *Wall Street Journal.* April 26, 2010.

Kenrick, Chris. "Caucasian Enrollment Dips Below 50 Percent: Palo Alto
Classrooms More Racially Diverse as Asian Enrollment Surpasses 36
Percent." *Palo Alto Weekly.* September 27, 2011.

———. "Gunn Student Remembered as 'Smart, Caring' Classmate Who
Loved Music, Video Games: JP Blanchard Wouldn't Have Wanted
People to Be Sad, Friend Says." *Palo Alto Online.* May 6, 2009.

———. "Gunn Students Offer Inspiring Stories Online: 'Gives Me Hope'
Website Draws Posts from Alums, Teachers, Parents, Kids." *Palo
Alto Online.* November 27, 2009. http://www.paloaltoonline.com
/news/2009/11/27/gunn-students-offer-inspiring-stories-online

————. "Religious Groups to Speak on Supporting Teens: Mayor Will Moderate Aug. 31 Panel Responding to Two Recent Suicides and an Attempt." *Palo Alto Online.* August 10, 2009. http://www .paloaltoonline.com/news/2009/08/10/religious-groups-to-speak-on -supporting-teens

————. "Sonya Raymakers' Services Set for Today." *Palo Alto Online.* June 5, 2009. http://www.paloaltoonline.com/news/2009/06/04 /sonya-raymakers-services-set-for-today

Kermode, Mark. "Falling Review—Swoon with a View: Carol Morley Joins the Ranks of Britain's Best Film-makers with This Enigmatic Tale of Apparent Mass Hysteria at a Girls' School." *Guardian.* April 26, 2015.

Khazan, Olga. "The Psychology of Irrational Fear: Why We're More Afraid of Sharks Than Car Accidents, and of Ebola Than Flu." *Atlantic.* October 31, 2014.

Khurana, Rakesh. "The Curse of the Superstar CEO." *Harvard Business Review.* September 2002.

Kilmann, Ralph H., Linda A. O'Hara, and Judy P. Strauss. "Developing and Validating a Quantitative Measure of Organizational Courage." *Journal of Business and Psychology* 25, no. 1 (2010), 15–23.

Kim, Bryan S. K., Donald R. Atkinson, and Peggy H. Yang. "The Asian Values Scale: Development, Factor Analysis, Validation, and Reliability." *Journal of Counseling Psychology* 46, no. 3 (1999), 342–52.

Kim, Meeri. "Study Finds That Fear Can Travel Quickly Through Generations of Mice DNA." *Washington Post.* December 7, 2013.

Kirchner, Lauren. "Breaking Down the Broken Windows Theory: As Rudy Giuliani's Old Police Commissioner William Bratton Returns to New York City, New Research Still Fuels a Debate over Their Pet Policy." *Pacific Standard.* January 7, 2014.

Kirkpatrick, Kayla. "The Social Contagion of Violence." Graduate thesis, California Polytechnic State University, 2012.

Kirsch, I., and W. Braffman. "Imaginative Suggestibility and Hypnotizability." *Current Directions in Psychological Science* 4, no. 2 (2001), 57–61.

Klein, Christopher. "Before Salem, the First American Witch Hunt." www .history.com. October 31, 2012. http://www.history.com/news/before -salem-the-first-american-witch-hunt

Klibert, Jeffrey, Jennifer Langhinrichsen-Rohling, Amy Luna, and Michelle Robichaux. "Suicide Proneness in College Students: Relationships with Gender, Procrastination, and Achievement Motivation." *Death Studies* 35, no. 7 (2011), 625-45.

Klump, Kelly L., Jessica L. Suisman, S. Alexandra Burt, Matt McGue, and William G. Iacono. "Genetic and Environmental Influences on Disordered Eating: An Adoption Study." *Journal of Abnormal Psychology* 118, no. 4 (2010), 797–805.

Knight, James A., Theodore I. Friedman, and Julie Sulianti. "Epidemic Hysteria: A Field Study." *American Journal of Public Health* 55. no. 6 (1965), 858–65.

Knowles, David. "Is Teen Suicide Contagious?" AOL News. November 3, 2009. http://www.aolnews.com/2009/11/03/is-teen-suicide-contagious/

Knox, Shanley. "Trauma Is Contagious: Shortly After We Moved in Together, My Boyfriend's Experiences in Afghanistan Began Affecting Me in Strange and Terrifying Ways." *Atlantic*. February 28, 2014.

Kolata, Gina. "Epidemic of Dangerous Eating Disorder May Be False Alarm." *New York Times*. August 25, 1988.

Kordova, Shoshana. "There's a Simple Theory That Explains New Bloodshed in the Middle East." *Quartz*. October 21, 2015. http://qz.com/529760/the-sociology-theory-that-explains-new-bloodshed-in-the-middle-east/

Kotchemidova, Christina. "From Good Cheer to 'Drive-by-Smiling': A Social History of Cheerfulness." *Journal of Social History* 39, no. 1 (2005), 5–37.

Kotte, Markus, and Volker Ludwig. "Intergenerational Transmission of Fertility Intentions and Behavior in Germany." *Vienna Yearbook of Population Research* 9 (2011), 207–226.

Kotz, Deborah. "Why Americans Have Irrational Ebola Fears." *Boston Globe*. October 23, 2014.

Kramera, Adam D. I., Jamie E. Guillory, and Jeffrey T. Hancock. "Experimental Evidence of Massive-Scale Emotional Contagion Through Social Networks." *Proceedings of the National Academy of Sciences* 111, no. 24 (2014), 8788–90.

Krieger, Lisa M., and Sharon Noguchi. "Palo Alto Train Death Opens Fresh Wound in a Community Searching for Solutions." *San Jose Mercury News*. March 9, 2015.

Kroski, Ellyssa. "The Hive Mind: Folksonomies and User-Based Tagging." InfoTangle, January 12, 2006.

Krysinska, Karolina, and Diego De Leo. "Suicide on Railway Networks:

Epidemiology, Risk Factors and Prevention." *Australian and New Zealand Journal of Psychiatry* 42 (2008), 763–71.

Kuziemko, Ilyana. "Is Having Babies Contagious? Estimating Fertility Peer Effects Between Siblings." Harvard University. June 2006. http://www.dis.xlibx.info/dd-economy/206474-1-ilyana-kuziemko-harvard-university-june-2006-kuziemko-nbero.php

Lauritsen, Janet L., Nicole White. "Seasonal Patterns in Criminal Victimization Trends." Special Report, Bureau of Justice Statistics, U.S. Department of Justice. NCJ 245959, June 2014.

La Ganga, Maria L. "Palo Alto Campus Searches for Healing After Suicides." *Los Angeles Times*. October 30, 2009.

Lancione, Marisa. "Suicide Isn't Contagious; We Need to Talk About It." Huffington Post. January 21, 2015. http://www.huffingtonpost.com/marisa-lancione/suicide-isnt-contagious-w_b_6497216.html

Lang, Larry H. P., and Rene M. Stulz. "Contagion and Competitive Intra-Industry Effects of Bankruptcy Announcements." *Journal of Financial Economics* 32 (1992), 45–60.

Lawrence, Sarah, and Gregory Shapiro. "Crime Trends in the City of East Palo Alto Report." Berkeley Center for Criminal Justice. November 2010. https://www.law.berkeley.edu/files/EPA_Main_Report_Final.pdf

Lawson, Carol. "Anorexia: It's Not a New Disease." *New York Times*. December 8, 1985.

Lee, Y. T. , and S. J. Tsai. "The Mirror Neuron System May Play a Role in the Pathogenesis of Mass Hysteria." *Medical Hypotheses* 74, no. 2 (2010), 244–45.

Lemonick, Michael D. "Deadly Delivery." *Time*. October 14, 2001.

Lew-Starowicz, Michal. "Shared Psychotic Disorder with Sexual Delusions." *Archive of Sex Behavior* 41, no. 6 (2012), 1515–20.

Lipman-Blumen, Jean. *The Allure of Toxic Leaders: Why We Follow Destructive Bosses and Corrupt Politicians—and How We Can Survive Them* (Cary, NC: Oxford University Press, 2004).

Lois, Daniel, and Oliver Arránz Becker. "Is Fertility Contagious? Using Panel Data to Disentangle Mechanisms of Social Network Influences on Fertility Decisions." *Advances in Life Course Research* 21 (2014), 123–34.

Ludwig, Jens, and Jeffrey R. Kling. "Is Crime Contagious?" *Journal of Law and Economics* 50, no. 3 (August 2007), 491-518.

Lynch, Aaron. *Thought Contagion: How Belief Spreads Through Society* (New York: Basic Books, 1996).

Lynch, Donal. "Suicide Is the Dark Side of Our Great Wealth." *Independent*. September 4, 2006.

Lythcott-Haims, Julie. *How to Raise an Adult* (New York: Henry Holt, 2015).

Martin, G., and J. Pear. *Behavior Modification: What It Is and How to Do It* (Upper Saddle River, NJ: Prentice-Hall, 2003).

Max-Planck-Gesellschaft. "Your Stress Is My Stress; Merely Observing Stressful Situations Can Trigger a Physical Stress Response." Max Planck Institute press release. April 2014. http://neurosciencenews.com/cortisol-hpa-axis-stress-psychology-1007/

Macdonald, Nancy. "Welcome to Winnipeg: Where Canada's Racism Problem Is at Its Worst." *Maclean's*. January 22, 2015.

MacLeod, Nancy. "Deal Killers: Superstitions and Core Beliefs." *Palo Alto Weekly*. January 23, 2013.

Makino, Maria, Koji Tsuboi, and Lorraine Dennerstein. "Prevalence of Eating Disorders: A Comparison of Western and Non-Western Countries." *MedGenMed (Medscape General Medicine)* 6, no. 3 (2004), 49.

Malkin, Elizabeth. "At a School for the Poor, a Mysterious Illness." *New York Times*. April 16, 2007.

Manzaria, Johnnie, and Jonathon Bruck. "Media's Use of Propaganda to Persuade People's Attitude, Beliefs and Behaviors." EDGE (Ethics of Development in a Global Environment). No date. https://web.stanford.edu/class/e297c/war_peace/media/hpropaganda.html

Martin, Claire. "Wearing Your Failure on Your Sleeve." *New York Times*. November 8, 2014.

Mathis, Sommer. "Overall, Americans in the Suburbs Are Still the Happiest." *Atlantic* Citylab. August 25, 2014. http://www.citylab.com/politics/2014/08/overall-americans-in-the-suburbs-are-still-the-happiest/378964/

Mathis, Sommer, and Ron Brownstein. "Who's Happiest? Atlantic Media/Siemens State of the City Poll Finds Suburbanites Express Most Overall Satisfaction." Siemens. August 25, 2014. http://news.usa.siemens.biz/press-release/corporate-and-cross-sector/whos-happiest-atlantic-mediasiemens-state-city-poll-find-s

Mayer, John D., Richard D. Roberts, and Sigal G. Barsade. "Human Abilities: Emotional Intelligence." *Annual Review of Psychology* 59 (2008), 507–536.

Mendoza, Martha. "In Silicon Valley, Economic Recovery Has Left Many in the Dust." Associated Press. May 11, 2013. http://www.dailyfinance.com/2013/03/11/silicon-valley-poverty-economic-recovery/

McCormick, Joe. "What Is Collective Hysteria?" Stuffyoushouldknow .com. November 20, 2014. http://www.stuffyoushouldknow.com/pod casts/what-is-collective-hysteria/

Mercy, James A., Marcie-jo Kresnow, Patrick W. O'Carroll, and Roberta K. Lee. "Is Suicide Contagious? A Study of the Relation Between Exposure to the Suicidal Behavior of Others and Nearly Lethal Suicide Attempts." *American Journal of Epidemiology* 154, no. 2 (2001), 120–54.

Mikita, Carole. "'Contagious' Brain Disorder Not Just for the Masses Anymore." KSL.com. February 29, 2012. https://www.ksl.com/?sid=19415888

Miller, William Ian. *The Mystery of Courage* (Cambridge, MA: Harvard University Press, 2000).

Mines, Robert A., and Cheryl A. Merrill. "Bulimia: Cognitive-Behavioral Treatment and Relapse Prevention." *Journal of Counseling and Treatment* 65 (1987), 562–64.

Mishra, Arul. "Influence of Contagious Versus Noncontagious Product Groupings on Consumer Preferences." *Journal of Consumer Research* 36, no. 1 (2009), 73–82.

Moore, Linda Wright. "AIDS Hospice? Proposal Divides West Mt. Airy." *Philadelphia Daily News.* May 4, 1989.

Morris, Kelly. "Bulimia: The Princess Diana Eating Disorder." Mirror Mirror. 2007. http://www.mirror-mirror.org/princess-diana-eating -disorder.htm

Moynihan, Colin, and Sewell Chan. "Recalling a City in Fear During the Year of 'Son of Sam.'" *New York Times.* August 7, 2007.

Murn, Lindsay T. "Group Therapies for the Treatment of Bulimia Nervosa." *Inquiries Journal* 2, no. 12 (2010).

Nadella, Satya. "Indian Immigrants Are Tech's New Titans." *Los Angeles Times.* August 11, 2015.

Nadworny, Elissa. "Preventing Suicide with a 'Contagion of Strength.'" NPR. February 25, 2015. http://www.npr.org/sections/ed/2015/02/25/385418961 /preventing-suicide-with-a-contagion-of-strength

Nauert, Rick. "Seasonal Patterns Found in Online Mental Illness Searches." PsychCentral. April 10, 2013. http://psychcentral.com /news/2013/04/10/seasonal-patterns-found-in-online-mental-illness -searches/53647.html

Neal, Meghan. "Stress Levels Soar in America by up to 30% in 30 Years." *New York Daily News.* June 16, 2012.

Nelson, Eric. "Conquering the Contagion of Fear: Simply Seeing Another

Patient Suffering Pain Can Make a Treatment Hurt More." Palo Alto Patch. March 16, 2015. http://patch.com/california/paloalto/conquering-contagion-fear

Ness, John. "100 Stories About Gun Violence Since Newtown." Durham Patch. December 14, 2013. http://patch.com/connecticut/durham/100-stories-about-gun-violence-since-newtown

Neumayer, Eric, and Thomas Plumper. "Galton's Problem and Contagion in International Terrorism Along Civilizational Lines." *Conflict Management and Peace Science* 27, no. 4 (2010), 308–325.

New, Jake. "Postvention: Tulane, Appalachian State Grapple with Clusters of Suicides on Campus." Slate. February 16, 2015. http://www.slate.com/articles/life/inside_higher_ed/2015/02/student_suicide_clusters_at_tulane_appalachian_state_universities_can_respond.html

Ngui, André Ngamini, Philippe Apparicio, Elena Moltchanova, and Helen-Maria Vasiliadis. "Spatial Analysis of Suicide Mortality in Québec: Spatial Clustering and Area Factor Correlates." *Psychiatry Research* 220, no. 1 (2014), 20-30.

Nguyen, Steve. "The True Financial Cost of Job Stress." Workplace Psychology. January 9, 2011. https://workplacepsychology.net/2011/01/09/the-true-financial-cost-of-job-stress/

Noguchi, Sharon. "Teen Health: Depression, Anxiety and Social Phobias Rising in Kids, Educators Say." *San Jose Mercury News*. February 5, 2014.

Nuwer, Rachel. "Sorry, Malcolm Gladwell: NYC's Drop in Crime Not Due to Broken Window Theory." Smithsonian.com. February 6, 2013. http://www.smithsonianmag.com/smart-news/sorry-malcolm-gladwell-nycs-drop-in-crime-not-due-to-broken-window-theory-12636297/

Ohnuma, Tohru, and Heii Arai. "Case Report: Genetic or Psychogenic? A Case Study of 'Folie à Quatre' Including Twins." *Case Reports in Psychiatry* (2015), doi: 10.1155/2015/983212

Olson, Samantha. "High School Students Are Stressed Out About College Admissions; The Reality of Burning Out Before College." Medical Daily. August 12, 2015. http://www.medicaldaily.com/high-school-students-are-stressed-out-about-college-admissions-reality-burning-out-347476

Palmer, Brian. "Two Flew Over the Cuckoo's Nest: Can a Married Couple Like Randy and Evi Quaid Go Insane Together?" *Explainer*. October 25, 2010. http://www.slate.com/articles/news_and_politics/explainer/2010/10/two_flew_over_the_cuckoos_nest.html

Park, Alice. "The Two Faces of Anxiety." *Time*. December 5, 2011.

Park, Jessica. "Palo Alto Teen Suicides Spark Fresh Debate on Stressful Student Life." *Peninsula Press*. December 19, 2014.

Parker-Pope, Tara. "Suicide Rates Rise Sharply in U.S." *New York Times*. May 2, 2013.

———. "Teacher Burnout? Blame the Parents." *New York Times*. January 2, 2008. http://well.blogs.nytimes.com/2008/01/02/teacher-burnout -blame-the-parents/?hp&_r=0

Parker, Ryan. "Colorado Background-Check Submissions for Guns Break All Records." *Denver Post*. December 17, 2012.

Pazorni, Amanda. "Grappling with Teen Suicide: Religious Leaders Offer Solace After Three Die on Palo Alto Tracks." *J-Weekly*. September 3, 2009.

Perner, Josef, Ted Ruffman, and Susan R. Leekam. "Theory of Mind Is Contagious: You Catch It from Your Sibs." *Child Development* 65 (1994), 1228–38.

Phillips, Owen. "Revolving Door of Teachers Costs Schools Billions Every Year." NPR. March 30, 2015.

Pied Type. "Insanity Is Contagious." Pied Type. December 18, 2012. https:// piedtype.com/2012/12/18/insanity-is-contagious/

Plumridge, Nicole. "How the Rise in Television Lead to Disordered Eating in Fiji." Psych.com. May 13, 2013. http://psychminds.com/how-the -rise-in-television-lead-to-disordered-eating-in-fiji/

Polanski, Norman, Ronald Lippitt, and Fritz Redl. "Investigation of Behavioral Contagion in Groups." *Human Relations* 3 (1950), 319–48.

Pompili, Maurizio, Monica Vichi, Diego De Leo, Cynthia Pfeffer, and Paolo Girardi. "A Longitudinal Epidemiological Comparison of Suicide and Other Causes of Death in Italian Children and Adolescents." *European Child and Adolescent Psychiatry* 21, no. 2 (2012), 111–21.

Popova, Maria. "Stay: The Social Contagion of Suicide and How to Preempt It." *Brain Pickings*. November 18, 2013. https://www.brainpick ings.org/2013/11/18/stay-suicide-hecht/

Preuitt, Lori. "Caltrain Suicide Leaves Palo Alto High School Grieving: School Starts Tuesday." NBC Bay Area. August 24, 2009. http://www.nbcbayarea.com/news/local/Weekend-Suicide-Sparks -Caltrain-to-Act-54545452.html

———. "Suicide High School Gets Relief from Ranking." NBC Bay Area. June 10, 2009. http://www.nbcbayarea.com/news/local/Suicide -High-School-Gets-Relief-From-Ranking.html

Provine, Robert R. "Contagious Laughter: Laughter Is a Sufficient Stimulus for Laughs and Smiles." *Bulletin of the Psychonomic Society* 30, no. 1 (1992), 1–4.

———. "Yawning: The Yawn Is Primal, Unstoppable and Contagious, Revealing the Evolutionary and Neural Basis of Empathy and Unconscious Behavior." *American Scientist* 93, no. 6 (2005), 532–39.

Purdum, T. "Sexual Abuse Is Investigated at 3 More Day-Care Centers." *New York Times.* August 9, 1984.

Qijin Cheng, Qijin, Hong Li, Vincent Silenzio, and Eric D. Caine. "Suicide Contagion: A Systematic Review of Definitions and Research Utility." *PLoS One* 9, no. 9 (September 26, 2014).

Rabinowitz, Dorothy. "A Darkness in Massachusetts." *Wall Street Journal.* January 30, 1995.

Radford, Benjamin. "Strange History: Mass Hysteria Through the Years." *Seeker.* February 6, 2012. http://news.discovery.com/history/history -mass-hysteria-120206.htm

Radio Lab. "Laughter." WYNC Radio/Radio Lab. February 25, 2008. http://www.radiolab.org/2008/feb/25.

Rampell, Catherine. "How Baby Fever Spreads Through Offices." *New York Times.* September 1, 2010. http://economix.blogs.nytimes .com/2010/09/01/how-baby-fever-spreads-through-offices/

Randerson, James. "The Smell of Fear Is Real, Say Scientists." *Guardian.* December 3, 2008.

Rankin, A. M., and P. J. Philip. "An Epidemic of Laughing in the Bukoba District of Tanganyika." *Central African Journal of Medicine* 9 (1963), 167–70.

Reaney, Patricia. "Urban Living Linked to Higher Rates of Bulimia." Reuters. December 1, 2006. http://www.medicineonline.com/news/12/7071 /Urban-living-linked-to-higher-rates-of-bulimia.html

Rettner, Rachael. "Apple Obsession: The Science of iPad Fanaticism." *Science.* May 2, 2010.

Reuters. "Are Eating Disorders Contagious?" Huffington Post. April 26, 2008. http://www.huffingtonpost.com/2008/04/18/are-eating -disorders-cont_n_97463.html

———. "Goldman Sachs Pays $272M to Settle Suit over Mortgage-Backed Securities." NBC News. August 13, 2015. http://www.nbcnews.com /business/business-news/goldman-sachs-pays-272m-settle-suit-over -mortgage-backed-securities-n409366

Ribeiro, Jessica D., and Thomas E. Joiner. "The Interpersonal-Psychological Theory of Suicidal Behavior: Current Status and Future Directions." *Journal of Clinical Psychology* 65, no. 12 (2009), 1291–99.

Richtel, Matt. "Push, Don't Crush, the Students." *New York Times*. April 24, 2015.

Riggs, Liz. "Why Do Teachers Quit? And Why Do They Stay?" *Atlantic*. October 18, 2013.

Robbins, Mel. "'Fear-bola' Hits Epidemic Proportions." CNN.com. October 15, 2014. http://www.cnn.com/2014/10/15/opinion/robbins-ebola -fear/

Robinson, Hadley. "As Facebook Moves In, Hopes That Progress Follows." The Bay Citizen. *New York Times*. August 12, 2011.

Rockmann, Kevin W., and Michael G. Pratt. "Contagious Offsite Work and the Lonely Office: The Unintended Consequences of Distributed Work." *Academy of Management Discoveries* 1, no. 2 (2015), 150–64.

Rodriguez, Tori. "Descendants of Holocaust Survivors Have Altered Stress Hormones." *Scientific American*. February 12, 2015.

———. "The Odd (but Awesome) Way Happiness Is Contagious." *Prevention*. July 7, 2014.

Romer, Daniel, Patrick E. Jamieson, and Kathleen H. Jamieson. "Are News Reports of Suicide Contagious? A Stringent Test in Six U.S. Cities." *Journal of Communication* 56, no. 2 (2006), 253–70.

Roney, Marty. "Small Towns Susceptible to Terrorism." Memo from the District Attorney's Office, 19th Judicial Circuit (Alabama). 2002.

Rosen, Rebecca J. "Violence Is Contagious: What Goes Around Really Does Come Around." *Atlantic*. October 2013.

Rosin, Hanna. "Life Lessons." *New Yorker*. June 5, 2006.

———. "The Silicon Valley Suicides: Why Are So Many Kids Killing Themselves in Palo Alto?" *Atlantic*. December 2015.

Ross, Martha. "Teen Suicides: Survivors Reach Out to Offer Hope." *San Jose Mercury News*. April 15, 2015.

Rozin, Paul, and Edward B. Royzman. "Negativity Bias, Negativity Dominance, and Contagion." *Personality and Social Psychology Review* 5, no. 4 (2001), 296–320

Rubin, Gretchen. *The Happiness Project: Or, Why I Spent a Year Trying to Sing in the Morning, Clean My Closets, Fight Right, Read Aristotle, and Generally Have More Fun* (New York: HarperCollins, 2009).

Russell, George. "Bulimia Nervosa: An Ominous Variant of Anorexia Nervosa." *Psychological Medicine* 9 (1979), 429–48.

Ryerson, William N. "The Effectiveness of Entertainment Mass Media in

Changing Behaviors." Population Media Center. No date. http://www.
populationmedia.org/wp-content/uploads/2008/02/effectiveness-of
-entertainment-education-112706.pdf

Sabido, Miguel. "Towards the Social Use of Commercial Television: Mexico's Experience with the Reinforcement of Social Values Through
TV Soap Operas." Paper presented at the annual conference of the
International Institute of Communications, Strasbourg, France,
1981.

Salas, Adriana. "Workforce Happiness Increases Morale." www.army.mil.
April 23, 2015. http://www.army.mil/article/147100/Workforce_hap
piness_increases_morale/

Samuels, Diana. "Palo Alto Faith Groups Organize Event on Teen Mental
Health." San Jose Mercury News. August 27, 2009.

Sanburn, Josh. "Why Suicides Are More Common in Richer Neighborhoods." Time. November 8, 2012.

Sanger Katz, Margo. "The Science Behind Suicide Contagion." New York
Times. August 13, 2014.

Schaffer, Amanda. "Tech's Enduring Great-Man Myth." MIT Technology
Review. August 4, 2015.

Schaufeli, Wilmar B., Michael P. Leiter, and Christina Maslach. "Burnout:
35 Years of Research and Practice." Emerald Insight 14, no. 3 (2008),
204–220.

Schwartz, Tony. "Emotional Contagion Can Take Down Your Whole
Team." Harvard Business Review. July 11, 2012.

Segran, Elizabeth. "Ivy League for Free: What One Man Learned by
Crashing Elite Colleges for 4 Years." Fast Company. March 3, 2015.

Self, Will. The Quantity Theory of Insanity (New York: Vintage, 1995).

Shang, Li, Jian Li, Yan Li, Tao Wang, and Johannes Siegrist. "Stressful Psy-
chosocial School Environment and Suicidal Ideation in Chinese Adolescents." Social Psychiatry Psychiatric Epidemiology 49, no. 2 (February
28, 2014), 205–210.

Showalter, Elaine. Hystories: Hysterical Epidemics and Modern Media.
(New York: Columbia University Press, 1997.)

Siegel-Itzkovich, Judy. "Inherited Nightmares: A New Book Examines
How Holocaust Trauma Can Haunt Even the Grandchildren of Survivors." Jerusalem Post. March 21, 2010.

Sifferlin, Alexandra. "The Most Stressed-out Generation? Young Adults."
Time. February 7, 2013.

Simone, Alina. "The Magical Law of Contagion: Why People Pay Silly

Money for Strange Celebrity Memorabilia." Slate. October 3, 2014. http://www.slate.com/articles/health_and_science/science/2014/10 /celebrity_memorabilia_market_the_magical_law_of_contagion_ex plains_high.html

Simons, Ronald L., and Phyllis I. Murphy. "Sex Differences in the Causes of Adolescent Suicide Ideation." *Journal of Youth and Adolescence* 14, no. 5 (1985), 423–34.

Singhal, Arvind, and Everett M. Rogers. *Entertainment Education: A Communication Strategy for Social Change* (New York: Routledge, 2011).

Sinyor, Mark, Ayal Schaffer, and Amy H. Cheung. "An Observational Study of Bullying as a Contributing Factor in Youth Suicide in Toronto." *Canadian Journal of Psychiatry* 59, no. 12 (2014), 632–38.

Sirois, François. "Epidemic Hysteria: School Outbreaks 1973–1993." *Medical Principles and Practice* 8 (1999), 12–25.

Slutkin, Gary. "Violence Is a Contagious Disease." *National Academy of Sciences* (2013), 94–111.

Small, Gary. "Mass Hysteria Can Strike Anywhere, Anytime: When Stressed Out, the Mind Can Make the Body Sick." *Psychology Today*. September 28, 2010. https://www.psychologytoday.com /blog/brainbootcamp/201009/mass-hysteria-can-strike-anywhere -anytime

Smith, Bryan. "The Cluster Conundrum: Copycat Teen Deaths in Lake Forest." *Chicago*. June 18, 2012.

Solon, Olivia. "Compassion over Empathy Could Help Prevent Emotional Burnout." *Wired* (UK edition). July 12, 2012.

Someah, Kathleen L. "Why Are College Students Vulnerable to Eating Disorders?" Eating Disorder Hope Foundation. August 6, 2012.

Somerville, William G. "The Psychology of Hysteria." *American Journal of Psychiatry* 73, no. 4 (1917), 639–53.

Sonneck, G., E. Etzerdorfer, and S. Nagel-Kuess. "Imitative Suicide on the Viennese Subway." *Social Science and Medicine* 38, no. 3 (1994), 453–57.

Sontag, Susan. "Susan Sontag on Courage and Resistance." *Nation*. May 5, 2003.

Soundy, T. J., A. R. Lucasa, V. J. Suman, and L. J. Melton. "Bulimia Nervosa in Rochester, Minnesota from 1980 to 1990." *Psychological Medicine* 25, no. 5 (1995), 1065–71.

Spettigue, Wendy, and Katherine A. Henderson. "Eating Disorders and the Role of the Media." *Canada Child Adolescent Psychiatric Review* 13, no. 1 (2004), 16–19.

Steimer, Thierry. "The Biology of Fear- and Anxiety-Related Behaviors." *Dialogues in Clinical Neuroscience* 4, no. 3 (2002), 231–49.

Steiner, Jakub, and Colin Stewart. "Contagion Through Learning." *Theoretical Economics* 3 (2008), 431–58.

Stromberg, Joseph. "What Is the Nocebo Effect? For Some Patients, the Mere Suggestion of Side Effects Is Enough to Bring on Negative Symptoms." *Smithsonian.* July 23, 2012.

Strunk, Bradley C., Paul Ginsburg, and Jon Gabel. "Tracking Health Care Costs." *Health Affairs* (September 26, 2001).

Sudak, Howard S., and Donna M. Sudak. "The Media and Suicide." *Academic Psychiatry* 29, no. 5 (2005), 495–99.

Surowiecki, James. *The Wisdom of Crowds* (New York: Anchor Books, 2004).

Swanson, Sonja A., and Ian Colman. "Association Between Exposure to Suicide and Suicidality Outcomes in Youth." *Canadian Medical Association.* May 21, 2013.

Takeda, Allison. "The Mystery of Mass Hysteria." *Everyday Health.* January 18, 2012. http://www.everydayhealth.com/healthy-living/0118/the -mystery-of-mass-hysteria.aspx

Ter Maat, Sue, and Lisa Black. "Student Deaths in Lake Forest Raise New Alarms: Some Mental Health Experts, Prevention Advocates Fear Recent Wave of Train Deaths May Be Related to 'Suicide Cluster.'" *Chicago Tribune.* April 1, 2012.

Tetyana. "Can Eating Disorders Be Contagious?" Science of Eating Disorders. August 22, 2012. www.scienceofeds.org/2012/08/22/Can-Eating -Disorders-Be-Contagious/

Thompson, T., J. A. Davidson, and J. G. Barber. "Self-worth Protection in Achievement Motivation: Performance Effects and Attributional Behavior." *Journal of Educational Psychology* 87, no. 4 (December 1995), 598–610.

Tomlinson, Mike. "Suicide and Young People: The Case of Northern Ireland." *Child Care in Practice* 13, no. 4 (2007), 435–43.

Topalli, Volkan, Richard Wright, and Robert Fornango. "Drug Dealers, Robbery and Retaliation Vulnerability, Deterrence and the Contagion of Violence." *British Journal of Criminology* 42, no. 2 (2002), 337–51.

Truong, Hoai-Thu, and Sharon Pereira. "Asian and Asian Indian Cultures:

Implications for Psychotherapy." Article for mental health professionals, 2007-2009. http://www.drhttruong.com/wp-content/uploads/2015/09/AsianCulturesPsychotherapy.pdf

Tschannen-Moran, Megan, Cynthia Uline, Anita Woolfolk Hoy, and Timm Mackley. "Creating Smarter Schools Through Collaboration." *Journal of Educational Administration* 38, no. 3 (2000), 247–72.

Turecki, Gustavo, Richard Brière, Karen Dewar, Tonino Antonetti, Alain D. Lesage, Monique Séguin, Nadia Chawky, Claude Vanier, Martin Alda, Ridha Joober, Chawki Benkelfat, and Guy A. Rouleau. "Prediction of Level of Serotonin 2A Receptor Binding by Serotonin Receptor 2A Genetic Variation in Postmortem Brain Samples from Subjects Who Did or Did Not Commit Suicide." *American Journal of Psychiatry* 156, no. 9 (1999), 1456–58.

Van Praag, Henriette, Gerd Kempermann, and Fred H. Gage. "Neural Consequences of Environmental Enrichment." *Neuroscience* 1 (December 2000), 191–98.

Vandereycken, Walter. "Can Eating Disorders Become 'Contagious' in Group Therapy and Specialized Inpatient Care?" *European Eating Disorders Review* 19, no. 4 (July-August 2011), 289–95.

———. "How 'Contagious' Can Eating Disorders Be in the Eyes of Patients?" *Eating Disorders Review* 23, no. 2 (March-April 2012).

Vargas, Jose Antonio. "Spring Awakening: How an Egyptian Revolution Began on Facebook." *New York Times.* February 17, 2012.

Virtue, Robert. "The Psychology of Fanaticism." ABC Newcastle, Australian Broadcasting Corporation. March 6, 2015.

Waldmeir, Patti. "The Asian Work Ethic Comes at a Price." *Financial Times.* March 4, 2014.

Walworth, Carolyn. "Paly School Board Rep: 'The Sorrows of Young Palo Altans.'" Palo Alto Online. March 25, 2015. http://www.paloaltoonline.com/news/2015/03/25/guest-opinion-the-sorrows-of-young-palo-altans

Wang, Long, Deepak Malhotra, and J. Keith Murnighan. "Economics Education and Greed." *Academy of Management Learning and Education* 10, no. 4 (2011), 643–60.

Wang, Shirley. "Contagious Behavior." *Association for Psychological Science* 19, no. 2 (2006).

Warrell, Margie. "Culture of Courage: Creating a Culture That Breeds Bravery." Forbes.com. August 31, 2014. http://www.forbes.com/sites/margiewarrell/2014/08/31/building-brave-people/

Warren, Jennifer. "E. Palo Alto Murder Rate Worst in U.S.; Drug Wars Blamed. *Los Angeles Times*. January 5, 1993.

Watkins, Gwynne. "Here's How You Sell a Haunted House." *Vulture*. October 22, 2014. http://www.vulture.com/2014/10/heres-how-you-sell -a-haunted-house.html

Watson, Rebecca. "The Science of Wind Turbine Syndrome." *Popular Science*. October 25, 2013. http://www.popsci.com/blog-network /unpopular-science/%E2%80%9Cscience%E2%80%9D-wind-turbine -syndrome

Weiner, Eric. *The Geography of Bliss: A Search for the World's Most Creative Places, From Ancient Athens to Silicon Valley* (New York: Simon & Schuster, 2016).

Wellcome Trust. "A Burst from the Blue—Is Bulimia Nervosa Really a Modern Disease?" BrainFacts.org. February 20, 2012. http://www .brainfacts.org/diseases-disorders/psychiatric-disorders/articles/2012 /burst-from-the-blue/

Wernau, Julie. "Wind Turbines Stir Up Bad Feelings, Health Concerns in DeKalb County: Proponents Point to Reduced Dependence on Foreign Oil, Say No Evidence of Physiological Harm." *Chicago Tribune*. March 14, 2010.

West, Jean. "Holocaust Survivors' Grandchildren Call for Action over Inherited Trauma." *Guardian*. August 3, 2015.

Wheeler, Ladd. "Toward a Theory of Behavioral Contagion." *Psychological Review* 76, no. 3 (1966), 179–92.

Wheelock, Angelique Marie. "Passion Is Catching: Emotional Contagion and Affective Action in Select Works by Shakespeare." Dissertation submitted to the Graduate School of the University of Maryland. 2011.

Whippman, Ruth. "America the Anxious." *New York Times*. September 22, 2012.

Widom, Cathy S., Michael G. Maxfield. "An Update on the "Cycle of Violence." *National Institute of Justice*. February 2001. https://www.ncjrs .gov/pdffiles1/nij/184894.pdf

Wieczner, Jen. "Is There a Suicide Contagion on Wall Street?" *Fortune*. February 27, 2014.

Wikipedia. "Day-care Sex-Abuse Hysteria." Wikipedia.com. https:// en.wikipedia.org/wiki/Day-care_sex-abuse_hysteria

Wilne, Andrew N. "An Explanation for Mass Hysteria?" Medscape.com. July 11, 2012. http://www.medscape.com/viewarticle/766971

Wilson, Mike. "A Search for Victims Quest Search for the Truth in California Child Abuse Case Has Cost the Taxpayers Six Years, $15 Million." *Miami Herald*. November 13, 1989.

Wilson, Robert A., and Frank C. Keil, "Magic and Superstition." *MIT Encyclopedia of Cognitive Science* (Cambridge, MA: MIT Press, 1999).

Winerman, Lea. "A Laughing Matter: Psychologists Are Finding That the Ancient Roots of Laughter Predate the Idea of 'Funny.'" *Monitor* 37, no. 6 (2006), 58.

Woodruff, Judy. "Army Program Aims to Build Troops' Mental Resilience to Stress." PBS NewsHour. December 14, 2011.

Woodruff, Mandi. "'Keeping Up with the Joneses' Could Lead to Suicide." Business Insider. November 12, 2012. http://www.businessinsider .com/link-between-wealth-and-suicide-rates-san-francisco-federal -reserve-2012-11

Yang, Shannon. "Gunn Students Voice Experiences at Student Forum." *Oracle* (Henry M. Gunn High School, Palo Alto, student newspaper). March 24, 2015. https://gunnoracle.com/2015/03/24/gunn-students -voice-experiences-at-student-forum/

Yoo, Aileen. "Third Gunn Student Attempts Suicide." *San Francisco Chronicle*. June 5, 2009. http://blog.sfgate.com/stew/2009/06/05 /third-gunn-student-attempts-suicide/

Young, Sandra. "New Study Supports Suicide 'Contagion' in Teens." CNN.com. May 21, 2013. http://thechart.blogs.cnn.com/2013/05/21 /new-study-supports-suicide-contagion-in-teens/

Young, Steve. "Why Are Young Lakota Killing Themselves? South Dakota Reservation's Suicide Rate Said to Be Among Highest in World." *Argus Leader*. September 20, 2008.

Young, Thomas W., Suzanna E. Wooden, Paul C. Dew, Gerald L. Hoff, and Jinwen Cai. "The Richard Cory Phenomenon: Suicide and Wealth in Kansas City, Missouri." *Journal Forensic Science* 50, no. 2 (April 2005), 443-47

Zadrozny, Brandy. "The Werther Effect: Teen Copycat Suicides Are a Real Phenomenon." Daily Beast. May 1, 2014. http://www.thedai lybeast.com/articles/2014/05/01/teen-copycat-suicides-are-a-real -phenomenon.html

Zenere, Frank J. "Suicide Clusters and Contagion: Recognizing and Addressing Suicide Contagion Are Essential to Successful Suicide Postvention Efforts." *Principal Leadership* (2009), 12–16.

Zepecki, Carol, and Wesley Cedros. "Responding to a Suicide Cluster: Palo Alto School District." *Lessons Learned* 5, no. 2 (2010).

Zimbardo, Philip. "What Makes a Hero?" *Greater Good*. January 18, 2011.

Zirpolo, Kyle. *"I'm Sorry: A Long-delayed Apology From One of the Accusers in the Notorious McMartin Pre-School Molestation Case."* *Los Angeles Times Magazine*. October 30, 2005.

ABOUT THE AUTHOR

LEE DANIEL KRAVETZ has a master's degree in counseling psychology and is a graduate of the University of Missouri-Columbia School of Journalism. He has written for *Psychology Today*, the *Huffington Post*, and the *New York Times*, among other publications. He lives in Northern California with his wife and children.